jQuery
A Beginner's Guide

About the Author

John Pollock (Huntsville, Texas) is employed as a Web Administrator during the day and works on Web sites and other projects in the evening. He runs a Web site devoted to Web development and design, www.scripttheweb.com. John is also a contributor to www.webxpertz.net, a help community for Web developers, and the author of four editions of *JavaScript: A Beginner's Guide.*

About the Technical Reviewer

Jaana Gilbert (Aurora, Colorado) is a Senior ColdFusion Developer with over 15 years of experience in building enterprise-level Web applications for clients around the world. She started as a front-end developer and expanded her skill set to back-end development and enjoys building complete Web applications from the ground up. She has worked with clients like the Tennis Industry Association, USTA, and Boston Scientific. Originally from Finland, she now resides in Aurora, Colorado, and enjoys spending time with her husband, Jim, and twin girls Alexis and Brianna.

jQuery
A Beginner's Guide

John Pollock

McGraw Hill Education

New York   Chicago   San Francisco
Athens   London   Madrid   Mexico City
Milan   New Delhi   Singapore   Sydney   Toronto

Cataloging-in-Publication Data is on file with the Library of Congress

McGraw-Hill Education books are available at special quantity discounts to use as premiums and sales promotions, or for use in corporate training programs. To contact a representative, please visit the Contact Us pages at www.mhprofessional.com.

jQuery: A Beginner's Guide

1 2 3 4 5 6 7 8 9 0 DOC DOC 1 0 9 8 7 6 5 4

ISBN   978-0-07-181791-2
MHID   0-07-181791-3

Sponsoring Editor   Brandi Shailer

Editorial Supervisor   Janet Walden

Project Manager   Charu Khanna, MPS Limited

Acquisitions Coordinator   Amanda Russell

Technical Editor   Jaana Gilbert

Copy Editor   Margaret Berson

Proofreader   Lisa McCoy

Indexer   Karin Arrigoni

Production Supervisor   Jean Bodeaux

Composition   MPS Limited

Illustration   MPS Limited

Art Director, Cover   Jeff Weeks

Cover Designer   Jeff Weeks

To my wife, Heather, daughters Eva and Elizabeth,
Bruce and Joy Anderson, and Dr. J.D. and Linda Andrews.

In memory of James D. and Livian Anderson, John William and Edith Hopkins,
Burley T. and Aline Price, "Doc" Flores, and Clifton Idom.

Contents at a Glance

Contents

Acknowledgments

I would like to thank my beautiful and wonderful wife, Heather Pollock, for all of her love, support, and encouragement in all I do. I love you! I would also like to thank my two daughters, Eva and Elizabeth Pollock. I love both of you!

I would like to thank my parents, Bruce and Joy Anderson, for their love and guidance, and for always supporting my endeavors.

I would like to thank Dr. J.D. and Linda Andrews for their love, guidance, and support.

In addition I would like to thank John and Betty Hopkins (grandparents), James D. and Livian Anderson (grandparents), Juanita Idom (grandmother), Richard Pollock and family (brother), Misty Castleman and family (sister), Warren Anderson and family (brother), Jon Andrews (brother) and family, Lisa and Julian Owens (aunt/uncle) and family, and every aunt, uncle, cousin, or other relation in my family. All of you have been a great influence in my life.

I would like to thank all of my editors at McGraw-Hill Professional for their outstanding help and support throughout the writing of this book. Thanks to Brandi Shailer, Amanda Russell, and to all of the editors who worked on this book to help make it better.

Thanks to my technical editor, Jaana Gilbert, for ensuring that the code was correct and that examples worked as expected. Most appreciated!

I would like to thank God for the ability he has given me to help and teach people through my writing. "Every good gift and every perfect gift is from above, and comes down from the Father of lights, with whom there is no variation or shadow of turning" (James 1:17).

Introduction

Welcome to *jQuery: A Beginner's Guide*! Several years ago, I noticed that there was a new popular term emerging on the Web: *jQuery*. Of course, I got curious and decided to go find out what this meant.

I quickly found out that this was a JavaScript library, but not just any library. This one provided the means to easily select elements and create dynamic effects with less code being required from the developer. Not only that, it also turned many of the cross-browser worries often encountered in JavaScript code into things that developers didn't need to pull their hair out about any more when using the library: It provided support even for older versions of Internet Explorer!

After seeing this, I felt this would be a helpful library to use when I needed to complete a JavaScript program that required support for older browsers such as Internet Explorer 6. Rather than worrying about the additional coding that would be needed to make the program compatible, the program could simply be written while jQuery made it consistent with each browser in the background. This made jQuery the perfect choice as my first library to learn in detail.

Why This Book?

Learning a new language or API (application programming interface) can be difficult even when great documentation is available. Many times, it is helpful to have a gentle introduction to the topic, especially if one is unfamiliar with the terms and practices that are used when talking about it. This book is designed to guide beginners to jQuery/JavaScript so that they can get started easily and learn all of the terms that will be needed to understand the topic fully.

Web designers, Web developers, or JavaScript programmers who want to learn to use jQuery from the beginning will find this a good place to start. With a gentle introduction and explanation of the terms often used, this guide provides a means for beginners to start using the jQuery library.

What This Book Covers

This book covers the basics of adding the jQuery library, element selection, event handling, animation, form validation, AJAX, use and creation of plugins, and more, and includes special features to help you along the way as you learn. These include

- **Key Skills & Concepts** Each chapter begins with a set of key skills and concepts that outline the topics you will want to understand by the end of the chapter.

- **Code** Code listings display the source code used with each example.

- **Callouts** Callouts point to specific lines or sections of code and provide helpful hints or notes about the code.

- **Notes, Tips, and Cautions** Notes, Tips, and Cautions call your attention to noteworthy statements that you will find helpful as you move through the chapters.

- **Ask the Expert** The Ask the Expert sections let you see what types of questions are commonly asked about certain topics, with responses from the author.

- **Try This** These sections get you to practice what you have learned using a hands-on approach. Each Try This section will have you code a script through step-by-step directions on what you need to do to in order to accomplish the goal. You can find solutions to each project on the McGraw-Hill Professional Web site at www.mhprofessional.com/computingdownload.

- **Self Test** Each chapter ends with a Self Test, which is a series of 15 questions to see if you have mastered the topics covered in the chapter. The answers to each Self Test can be found in the appendix.

Chapters 1 through 4 cover the very basics of jQuery, from including the library in an HTML document (Chapter 1) to element selection (Chapter 2), event handling (Chapter 3), and CSS style manipulation (Chapter 4).

Chapters 5 through 8 cover further basic principles, building on what you learned in Chapters 1 through 4. This begins with JavaScript and the DOM (Chapter 5), and continues with animation/effects (Chapter 6), the *Event* object (Chapter 7), and form validation (Chapter 8).

Chapters 9 through 12 cover intermediate concepts, such as AJAX (Chapter 9) and plugins (Chapters 10 and 11), and touches on more advanced techniques such as debugging and unit testing (Chapter 12).

At the end of this book, you should be able to use all the basics of the jQuery library and be ready to read more advanced material on the subject if you choose to pursue it further.

If you have any questions while working through this book, you can contact me via one of the following methods:

- E-mail me from my Web site: www.scripttheweb.com/about/contact/

- Contact on Twitter: @ScripttheWeb

Now, let's begin learning jQuery!

Chapter 1

Getting Started with jQuery

Key Skills & Concepts

- What You Need to Know
- What Is jQuery?
- Why jQuery Is Useful
- Begin Using jQuery
  - Downloading jQuery
  - Including jQuery in an HTML Document
- Your First jQuery Script

Welcome to *jQuery: A Beginner's Guide*! You've probably heard the word *jQuery* numerous times by now, and perhaps you've even been told you need to learn it for your job. This chapter discusses the things you should know before starting with jQuery, what jQuery is, and how to begin using it in your Web site code.

jQuery has become an immensely popular tool for adding dynamic effects to Web pages, such as adding, removing, or moving elements. It uses a syntax that is often easier to learn than JavaScript programming, since it makes use of HTML/CSS syntax as a basis for accessing page elements. This syntax is something most Web designers and developers are familiar with already, which is a nice feature when you are learning something new.

What You Need to Know

Before you begin using jQuery, you should have (or obtain) knowledge of the following:

- HTML and Cascading Style Sheets (CSS)
- Text editors and Web browsers
- Basic JavaScript

If you have been asked to learn jQuery, you likely have some or all of this knowledge already. If you don't know some or all of the aforementioned topics, a closer look at each of them may help you decide where to begin.

Basic HTML and CSS Knowledge

Ideally, you will want to have previous experience with HTML (Hypertext Markup Language) and CSS (Cascading Style Sheets), or at least have a basic understanding of how these languages work and how they help to build a Web page.

You will use HTML to create the structure of a Web page, and you will be adding, changing, or removing tags during the course of this book. For this reason, it is good to know the basics regarding the opening and closing of tags and how to add attributes to tags, as in the following code:

```
<div class="news">
```

If you don't know HTML, you can learn it fairly quickly by purchasing a book or reading a Web site. A good book is *HTML: A Beginner's Guide, Fourth Edition* by Wendy Willard (McGraw-Hill Professional, 2009). For good Web sites to learn HTML, try: www.scripttheweb .com/html5/ and www.w3.org/wiki/The_basics_of_HTML.

In this book, I will use HTML5 in the example code. You are free to use HTML4 or XHTML if necessary, or if you prefer to do so. You will just need to adjust the code as needed to fit the convention you will be using.

You will also need to know how to use CSS, particularly when it comes to using CSS selectors. Two good places to learn CSS are www.scripttheweb.com/css/ and www.w3.org/ wiki/CSS_basics.

Basic Text Editor and Web Browser Knowledge

Before jumping in and coding with JavaScript, you must be able to use a text editor or HTML editor, and a Web browser. You'll use these tools to code your scripts.

Text Editors

Any HTML/text editor can be used for jQuery code, just as with HTML, CSS, or JavaScript. Some examples include Adobe Dreamweaver (in code mode), NetBeans, or a plain text editor such as Notepad, TextPad, or Simple Text.

Web Browsers

jQuery is written to work in many different browsers, but the following are recommended since they will be more up to date with other technologies (such as HTML5 or CSS3):

- Microsoft Internet Explorer version 9.0 or later, or 8 if you are not able to upgrade on your operating system, for example, Windows XP (www.microsoft.com/ie)

- Mozilla Firefox version 14.0 or later (www.mozilla.com/firefox)

- Google Chrome version 20.0 or later (www.google.com/chrome/)

- Opera version 12.0 or later (www.opera.com)

New versions of these browsers continue to be produced, so when you download one, be sure to get the latest stable version available.

To give you an idea of what some of the aforementioned browsers look like when in use, Figure 1-1 shows a Web page when viewed in Microsoft Internet Explorer, and Figure 1-2 shows the same page when viewed in Mozilla Firefox.

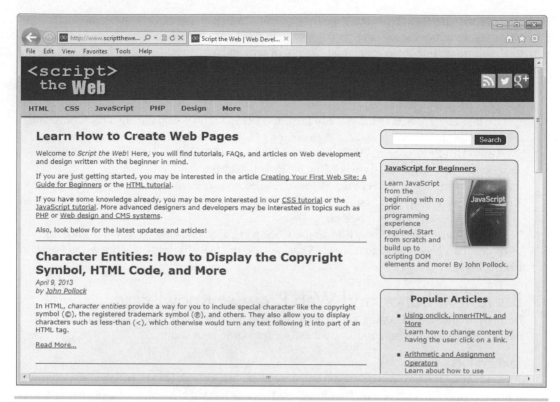

Figure 1-1 A Web page viewed in Microsoft Internet Explorer

Basic JavaScript Knowledge

jQuery is a JavaScript library, so it is helpful to know some of the basics of the JavaScript language, such as including JavaScript files in an HTML document, defining variables and functions, using conditional statements, and working with the dot (.) operator.

While jQuery makes many things easier, it does not always entirely replace the use of JavaScript code. For example, you may need to use an *if/else* statement or define a variable using JavaScript code. However, if you do not know these basics, I will provide some assistance in this book when they come up, as well as provide references for further reading.

If you decide that you would like to learn the basics of JavaScript first, these resources can help you:

- *JavaScript: A Beginner's Guide, 4th Edition* (McGraw-Hill Professional, 2013)
- www.scripttheweb.com/js/
- https://developer.mozilla.org/en-US/learn/javascript

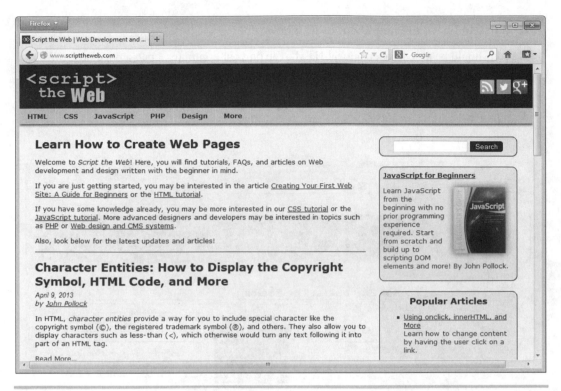

Figure 1-2   A Web page viewed in Mozilla Firefox

Since this is a beginner's guide, I will try to integrate other technologies as gently as possible into the text. However, if you don't know the absolute basics (such as what an HTML tag is), it will be best to begin by learning the basics of the topics using the resources provided earlier in the chapter.

Ask the Expert

Q: **What exactly do I need to know about using a text editor?**

A: As long as you know how to edit and save plain text files with different file extensions, you should have no problems. You will be using three different file extensions through this book (.html, .css, .js), which are typically included as options for you when you save your files in a text or HTML editor.

(continued)

Q: **What do I need to know about using a browser?**

A: You should be able to open a local HTML file on your computer, open a page on the Web, and reload a page. If you don't know how to open a local HTML file, open your browser and go to the File menu. Look for an option that says Open, Open File, or a similar phrase and select it. You can then browse for and open the file you need. The following illustration shows an example using Microsoft Internet Explorer:

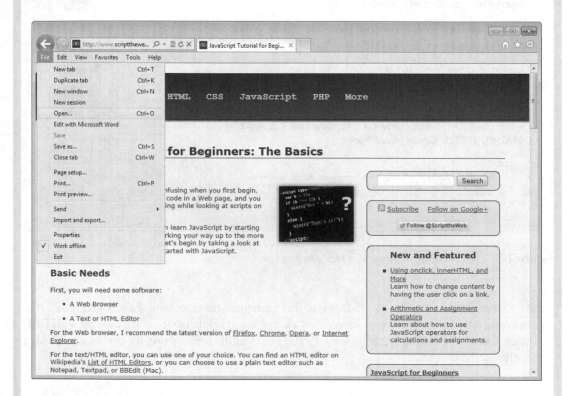

Q: **What if I don't know some of the required technologies?**

A: Since this is a beginner's guide, I will try to integrate other technologies as gently as possible into the text. However, if you don't know the absolute basics (such as what an HTML tag is), it will be best to begin by learning the basics of the specific topic using the resources provided earlier in the chapter.

Q: Since jQuery is a JavaScript library, can I just learn JavaScript instead?

A: Ultimately, that is up to you. If you decide to use JavaScript instead, the resources presented earlier in this chapter can help you learn it. jQuery, as you will see later in this chapter, makes many of the difficult aspects of dealing with a document much easier for you (such as selecting elements and making effects work cross-browser). Rather than needing to worry about what can be done to make an effect work in Internet Explorer, Chrome, Firefox, Opera, Safari, and others, you can simply write the jQuery code, which will handle the browser differences for you.

What Is jQuery?

Back in 2005, a programmer named John Resig came up with an idea that would streamline code in JavaScript libraries by using CSS selectors as a basis for accessing elements in the document and by creating syntax that would make event handling easier to implement. By 2006, he had implemented these ideas into his own JavaScript library, which was named jQuery.

The first stable version was released that year, and since then the library has become widely used by Web designers and developers all over the world. Additional features can be added to the library through jQuery plugins, which can be found on the jQuery Web site. Over the years, it has been optimized to be faster and more compact in order to help sites that use it load more quickly.

What Can jQuery Do?

The jQuery library can perform numerous tasks with its user-friendly access to scripting, including

- **Accessing elements**   CSS syntax is used to access elements, so you do not need to learn or use all of the necessary JavaScript coding necessary to do this consistently cross-browser.

- **Making changes to the document**   Changing the appearance of or content within elements is more intuitive than it is in JavaScript. For example, jQuery uses the *append()* method to add content to the end of an element, which is easy to remember when you need to perform the task.

- **Creating effects**   Numerous methods for creating animations to move, show, or hide elements are available to easily implement these effects cross-browser.

- **AJAX**   jQuery provides methods for retrieving information from the server to ease the burden of writing cross-browser code to do so in JavaScript.

In addition to this, jQuery has methods that allow you to easily work with arrays and other items in JavaScript. For example, the *jQuery.inArray()* method can be used to easily search for items in an array, which in JavaScript would require a special function to be written for older browsers that may not support the *indexOf()* method for arrays.

Who Can Use jQuery?

jQuery is open source, so it is free to be used by anyone. It has a dual license under both the GNU Public License, which allows it to be used on other open-source projects that are under the GNU Public License, and the MIT License, which allows it to be used on any Web site. This flexibility makes it an easy and cost-efficient tool to implement in order to assist with the coding of dynamic effects.

Why jQuery Is Useful

Many Web designers and developers do not have the additional time required to learn all of the details of JavaScript programming necessary to create dynamic changes or effects and have them work cross-browser.

Designers tend to be more focused on graphics, layout, HTML, and CSS. Design is a large job in itself, so it would certainly be handy to have a tool that made the addition of dynamic effects easier than outright JavaScript programming. Developers often have to know one or multiple server-side languages such as PHP, Ruby, Python, Java, and others, so it would be helpful not to be required to learn yet another language in order to perform client-side scripting tasks.

jQuery does a number of things to help those working on Web sites: It is accessible, it addresses browser inconsistencies, and it provides plugins for those who need additional functionality.

Accessible

jQuery addresses the needs of designers and developers alike by having syntax that is accessible to both programmers and nonprogrammers. Since most designers and developers are familiar with CSS code, using CSS selectors as the basis for accessing elements makes it much easier to begin adding dynamic effects without needing to work with yet another set of rules in JavaScript.

With jQuery, you can select elements via their element name, id, class name, or most any valid CSS selection method. For example, using the string "div.news-item" will select all <div> elements with a class name of *news-item*. This is much simpler than iterating through in JavaScript to find either all the elements with the class name of *news-item* and then finding the <div> elements within that set, or finding all of the <div> elements and then determining which ones have the *news-item* class name.

Browser Inconsistencies

While browsers have improved at the task of adhering to standards, there are still differences, which can often lead to headaches for designers and developers—especially when a client or employer wants a dynamic effect and needs it to work in all browsers. Often, an older version of a browser needs to be supported, which may require additional JavaScript coding to make a desired effect possible in that browser.

Instead of having the designer or developer bear this burden in a potentially unfamiliar language, jQuery handles the integration of coded effects into each browser so that they work consistently. As of this writing, jQuery supports most browsers in their current version and their previous version (Firefox, Chrome, Safari, and Opera). For Internet Explorer, jQuery 1.x supports version 6 and above, while jQuery 2.x supports version 9 and above.

Additional Functionality

When the core jQuery library lacks some functionality you need for your project, you can usually find that functionality available as a jQuery plugin. This flexibility allows you to extend the library when needed, while simply using the slim core library (a minified file of 32KB at the time of this writing) when additional functionality is not required.

Begin Using jQuery

To begin using jQuery, you will need to insert the script into an HTML document. You can do this by downloading the jQuery library and including the downloaded copy in your document, or you can simply include the script from a Content Delivery Network (CDN) and begin using it.

Obtaining jQuery

If you want to use your own copy of jQuery, which is advantageous if you are going to need to use it in an environment that isn't always connected to the Internet, then you will need to download it from the jQuery Web site.

Download the Library

First, go to the jQuery Web site at http://jquery.com/download/. You will be given two options: to download the compressed production version or to download the uncompressed development version. At this point, you may choose either one.

If you are curious and would like to see the code within the library, you can download the development version. However, before you place it live on a Web site, you will want to replace it with the production version so that the library will load faster for your visitors.

Inserting jQuery into a Document

Once you have it downloaded, you will need to insert it into the HTML code of any documents that will be using it. This is done in the same way that you insert any other JavaScript file into a document, by adding a <script> element that points to the jQuery file.

The following <script> element shows how this can be done when the jQuery file is located in the same directory as your HTML file:

```
<script src="jquery-1.9.1.min.js" type="text/javascript"></script>
```

If you keep your JavaScript files in a particular folder, you can adjust the src attribute as needed to point to the proper place.

The jQuery site recommends placing the <script> element that calls the jQuery library within the <head> element of a document. I would recommend placing it after your style sheets are included and before your other JavaScript files are included (at least before the JavaScript file you will use for writing your jQuery code). So, if you have a CSS file named *styles.css*, and you have a JavaScript file named *mycode.js* that you will use for your jQuery code, your HTML code would look similar to this test page:

```
<!DOCTYPE html>
<html>
<head>
  <meta charset="utf-8">
  <title>My Site</title>
  <link href="styles.css" rel="stylesheet">
  <script src="jquery-1.9.1.min.js" type="text/javascript"></script>
  <script src="mycode.js" type="text/javascript"></script>
</head>
<body>
<h1>My Site</h1>
<div class="main">
Welcome to my site! Obviously, this site is all about me! I probably
should think about others, but right now I am simply talking about me.
</div>
<div class="about-me">
<h2>About Me</h2>
I enjoy writing HTML, CSS, and jQuery. I also picked up a love of
flying kites when a friend of my told me to &quot;Go fly a kite!&quot;
I did, and it has been a hobby ever since.
</div>
</body>
</html>
```

As you can see, the CSS file is added via the <link> element, and then the jQuery file and the JavaScript file are included via the <script> element. The remainder of the page is simply HTML and content that can be manipulated using jQuery.

With this in place, you are now set up to use jQuery! All you will need to do is add code to your CSS file for styling and write jQuery code in your *mycode.js* file to begin. First, however, you will need to make sure you want to include jQuery using this method rather than using a CDN.

Using a CDN

An alternative to keeping your own copy of jQuery is to use a copy from a CDN, which is an external network that allows content to be delivered all over the world. The most widely used CDN for jQuery is Google, but there are numerous others, including Microsoft and MediaTemple.

Loading the jQuery library from a CDN offers two advantages:

● The file is loaded from the server that is closest to the user, improving the speed of the file download.

● If the user has downloaded the file from the same CDN previously, then it can be loaded from the browser's cache, eliminating the need to download it again.

The main disadvantage of this method is that an Internet connection is required (since the file will be downloaded from an external source). If you need to work offline for development, you will likely want to download your own copy as described in the previous section.

Loading from a CDN

To load the jQuery file from a CDN, you simply point the src attribute of the <script> element to the external file. For example, to load the latest version (at the time of this writing) from the Google CDN, you would use the following code:

```
<script src="//ajax.googleapis.com/ajax/libs/jquery/1.9.1/jquery.min.js">
</script>
```

To make sure you are loading the latest version, be sure to check the Google site at https://developers.google.com/speed/libraries/devguide#jquery.

If you choose to use the Microsoft or MediaTemple CDNs, the proper URL can be obtained from their sites, which are listed here:

● **Microsoft CDN**   www.asp.net/ajaxlibrary/cdn.ashx#jQuery_Releases_on_the_CDN_0

● **MediaTemple**   http://jquery.com/download/

Once you have the <script> element with the proper URL in place, you are ready to begin using jQuery from the chosen CDN!

Local or CDN: Which Method Should I Use?

The method you choose will depend on your particular needs. If you are mainly developing offline, then using a local copy will likely be the best solution. If you are distributing an application live on the Web to numerous users, then a CDN may be a better choice, since it can help speed up the loading of the application.

In this book, the examples will use a local copy of jQuery downloaded from the jQuery site. Once you have downloaded the file, you will be able to use the provided code whether or not you are currently connected to the Internet.

Your First jQuery Script

To begin, you will write a jQuery script that simply updates the style of a <div> element in an HTML document. First, the code for the HTML document:

```
<!DOCTYPE html>
<html>
<head>
  <meta charset="utf-8">
  <title>My Site</title>
```

```
            <link href="styles.css" rel="stylesheet">
            <script src="jquery-1.9.1.min.js" type="text/javascript"></script>
            <script src="mycode.js" type="text/javascript"></script>
</head>
<body>
<h1>My Site</h1>
<div class="main">
Welcome to my site! Obviously, this site is all about me! I probably
should think about others, but right now I am simply talking about me.
</div>
<div class="about-me">
<h2>About Me</h2>
I enjoy writing HTML, CSS, and jQuery. I also picked up a love of
flying kites when a friend of my told me to &quot;Go fly a kite!&quot;
I did, and it has been a hobby ever since.
</div>
</body>
</html>
```

Save this file as *index.html* and make sure the *jquery-1.9.1.min.js* file is saved in the same folder as the HTML file. You will also place your CSS and JavaScript files in this folder.

Next, save the following code in a file named *styles.css*:

```
.special { font-style:italic; }
```

This defines a single class named *special*, which you will add to one of the <div> elements using jQuery.

Finally, save the following code in a file named *mycode.js*:

```
$(document).ready(function() {
    $(".about-me").addClass("special");
});
```

In this file, you will be writing the code that makes use of the jQuery library. This is technically JavaScript code, but the jQuery library allows you to call special functions that make the syntax simpler than typical JavaScript code.

Open *index.html* in your Web browser and examine the resulting page. You will notice that most of the page displays with the default style settings of the browser, but the "About Me" section is italicized. The jQuery code added the special class to that particular <div> element, giving it additional styling. Figure 1-3 shows an example of the completed Web page when viewed in a browser.

Locating the Proper Element

As a starting point, you will look at the middle line of code from the *mycode.js* file:

```
$(".about-me").addClass("special");
```

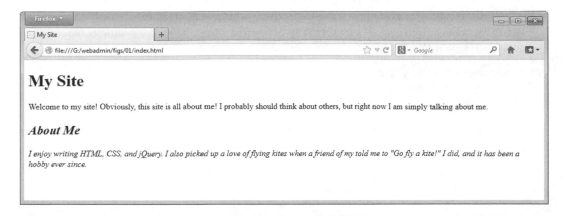

Figure 1-3   The *index.html* file when viewed in a Web browser

The line begins by using the $() function to make a selection from the document. This allows you to select one or more elements using CSS syntax, which is often more familiar than the corresponding JavaScript syntax. In this case, the *about-me* class is selected by passing the $() function a value of ".about-me". Since only one element is using the *about-me* class, that element is what is selected (the second <div> element).

Next, you will see a dot (.), which indicates that a method of the $() function will be called. The method is appropriately named *addClass*, since it will add the styles in the specified class to the selected element(s). In this case, the styles in the *special* class are applied to the selected <div> element (the one with the *about-me* class).

Waiting for the Document to Be Ready

The middle line of code by itself would likely have no effect when the page is loaded in a browser. The browser would try to run this code before the document has finished loading all of the necessary elements due to the code being placed within the <head> element. To avoid this problem, jQuery provides a method named *ready* that can be applied to the document.

In this script, the outer lines of code ensure that any code within them runs only after the document is ready for changes to be made to its elements:

```
$(document).ready(function() {
    // code
});
```

As you can see, the *ready* method allows you to define a function that will be run once the elements of the document have been loaded.

When using the *ready* method, you can provide what is called an *anonymous function* (like the one you have been using) or a previously defined function name. For example, here is the code you implemented, which uses an anonymous function:

```
$(document).ready(function() {
    $(".about-me").addClass("special");
});
```

To perform the same task by providing a defined function, you could instead use the following code:

```
function makeSpecial() {
  $(".about-me").addClass("special");
}
$(document).ready(makeSpecial);
```

Here, a typical JavaScript function is defined, which uses the jQuery code to perform the same task. The function is then called by using the function name in the *ready* method.

The main difference between the two approaches is that an anonymous function is most often used when the function code is not reusable, while a defined function is used when the function will be reused at a later time.

Try This 1-1   Add Another Class

```
index.html
styles.css
mycode.js
```

This project allows you to practice adding a class using jQuery. In this case, you will add another line of code to add another class to an element on the *index.html* page you have been using.

Step by Step

1. Use your current *index.html* page for the HTML code.

2. In the *styles.css* file, update the file to add a new class named *main-text* that will set the font size to 1.3em. Save the file. When complete, it should look like this code:

```
.special { font-style:italic; }
.main-text { font-size:1.3em; }
```

3. In the *mycode.js* file, add jQuery code that will add the *main-text* class to the div element that has a class of *main*. Save the file. When complete, the code should look like this:

```
$(document).ready(function() {
    $(".about-me").addClass("special");
    $(".main").addClass("main-text");
});
```

4. Open the *index.html* file in your Web browser. You should see an increased font size for the text underneath the level one heading.

Try This Summary

In this project, you added a class to another <div> element, which gave the text within it a larger font size. This added another line to your CSS and your jQuery code. In the next chapter, you will learn more about using the $() function to select elements and how you can use CSS syntax to make element selection easier for you.

Resources for Help

If you find you need additional help while progressing through this book, the following resources may be useful to you:

- ● **www.webxpertz.net/forums**   A community of developers that allows you to ask questions and discuss various Web development topics.

- ● **www.scripttheweb.com/about/contact/**   To contact me, you can send me an e-mail from this page.

- ● **@ScripttheWeb**   To contact me on Twitter, use this handle.

✔ *Chapter 1 Self Test*

1. Which of the following is not something you should be familiar with before beginning with jQuery?

   A. CSS

   B. C#

   C. HTML

   D. Text editors

2. Which of the following is something you should have to use jQuery?

   A. A Web browser

   B. A Java compiler

   C. A 500GB flash drive

   D. Angry Birds

3. A programmer named _____ began the jQuery library.

    A. John Walker

    B. John Pollock

    C. John Resig

    D. John Wayne

4. jQuery uses CSS selectors as a basis for accessing elements in the document.

    A. True

    B. False

5. jQuery is licensed under both the GNU Public License and the _____.

    A. Common Project Open License

    B. BSD License

    C. Open Software License

    D. MIT License

6. jQuery does not provide plugins for those who need additional functionality.

    A. True

    B. False

7. You can include jQuery in a document by using the _____ element.

    A. <link>

    B. <script>

    C. <meta>

    D. <style>

8. The jQuery site recommends placing the call to the jQuery library within the _____ element of a document.

    A. <head>

    B. <body>

    C. <link>

    D. <footer>

9. Which of the following would correctly call a locally stored version of jQuery 1.9.1?

    A. <script file="jquery-1.9.1.min.js" type="text/javascript"></script>

    B. <script src="jquery-1.6.0.min.js" type="text/javascript"></script>

    C. <script src="jquery-1.9.1.min.html" type="text/html"></script>

    D. <script src="jquery-1.9.1.min.js" type="text/javascript"></script>

10. Which of the following is an advantage of loading jQuery from a CDN?

    A. It will work even when you are not connected to the Internet.

    B. The file is loaded from the server that is closest to the user, improving the speed of the file download.

    C. It is never cached in the user's browser.

    D. You don't have to use the <script> element to load it.

11. The _____ function allows you to select one or more elements in the document by using CSS syntax.

    A. select()

    B. #()

    C. $()

    D. cssSelect()

12. The *ready* method allows you to define a function that will be run once the elements of the document have been loaded.

    A. True

    B. False

13. When using the *ready* method, you can provide a previously defined function name or a(n) _____.

    A. variable

    B. array

    C. anonymous function

    D. property

14. The _____ method will add the styles in the specified class to the selected element(s).

    A. addClass

    B. insertClass

    C. classAdd

    D. add

15. An anonymous function is most often used when the function code is not _____.

    A. stable

    B. correct

    C. reusable

    D. happy with anyone knowing its real name

Chapter 2

Selecting Elements in the Document

Key Skills & Concepts

- The $() Function
- CSS Basics
- Using CSS Selectors
- Using Extended jQuery Selectors

Element selection is a fundamental part of using jQuery. This chapter will cover the basics of selecting elements by covering the $() function, basic CSS, CSS selectors, and extended selectors. First, you will take a look at the $() function and how it works.

The $() Function

The $() function is used to select one or more elements in the document. It returns a collection of elements that match the specified selection. $() is actually an alias for the full function name, jQuery().

TIP
If you find that jQuery is in conflict with another JavaScript library that also uses the $() alias, you can use jQuery() in place of $() to fix the issue.

More technically, the $() function returns a jQuery object that points to all of the selected elements. When you call a jQuery method such as *addClass()*, it is run for all of the selected elements automatically, which keeps you from adding JavaScript loops to the code in order to run the method for each element. This is a very useful feature that keeps extra coding to a minimum and allows you to concentrate more on constructing the proper selectors and calling the jQuery methods you want to use.

jQuery uses CSS selector syntax and also has a number of extended selectors that can be passed to the $() function. To begin using CSS selectors, you will first want to understand the basics of CSS and how it is used to select elements.

NOTE
If you already know CSS, you may skip the "CSS Basics" section.

CSS Basics

While HTML is used to create the structure of a document, Cascading Style Sheets (CSS) is used to shape the presentation of a document. For example, recall the plain HTML code from the example page you have been using (*index.html*):

```
<!DOCTYPE html>
<html>
<head>
  <meta charset="utf-8">
  <title>My Site</title>
  <link href="styles.css" rel="stylesheet">
  <script src="jquery-1.9.1.min.js" type="text/javascript"></script>
  <script src="mycode.js" type="text/javascript"></script>
</head>
<body>
<h1>My Site</h1>
<div class="main">
Welcome to my site! Obviously, this site is all about me! I probably
should think about others, but right now I am simply talking about me.
</div>
<div class="about-me">
<h2>About Me</h2>
I enjoy writing HTML, CSS, and jQuery. I also picked up a love of
flying kites when a friend of my told me to &quot;Go fly a kite!&quot;
I did, and it has been a hobby ever since.
</div>
</body>
</html>
```

A CSS file named *styles.css* is included here.

On its own, this would display as a plain page with very little design. The only presentation is based on the browser default settings for displaying particular HTML elements. Figure 2-1 shows how this plain page would look in a Web browser. To give the page a more interesting presentation and design, you can use CSS.

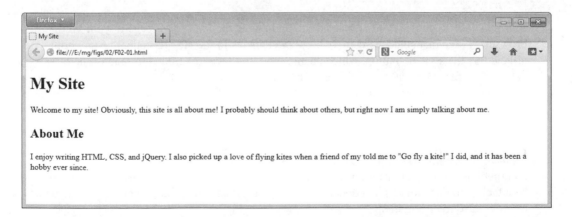

Figure 2-1   An HTML page with no CSS applied

Notice that the HTML code already includes a style sheet via the *href* attribute of the <link> tag (*styles.css*). Updating the *styles.css* file will allow you to select elements in the HTML document and define how they should look and where they should appear. Including the same CSS file in each page of a site like this enables you to make numerous presentational changes for the entire Web site by simply editing that single CSS file. This makes CSS (and, by extension, jQuery) an especially helpful tool to use when designing and developing your Web sites.

Selecting Elements

In order to change the presentation of the document, you will need to select elements and give them style declarations. This is a basic building block that will be used as the selection syntax in jQuery, so once you know how to select elements in CSS, you can easily migrate that knowledge over to your jQuery scripts.

CSS has numerous methods that can be used to select elements. Since many of these techniques will be covered later in this chapter when discussing jQuery CSS selectors, you will simply learn some basic CSS selectors at this time.

First, suppose you want to alter the look of the <h1> element on the *index.html* page. An easy way to select this would be to use the element name (h1). You can then apply style definitions to this by including them within a set of curly braces, as shown in the following code:

```
h1 { color:#009; font-size:1.7em; }
```

In this case, the lone <h1> element is selected and the style definitions within the curly braces will be applied to that element. Had there been more than one <h1> element on the page, this would have selected and applied the styles to *all* of them.

As an example of this, you can select all of the <div> elements in the document by using the element name as the selector:

```
div { font-family:Verdana; }
```

Add this code to your *styles.css* file, save it, and reload the *index.html* page in your Web browser. Notice that since there are two <div> elements in the HTML code, they are both affected by the style definition, which changes the font face to Verdana instead of the browser's default font face (typically a serif face such as Times New Roman).

Figure 2-2 shows the result of opening the page in a Web browser after these changes have been made.

Selecting Elements Using IDs and Classes

Another basic selection method is to use an id or class name to select elements. An id can only be attached to one element in a document, while a class can be applied to numerous elements to provide style information.

An id can be used if you know you need to select one particular element from the document, while a class can be used if you need to style more than one element (but can also be used on a single element if desired). In CSS, you select an id by preceding it with #, while

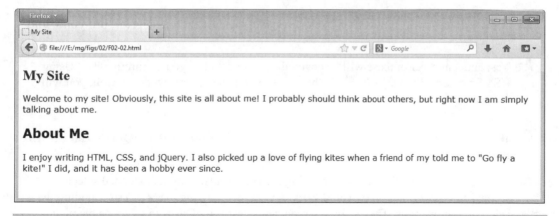

Figure 2-2   All text within all <div> elements uses the Verdana font.

a class name is preceded by a dot (.). For example, the following code shows both an id and a class name being selected:

```
#author-bio { font-size:0.8em; }  ◄──────────── An id is selected
.description { font-size:1em; }  ◄──────────── A class is selected
```

As an example of this, you can refer back to the *index.html* page you have been using. It contains two classes: *main* and *about-me*. If you decide that any text with a class of *main* should use the Verdana font, you could simply use the following code in your CSS file:

```
.main { font-family:Verdana; }
```

Now that you know how to perform basic selections in CSS, you can now learn how to select elements in jQuery and how to use more advanced CSS selectors.

Ask the Expert

Q: The CSS lesson did not cover much. Is there more to learn?

A: At this point, the most important thing you need to understand is how CSS is used to select one or more elements. The "CSS Basics" section is simply an overview of this process and does not replace a more thorough tutorial or book on CSS; however, it will help you get started with jQuery if you are not able to delve into it in more detail right now.

(continued)

Q: Aren't there more complex CSS selectors, like the descendant selector, nth-child, and others?

A: Yes, and a number of these will be covered in more detail as you go through the "Using CSS Selectors" section next. Since they are used for the jQuery syntax as well, you will only need to cover them once to use them in your jQuery scripts.

Q: If I want to use more advanced selectors in CSS code rather than jQuery, can I learn how?

A: Yes! jQuery uses CSS syntax for selecting elements (outside of the extended selectors), so the same selection syntax would work in CSS by removing the $(" ") surrounding the selector. For example, The use of a descendant selector in jQuery to select an element is shown here:

```
$("div p")
```

In CSS, the same selector can be used by simply removing the jQuery code around the selector, as shown in the following code:

```
div p
```

You can then add any style declarations after the selector to complete the CSS for that selection, as demonstrated in the following code:

```
div p { font-size:1.1em; }
```

If you decide you want to learn CSS itself in more detail, you can go to an online CSS tutorial or grab a book on CSS. Some resources are listed here if you want to pursue them:

- www.scripttheweb.com/css3/
- www.w3.org/Style/Examples/011/firstcss
- https://developer.mozilla.org/en-US/docs/Web/Guide/CSS/Getting_started
- *Beginning CSS: Cascading Style Sheets for Web Design* (Wrox, 2011)

Using CSS Selectors

Most of the selectors available in the CSS Level 3 Recommendation (www.w3.org/TR/css3-selectors/) are available for use in jQuery. This makes jQuery much easier to use than JavaScript for those who already are familiar with CSS syntax.

The official jQuery site lists all of its supported selectors at http://api.jquery.com/category/selectors/. Most of these are CSS selectors, but there are also a number of extended selectors available in jQuery that are not part of the CSS specification.

To begin, Table 2-1 lists the CSS selectors that can be used with the jQuery library. Extended selectors will be covered in the "Using Extended jQuery Selectors" section later in this chapter.

Name	Syntax	Description
All	*	Selects all of the elements in the document
Attribute Contains Prefix	[attribute-name|= 'value']	Selects all elements that have the attribute-name attribute where the value of the attribute is equal to the specified string *value* or begins with the specified string *value* followed immediately by a hyphen (-)
Attribute Contains	[attribute-name*= 'value']	Selects all elements that have the attribute-name attribute where the value of the attribute contains the specified *value*
Attribute Contains Word	[attribute-name~= 'value']	Selects all elements that have the attribute-name attribute where the value of the attribute contains the specified *value* as its own word (separated by spaces)
Attribute Ends With	[attribute-name$= 'value']	Selects all elements that have the attribute-name attribute where the value of the attribute ends with the specified *value*
Attribute Equals	[attribute-name= 'value']	Selects all elements that have the attribute-name attribute where the value of the attribute is equal to the specified *value*
Attribute Starts With	[attribute-name^= 'value']	Selects all elements that have the attribute-name attribute where the value of the attribute starts with the specified *value*
Checked	:checked	Selects all elements that are checked (checked check boxes and radio buttons)
Child	parent>child	Selects all elements that are child elements of the specified *parent* element
Class	.class-name	Selects all elements that have the specified *class-name*
Descendant	ancestor descendant	Selects all elements that are descendants of the specified *ancestor* element
Disabled	:disabled	Selects all disabled elements
Element	element-name	Selects all of the *element-name* elements in the document
Empty	:empty	Selects all elements that have no child nodes *(continued)*

Table 2-1   CSS Selectors

Name	Syntax	Description
Enabled	:enabled	Selects all enabled elements
First Child	:first-child	Selects all elements that are the first child of their parent node
First of Type	:first-of-type	Selects all elements that are the first sibling of the same element name
Focus	:focus	Selects the element that is currently in focus
Has Attribute	[attribute-name]	Selects all elements that have the attribute-name attribute
ID	#id	Selects the element with the specified *id*
Language	:lang	Selects all elements that use the specified language
Last Child	:last-child	Selects all elements that are the last child of their parent node
Last of Type	:last-of-type	Selects all elements that are the last sibling of the same element name
Multiple Attribute	[attribute-name= "value"] [attribute-name= "value"]	Selects all elements that match all of the attribute selections
Multiple	selector, selector	Selects all elements that match at least one of the specified selectors
Next Adjacent	prev + next	Selects all <next> elements that immediately follow the sibling <prev> element
Next Siblings	prev ~ siblings	Selects all elements that are next siblings
Not	:not()	Selects all elements that do not match the specified selector
Nth Child	:nth-child()	Selects all elements that are the nth child of their parent node
Nth Last Child	:nth-last-child	Selects all elements that are the nth child of their parent node, starting from the last element and going in reverse
Nth Last of Type	:nth-of-type()	Selects all elements that are the nth child of their parent node and are the same element name
Only Child	:only-child	Selects all elements that are the only child of their parent node
Only of Type	:only-of-type	Selects all elements that do not have sibling nodes of the same element name
Root	:root	Selects the root element of the document
Target	:target	Selects the specified target element

Table 2-1 CSS Selectors (*continued*)

Notably, there are numerous selectors from which you can choose. We will go over a number of the most used selectors in more detail here, but you can always make use of any of the others if the situation calls for it.

The All, Element, Class, and ID Selectors

The all, element, class, and id selectors provide some basic selections for you in jQuery (and CSS). For example, look at this code:

Adds the *special* class to *all* elements in the document

Adds the *special* class to all <div> elements in the document

```
$("*").addClass("special");
$("div").addClass("special");
$(".about-me").addClass("special");
$("#author-bio").addClass("special");
```

Adds the *special* class to all elements that have the *about-me* class

Adds the *special* class to the element with an id of *author-bio*

The most inclusive selector is the all selector, which selects all of the elements in the document, regardless of what they are or what class or id is used. This selector is not used often, since it does not select anything more specific—you will almost always want to select one element or a particular group of elements rather than every one of them.

The element selector simply selects all elements of the specified tag name. This means that $("div") will select all <div> elements, $("a") will select all <a> elements, and so on.

The class selector selects all elements that have the specified class name, regardless of the tag name. This means that $(".about-me") would select any of the elements shown in the following code:

```
<div class="about-me">content...</div>
<p class="about-me">content...</p>
<img class="about-me bio-image" src="me.jpg" alt="Me!">
```

Each element is different, but all of them have the *about-me* class. The <img> element has two classes, one of which is *about-me*. This will still be part of the selection, since it does indeed have the *about-me* class. As you get further into the selectors in this chapter, you will see how you can be more specific about which elements to select, rather than relying solely on an element or class name alone.

Finally, the id selector is used to select a single element in the document—the one with the specified id. Rather than selecting multiple elements like the others mentioned here, it very specifically selects a single element.

When you want to be sure only one element is selected for something, you can give it an id in your HTML code and select it using the id selector. Thus, $("#author-bio")

will select only the element whose id is *author-bio*. The following code shows an example for you:

This element will be selected

```
<div id="author-bio">I write for various Web sites.</div>
<div id="bio-link"><a href="http://www.mysite.com">My Site</a></div>
<p class="author-bio">More about me...</p>
```

These elements will not be selected

In this case, only the first <div> element will be selected. The second element is also a <div>, but does not have the correct id. The third element, even though it uses *author-bio* as a class name, will not be selected because it, too, does not have the correct id.

NOTE

Only one element can be assigned a given id. If more than one element uses the same id, then only one of them (typically the first one) will be recognized.

The Descendant Selector

One way to be more specific about which elements to select is through the use of the descendant selector. This can be used in conjunction with the element, class, and id selectors to find elements that *descend* from a particular selection.

As an example, consider the following HTML code snippet:

These <p> elements descend from both the <div> element and the *about-me* class

```
<div class="about-me">
  <p>I do many things, some of them are interesting.</p>
  <p>If you want to know more, contact me.</p>
</div>
<div class="share">
  <p>If you like my site, please share it with others!</p>
  <p>I will also recommend your site to others as well.</p>
</div>
```

These <p> elements descend from both the <div> element and the *share* class

Any element within another element is a descendant of the outer element. In this case, all of the <p> elements are descendants of <div> elements. For instance, the following code shows three different collections of <p> elements that can be selected using the descendant selector.

Selects all of the <p> elements that are within <div> elements (all four in this case)

```
$("div p")
$(".about-me p")
$(".share p")
```

Selects all <p> elements are within elements that have the *about-me* class (the first two in this case)

Selects all <p> elements that are within elements that have the *share* class (the last two in this case)

One thing you will need to watch when using the descendant selector is that it selects *all* descendants, regardless of nesting. This can lead to some unexpected results when dealing with nested lists, div elements, or other items. For example, consider the following HTML code:

```
<!DOCTYPE html>
<html>
<head>                                    A nested list
  <meta charset="utf-8">
  <title>My Site</title>
  <style type="text/css">
    ul {list-style-type:disc;}
    .items { list-style-type:square; }
  </style>
  <script src="jquery-1.9.1.min.js" type="text/javascript"></script>
  <script src="desc.js" type="text/javascript"></script>
</head>
<body>
<ul class="supplies">
  <li>Pencils</li>
  <li>Paper</li>
  <li>Books
    <ul>
      <li>Science Book</li>
      <li>History Book</li>
    </ul>
  </li>
</ul>
</body>
</html>
```

Save this file as *desc.html*. Notice that this list includes one nested list and a class named *items* within <style></style> tags that can be added to the list items using jQuery. You can use the descendant selector to add the class, as shown in the following code:

```
$(document).ready(function() {
  $(".supplies li").addClass("items");
});
```

Save this file as *desc.js* and then open *desc.html* in your browser. Figure 2-3 shows what this page will look like.

Notice that every list item uses a square marker, even the nested list items. This may be all you require, but you may decide later that you only want the items in the outer list to display the square marker. This can be done using the child selector, discussed next.

The Child Selector

The child selector selects all specified elements that are children of the given parent element. For example, review the code in your *desc.html* file. Suppose you want to select only the list

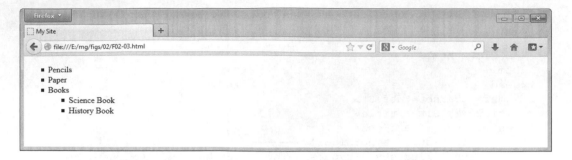

Figure 2-3 The descendant selector affects all of the list items.

items in the outer list and have them display a square marker. This can be done by changing your jQuery code in *desc.js* to the following:

```
$(document).ready(function() {
  $(".supplies").addClass("items");
});
```

Save the change to the *desc.js* file and then reload the *desc.html* file in your browser. Figure 2-4 shows the result of using the child selector on the list.

CAUTION

Some style rules, such as font colors, font weights, text decorations, and others, will still be inherited by the parent element's grandchildren, great-grandchildren, and so on even though the child selector is used. For more about this, see www.stackoverflow .com/questions/14789094/does-child-combinator-css-affects-sibling-elements.

The First Child, Last Child, and Nth Child Selectors

The first child, last child, and nth child selectors allow you to select particular elements based on their location within the parent element.

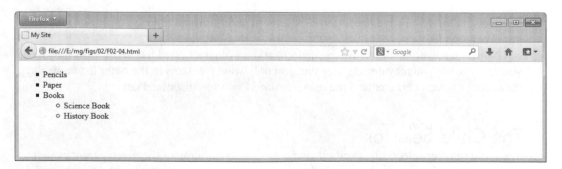

Figure 2-4 Using the child selector allows only the top-level list to use the square markers.

The first-child Selector

Going back to the *desc.html* file you have been using, notice that the <li> elements are all children of <ul> elements. The relevant portion of the HTML is displayed again in the following code:

```
<ul class="supplies">
  <li>Pencils</li>
  <li>Paper</li>
  <li>Books
    <ul>
       <li>Science Book</li>
       <li>History Book</li>
    </ul>
  </li>
</ul>
```

Suppose that you wanted any <li> element that is the first child of a <ul> element to have a square marker. In this case, that would select both the "Pencils" and "Science Book" list items, since they are first children of <ul> elements.

To make the selection, you can use the following code:

```
$("ul li:first-child")
```

Notice the colon between *li* and *first-child*. Basically, this selection tells jQuery to look for all <li> elements that descend from <ul> elements, but only if the <li> element is a first child of the <ul> element. With this in place, you can alter the code in your *desc.js* file as follows:

```
$(document).ready(function() {
  $("ul li:first-child").addClass("items");
});
```

Save these changes and reload the *desc.html* page in your browser. Figure 2-5 shows the result.

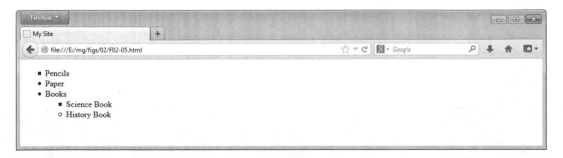

Figure 2-5 Only the first children of each unordered list are changed to have a square marker.

The last-child Selector

You can use the same process for last-child to select the last items in each list, which will be "Books" and "History Book" in this case. Simply change the selection to use last-child instead, as in the following code:

```
$("ul li:last-child").addClass("items");
```

The nth-child Selector

When using nth-child, you will need to supply an index number for the element you are seeking. This is done in parentheses at the end, as in the following code (which selects all <li> elements that are the second child of <ul> elements):

```
$("ul li:nth-child(2)")
```

In this case, you would be selecting the "Paper" and "History Book" list items. To see this in action, you can alter your *desc.js* file to use the following code:

```
$(document).ready(function() {
  $("ul li:nth-child(2)").addClass("items");
});
```

Figure 2-6 shows the result of reloading the page in your browser. Notice that the second item in each list uses the square list marker.

The Not Selector

The not selector allows you to select elements that do *not* match a selection. For example, consider the following HTML code:

```
<p class="cool">I am cool.</p>
<p>I don't feel very cool.</p>
<p class="uncool">Not cool.</p>
<p class="cool">Nice and cool here!</p>
<p class="cool">Very cool indeed!</p>
```

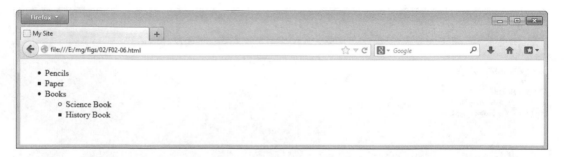

Figure 2-6 The use of nth-child allows the second item in each list to have a square marker.

Notice that several of the <p> elements have a class of *cool*. There are two other <p> elements that are not part of that class: One has no class and the other has a class of *uncool*.

While you can easily select any element with a class of *cool*, it may not be so easy to find the remaining elements and select them. The use of not allows you to select those elements easily. For example, to select all of the <p> elements that do not have a class of *cool*, you can use the following selection:

```
$("p:not(.cool)")
```

Notice that you provide a selection within the parentheses. In this case, it eliminates any <p> elements that do not have the *cool* class.

Attribute Selectors

Attribute selectors allow you to select elements based on the value of a particular attribute (or whether an element actually has the specified attribute). This gives you another helpful tool to select the elements you need.

The Has Attribute Selector

First, you can select elements that have a particular attribute. For example, you may want to select all <p> elements that have a class attribute. You could do this using the following code:

```
$("p[class]")
```

Consider the following HTML code:

```
<p class="blah">I have class!</p>
<p>I have no class.</p>
<p class="blah blah">I have plenty of class!</p>
```

Here, $("p[class]") would select the first and the last paragraph, but would leave out the second, since there is no class attribute.

You can combine this with other selectors as well. By combining it with the not selector, you could build a quick jQuery script to highlight images that are missing an alt attribute. First, you will need an HTML page, so use the following code and save the page as *noalt.html*:

```
<!DOCTYPE html>
<html>
<head>
  <meta charset="utf-8">
  <title>My Site</title>
  <style type="text/css">
     .needs-alt { border:5px solid #F00; }
  </style>
  <script src="jquery-1.9.1.js" type="text/javascript"></script>
  <script src="noalt.js" type="text/javascript"></script>
</head>
<body>
```

A class named *needs-alt* is defined, which will be added to any image missing an alt attribute

```
<p><img src="image1.jpg" width="100" alt="" /></p>
<p><img src="image2.jpg" width="100" alt="cool" /></p>
<p><img src="image3.jpg" width="100" /></p>
<p><img src="image4.jpg" width="100" alt="cool beans" /></p>
</body>
</html>
```

This <img> element has no alt attribute and needs to be highlighted

Next you will need to write your jQuery code. Use the following code and save the file as *noalt.js*:

```
$(document).ready(function() {
  $("img:not([alt])").addClass("needs-alt");
});
```

Here, *not* is applied to the <img> elements to determine which ones are missing alt attributes. Any of them that are found will have the *needs-alt* class applied to them, which will place a 5-pixel colored border around any images missing an alt attribute. In this case, the third image should be highlighted once the *noalt.html* page is opened in your browser. Figure 2-7 shows how this looks when run.

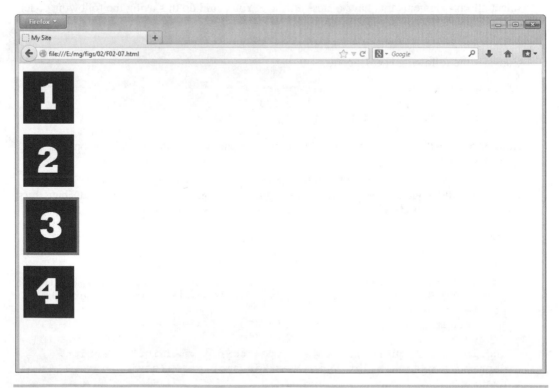

Figure 2-7 The highlighted image needs an alt attribute!

The Attribute Equals Selector

The attribute equals selector will select all elements that have the attribute and its value is equal to a specified value. For example, to select all <img> elements that have an alt attribute with a value of *cool*, you could use the following code for the $() function:

```
$("img[alt='cool']")
```

Notice that you need to use quote marks around the value of the attribute. Since you already have double quotes around the selection, you cannot place another set of double quotes inside of it. You either need to use single quotes (as in the code example) or escape the inner set of double quotes using a backslash (\).

When dealing with quotes, jQuery uses the same rules as JavaScript. If you have one set of quote marks within another set of quote marks, you need to alternate quote mark types (single quotes within double quotes, double quotes within single quotes) or escape the same quote mark type using the backslash character (which will be the only alternative if you have to go more than one level deep). In the case of this example, you can alternate the quote mark types as mentioned previously, or use the backslash to escape another set of double quotes, as shown in this code:

```
$("img[alt=\"cool\"]")
```
◀───── Notice the backslashes, which escape the inner set of quote marks

The attribute equals selector could be used with the code from the previous section (your *noalt.html* and *noalt.js* files), which had four images that needed alt attributes. Recall the original HTML code for the images, shown in the following code listing:

```
<p><img src="image1.jpg" width="100" alt="" /></p>
<p><img src="image2.jpg" width="100" alt="cool" /></p>
<p><img src="image3.jpg" width="100" /></p>
<p><img src="image4.jpg" width="100" alt="cool beans" /></p>
```

Since the last script located the image with no alt attribute (the third one), you can now fix it, as in the following code:

```
<p><img src="image1.jpg" width="100" alt="" /></p>
<p><img src="image2.jpg" width="100" alt="cool" /></p>
<p><img src="image3.jpg" width="100" alt="cool" /></p>
<p><img src="image4.jpg" width="100" alt="cool beans" /></p>
```

Suppose you now want to run a test to be sure that no images have a particular value for their alt attributes. You could change the code in your *noalt.js* file to the following:

```
$(document).ready(function() {
  $("img[alt='cool']").addClass("needs-alt");
});
```

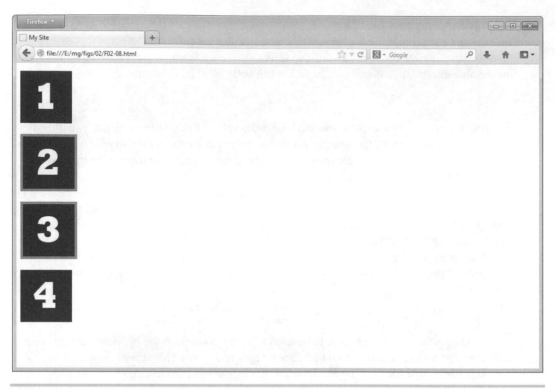

Figure 2-8 The second and third images have *cool* as the alternative text.

Save the changes and then reload the *noalt.html* file in your browser. Notice that it will now highlight the second and third images, which both have alt values of *cool*. You now know that you will need to change these values if you want to use more meaningful text. Figure 2-8 shows the results when run in a browser.

A script like this could save you quite a bit of time if you were to search a page with numerous images and wanted to eliminate generic alternative text such as "photo," "pic," "image," and so on.

The Remaining CSS Selectors

The other selectors mentioned in the table are also available, but will not be covered in detail here. As they come up for use in the book, however, they will be explained at that time.

This section gave an overview of the most used selectors for those who need to dive in quickly, but it is a good idea to study CSS in more detail as you have time in order to become more familiar with the other selectors and what they do.

Try This 2-1 Add Another Class

pr02-01.html
pr02-01.js

This project allows you to practice using jQuery CSS selectors to select items and add a class to the selected items.

Step by Step

1. Place the following HTML code into your editor and save the file as *pr02-01.html*:

```
<!DOCTYPE html>
<html>
<head>
  <meta charset="utf-8">
  <title>Project 2-1</title>
  <style type="text/css">
    .intro { font-style:italic; color:#AA0000; }
      .main { font-family:Arial; }
      .end { font-family:monospace; }
  </style>
  <script src="jquery-1.9.1.js" type="text/javascript"></script>
  <script src="pr02-01.js" type="text/javascript"></script>
</head>
<body>
<p class="main-text">I am the first paragraph! Howdy!</p>
<p class="main-text">I am the second paragraph. I just sit here
under the first one.</p>
<p class="end-text">I am the third and last paragraph on this page!
</p>
</body>
</html>
```

2. In the *pr02-01.js* file, add jQuery code that will add the *intro* class to the first <p> element within the <body> element.

3. Add the *main* class to any element in the document that has the *main-text* class.

4. Add the *end* class to any element that has the *end-text* class.

5. Save the file. When complete, the code should look like this:

```
$(document).ready(function() {
  $("body p:first-child").addClass("intro");
  $(".main-text").addClass("main");
  $(".end-text").addClass("end");
});
```

(continued)

6. Open the *pr02-01.html* file in your Web browser. You should see the first paragraph displaying in italic, Arial font. The second should display in an Arial font without italics. The last paragraph should display in a monospace font.

Try This Summary

In this project, you added classes to selected elements using the jQuery $() function and CSS selectors to select those elements. You were able to practice your selection techniques using the first-child and class selectors.

Using Extended jQuery Selectors

In addition to standard CSS selectors, jQuery offers its own extensions in order to provide additional methods for you to easily select elements. Table 2-2 lists the jQuery extended selectors.

Name	Syntax	Description
Animated	:animated	Selects all of the elements in the document that are currently animated
Attribute Not Equal	[attribute-name!= 'value']	Selects all elements that have the attribute-name attribute where the value of the attribute is not equal to the specified *value*
Button	:button	Selects all of the button elements (both button elements and input elements of the button type)
Check Box	:checkbox	Selects all check boxes
Contains	:contains()	Selects all elements that contain the text specified
Element at Index	:eq()	Selects the element at the specified index (zero-based) from a collection of elements
Even	:even	Selects all even elements from a collection of elements (zero-based index)
File	:file	Selects all file elements
First	:first	Selects the first element from a collection of elements
Elements at Index Greater Than	:gt()	Selects all elements at an index greater than the specified index (zero-based)

Table 2-2 Extended jQuery Selectors

Name	Syntax	Description
Has	:has()	Selects all elements that contain one or more matches for the specified selector
Header	:header	Selects all heading elements (h1, h2, h3, and so on)
Hidden	:hidden	Selects all hidden elements
Image	:image	Selects all image elements
Input	:input	Selects all input elements (includes input, textarea, select, and button)
Last	:last	Selects the last element from a collection of elements
Elements at Index Less Than	:lt()	Selects all elements at an index less than the specified index (zero-based)
Odd	:odd	Selects all odd elements from a collection of elements (zero-based index)
Parent	:parent	Selects all elements that contain one or more child nodes
Password	:password	Selects all password elements
Radio	:radio	Selects all radio elements
Reset	:reset	Selects all reset elements
Selected	:selected	Selects all elements that are selected (from a select list)
Submit	:submit	Selects all submit elements
Text	:text	Selects all text elements
Visible	:visible	Selects all visible elements

Table 2-2   Extended jQuery Selectors (*continued*)

You will now look at some of these in more detail to see how they can assist you in making selections in jQuery.

The Attribute Not Equal Selector

The attribute not equal selector provides you with a way to perform the opposite action of the CSS attribute equals selector: It will select all elements that have the attribute but where the value is *not* equal to the specified value.

In the example *noalt.html* and *noalt.js* files you have been using, you could use this selector to select any elements where the value of the alt attribute is not equal to *cool*. Recall the images in the HTML, which are shown in the following code:

```
<p><img src="image1.jpg" width="100" alt="" /></p>
<p><img src="image2.jpg" width="100" alt="cool" /></p>
<p><img src="image3.jpg" width="100" alt="cool" /></p>
<p><img src="image4.jpg" width="100" alt="cool beans" /></p>
```

Change your *noalt.js* file to use the following code:

```
$(document).ready(function() {
  $("img[alt!='cool']").addClass("needs-alt");
});
```

Save your changes and reload the HTML file in your browser. It should now highlight the first and fourth images, which do not have *cool* as the alternative text. Figure 2-9 shows the results of this script.

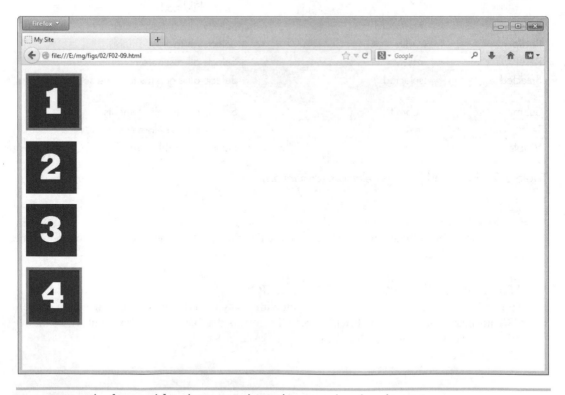

Figure 2-9 The first and fourth images do not have *cool* as the alternative text.

The First, Last, and Element at Index Selectors

The first, last, and element at index selectors allow you to select a single element from a collection. This can be useful, for instance, when you simply want the first <li> element within a <ul> element rather than including all of the first children of all of its inner <ul> elements as well.

You will be using your *desc.html* and *desc.js* files from earlier in this chapter to look at how these selectors work. For reference, here is the relevant HTML code from the page:

```
<ul class="supplies">
  <li>Pencils</li>
  <li>Paper</li>
  <li>Books
    <ul>
      <li>Science Book</li>
      <li>History Book</li>
    </ul>
  </li>
</ul>
```

Recall also that the CSS code included a class named *items*, which would make any selected list item use a square marker. You will alter the *desc.js* file as necessary in the examples in order to use the selectors.

The first Selector

The first selector will select the first element that matches a selection, based on the order the elements appear in the HTML code. For example, if you want to select the first list item from the supplies list in your *desc.html* file, alter your *desc.js* file to use the following code:

```
$(document).ready(function() {
  $(".supplies li:first").addClass("items");
});
```

Rather than selecting all the first children the way the first-child selector does, first simply selects the first one—and that's it. Figure 2-10 shows the result of this script when run in a

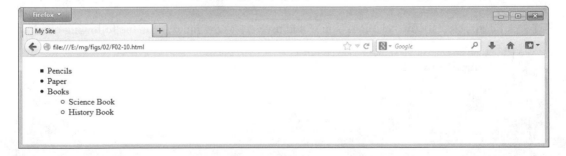

Figure 2-10 Only the first element is affected when using the first selector.

browser. Notice that only the first list item ("Pencils" in this case) displays with the square list item marker.

The last Selector

The last selector will select the last element that matches a selection. For example, you can alter your *desc.js* file to use the following code:

```
$(document).ready(function() {
  $(".supplies li:last").addClass("items");
});
```

Save the updates and then reload *desc.html* in your Web browser. The last list item ("History Book") will use the square marker. Notice that this element is within a child <ul>, but is still the last <li> element within the selected list and thus is the element that is selected when using last.

The Element at Index Selector

The element at index selector selects the element at a specified index within the matched elements. For example, suppose you want to select the second element from the supplies list ("Paper"). You can do this by changing your *desc.js* files to use the following code:

The second element is selected with the index 1 rather than 2!

```
$(document).ready(function() {
  $(".supplies li:eq(1)").addClass("items"); ◄
});
```

Notice that the syntax is eq(*n*), where *n* is the index of the element you want to select. However, this selector uses a zero-based index, meaning that it starts counting from zero rather than one. As a result, you will need to remember to specify the index number as one *less* than expected (if you are familiar with JavaScript arrays, this works the same way since they also use a zero-based index). Here, the second matched element is selected by specifying 1 as the index.

So, to select the first element, you would use zero as the index, as in the following code:

```
$(document).ready(function() {
  $(".supplies li:eq(0)").addClass("items"); ◄
});
```

This selects the first matching <li> element

The Even and Odd Selectors

The even and odd selectors allow you to select either the even-numbered items or odd-numbered items within a collection of matched elements. Often, this is used for structures such as tables, where you may want to change the background color on every other row to make it easier to read. For example, consider the following code:

```
<!DOCTYPE html>
<html>
<head>
  <meta charset="utf-8">
  <title>My Site</title>
  <style type="text/css">
    .emp-alt { background-color:#DDD; }  ◄——— This class will be added to every
  </style>                                      other row in the table
  <script src="jquery-1.9.1.js" type="text/javascript"></script>
  <script src="pr02-02.js" type="text/javascript"></script>
</head>
<body>
<table class="employees">
<tr>
  <th>Name</th>
  <th>ID</th>
</tr>
<tr>
  <td>John</td>
  <td>12345</td>
</tr>
<tr>
  <td>James</td>
  <td>12346</td>
</tr>
<tr>
  <td>Heather</td>
  <td>12347</td>
</tr>
<tr>
  <td>Jerry</td>
  <td>12348</td>
</tr>
</table>
</body>
</html>
```

This creates a simple table to display employee names and id numbers. To make it easier to read, you could use the even selector to add the *emp-alt* class to each even row of the table. Note, however, that this uses a zero-based index, so the first row of the table will be row zero, and thus even.

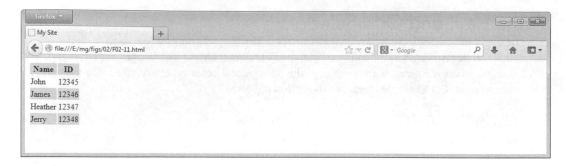

Figure 2-11 The table uses alternating row colors to make it easier to read.

The following code will add the class to the even rows:

```
$(document).ready(function() {
  $(".employees tr:even").addClass("emp-alt");
});
```

This will make the first (index 0), third (index 2), and fifth (index 4) rows display with a light gray background, while the others continue to use the default background color. Figure 2-11 shows how this will look when viewed in a browser.

Try This 2-2 More Selection Practice

```
pr02-02.html
pr02-02.js
```

This project allows you to practice selecting elements using the extended jQuery selectors in combination with CSS selectors so that you can create a data table with a unique heading row and alternate the color of each data row.

Step by Step

1. Insert the following HTML code into your editor and save the file as *pr02-02.html*:

```
<html>
<head>
  <meta charset="utf-8">
  <title>Project 2-1</title>
  <style type="text/css">
    .emp-head { background-color:#005; color:#FFF; }
    .emp-alt { background-color:#DDD; }
  </style>
  <script src="jquery-1.9.1.min.js" type="text/javascript"></script>
  <script src="pr02-02.js" type="text/javascript"></script>
```

```
  </head>
  <body>
  <table class="employees">
  <tr>
    <th>Name</th>
    <th>ID</th>
  </tr>
  <tr>
    <td>John</td>
    <td>12345</td>
  </tr>
  <tr>
    <td>James</td>
    <td>12346</td>
  </tr>
  <tr>
    <td>Heather</td>
    <td>12347</td>
  </tr>
  <tr>
    <td>Jerry</td>
    <td>12348</td>
  </tr>
  </table>
  </body>
  </html>
```

2. In the *pr02-02.js* file, add jQuery code that will add the *emp-head* class to the first table row element.

3. For every other row after the first, add the *emp-alt* class using the even selector. Hint: You can use the not selector to keep the first row from being affected.

4. Save the file. When complete, the code should look like this:

```
$(document).ready(function() {
  $(".employees tr:first").addClass("emp-head");
  $(".employees tr:even:not(tr:first)").addClass("emp-alt");
});
```

5. Open the *pr02-02.html* file in your Web browser. You should see the table display with a dark blue background and white text on the header row, and every other row after that should display with a light gray background.

(continued)

Try This Summary

In this project, you used your knowledge of CSS and extended selectors to style a data table to be easier to read and have a unique header row. This allowed you to combine your skills from the CSS selectors and extended selectors sections in this chapter.

Chapter 2 Self Test

1. The $() function returns a jQuery _____, which points to all of the selected elements.

2. In CSS, what encloses style definitions?

 A. Square braces []

 B. Curly braces { }

 C. Quotation marks ""

 D. Text editors

3. What is the # character used for in CSS?

 A. It selects elements by id.

 B. It selects elements by class name.

 C. It separates rules and definitions.

 D. It is not used at all.

4. The * selector will select _____ elements in a document.

 A. h1

 B. div

 C. all

 D. p

5. Using a tag name in the $() function will select all elements of that type.

 A. True

 B. False

6. Which of the following properly selects all elements that have a class named *more* in a document and adds the *even-more* class to them?

    A. $(".more").addClass("even");

    B. $(".even-more").addClass("more");

    C. $(".more").addClass("even-more");

    D. $("#more").addClass("even-more");

7. *$("#mydivs")* will select all <div> elements in a document.

    A. True

    B. False

8. Which of the following would properly select all <p> elements within a <div> element?

    A. $("div p")

    B. $("p div")

    C. $("div.p")

    D. $("div#p")

9. The _____ symbol is used to select all children of a specified parent element.

    A. <

    B. >

    C. ,

    D. |

10. Which of the following properly selects all <p> elements that do not have the *about-me* class?

    A. $("about-me:NOT(p)")

    B. $("p:not(me)")

    C. $("not about-me")

    D. $("p:not(.about-me)")

11. Which of the following would select all <img> elements that have an alt attribute?

    A. $(p[alt])

    B. $("img[alt]")

    C. $("p|alt")

    D. $(p:alt)

12. If you want to find all elements that have a particular value for an attribute, you can use the _____ selector.

    A. attribute equals

    B. attribute is

    C. attribute not equal

    D. attribute value is

13. Using :even will select all even elements within a collection, using a one-based index.

    A. True

    B. False

14. Using :last will select the last element in a collection.

    A. True

    B. False

15. The _____ selector selects the nth element within a collection using a zero-based index.

    A. element at spot

    B. element at index

    C. indexOf

    D. array

Chapter 3

Event Handling

Key Skills & Concepts

- Waiting for the Document to Be Ready
- Handling an Event
- jQuery Events
- Triggering Events

Events are a fundamental aspect of creating dynamic and responsive scripts. Typically, an event occurs when a user performs some type of action such as a mouse click, key press, or form submission. Some events can also be triggered by calling them programmatically, which can be helpful when you need to perform a task automatically.

The jQuery library offers a number of features that make handling events an easier task than when using JavaScript, especially when it comes to handling browser differences. Rather than worrying about using *addEventListener()*, *attachEvent()*, and DOM Level 0 event handlers based on the capabilities of different browsers, you can use something as simple as *click()* or *keydown()* to handle an event, and jQuery will do the rest of the work for you.

Waiting for the Document to Be Ready

As you will remember from previous chapters, jQuery offers you the *ready()* function so that you can be sure that all the elements in the document are loaded before running jQuery code on them. This is certainly important when you are reacting to a user event, since you do not want the user to receive JavaScript errors when interacting with your Web site or application.

ready() vs. load()

In JavaScript, you will see a number of scripts use the *load* event on the window object to determine when all the elements have been completely loaded. For example, you may see something similar to the following code:

```
window.onload = function() {
  // Code to execute when elements have loaded
}
```

Alternatively, you might see a more modernized version, using the *addEventListener()* function, as in the following code:

```
window.addEventListener("load", function() {
  // Code to execute when elements have loaded
}, false);
```

Notice the similarity to using *ready()* in jQuery, shown in the following code:

```
$(document).ready(function() {
    // Code to execute when elements have loaded
});
```

What Is the Difference?

There is an important difference between the two methods. The *ready()* method allows you to begin running your script as soon as all of the elements have been loaded, but it does not wait for images or other media to finish loading. The JavaScript *load* event waits for the document and all media to be loaded before it is triggered.

Many scripts can be run without worrying about whether images or other media have loaded, which allows *ready()* to give you access to the elements in the document more quickly than the *load* event. This gives the users a better experience when media isn't essential to the script, allowing them to more quickly interact with your Web site or application.

On the other hand, when running a script that works with images (such as a slideshow), using *ready()* could cause unexpected results. If the script needs to show an image that has not yet loaded, it could show a broken image or nothing at all. In cases like this, it is better to wait for the load event to ensure that all of the media has been loaded before being manipulated.

When you need to wait for the *load* event, jQuery provides you its own *load* method, which does the cross-browser work for you. The following code uses the jQuery *load* function:

```
$(window).load(function () {
    // Code to execute when elements and media have loaded
});
```

Throughout the remainder of the book, you will see *ready()* used for most scripts, while the *load* method will be used when necessary to wait for other media to load.

Using the $ Argument with ready()

The *ready()* method also performs one more helpful task for you. Suppose you are using jQuery as well as another JavaScript library (such as prototype) that uses the $ identifier to shorten the code. Rather than replacing all instances of $ with jQuery, you can call *jQuery(document).ready()* and include all of your jQuery code within the *ready()* method and send $ as an argument, as in the following code:

```
jQuery(document).ready(function($) {
    // Code to execute. $ can be used as expected in here.
});
```

This allows the other library to use the $ identifier and allows you to use it with your jQuery code. One problem can still exist, though.

When using more than one library that uses the $ identifier, the last one included in the HTML code will take control of it, making $ buggy or unusable for the other libraries. In addition to sending the $ argument to ready, jQuery provides the *noConflict( )* method to ensure that it does not take control of the $ identifier.

Suppose you had the following code in the head section of your HTML document:

The prototype library is included, and controls the $ identifier

```
<script type="text/javascript" src="prototype.js"></script>
<script type="text/javascript" src="jquery-1.9.1.min.js"></script>
<script type="text/javascript" src="yourcode.js"></script>
```

Your own JavaScript file, which now cannot use $ with both libraries

The jQuery library is included, and takes control of the $ identifier from prototype!

Notice that prototype will initially control the $ identifier, but this is quickly taken away on the next line by the inclusion of jQuery. To fix this, you can use jQuery's *noConflict( )* method, as in the following code:

```
<script type="text/javascript" src="prototype.js"></script>
<script type="text/javascript" src="jquery-1.9.1.min.js"></script>
<script type="text/javascript">
jQuery.noConflict();
</script>
<script type="text/javascript" src="yourcode.js"></script>
```

Calling the *noConflict()* method immediately after jQuery is loaded will give control of the $ identifier back to the prototype library

This will now allow $ to be used by prototype. As an added bonus, you can still use $ with your jQuery code by sending the *ready( )* method the $ argument, as described previously!

NOTE
You can call the *noConflict()* method in your own JavaScript file (*yourcode.js* in this case) if you prefer; just be sure to place it on the first line of your code.

Now that you know when to begin reacting to events, it's time to learn how to handle those events.

Handling an Event

The jQuery library provides several methods for handling events. For the most common events, jQuery has its own shorthand functions to make it easy to react to a user event. Other events can be added using the *on( )* method, which will be discussed later in this chapter. First, you will look at basic event handling using one of the jQuery shorthand functions.

Basic Event Handling

Suppose you need to perform an action when the user clicks an element. jQuery provides the *click()* method to handle this event. For example, if you had an element with an id of *change-size*, you could use the following code:

```
$("#change-size").click(function() {
  // Code to execute when element is clicked
});
```

The *click()* method calls a function that will be run when the event occurs. The code within the function will then execute and react to the *click* event.

Since this script will not require media to be loaded, you can place everything inside of the *ready()* function, as in the following code:

```
$(document).ready(function() {
   $("#change-size").click(function() {
      // Code to execute when element is clicked
   });
});
```

The *ready()* function surrounds all of the code to be executed

The *click* event is handled with the inner function

Using the click Event

Now that you have seen the basic syntax, you can apply it to a Web page to react to a *click* event. Place the following HTML code into a file and save it as *size.html*:

```
<!DOCTYPE html>
<html>
<head>
   <meta charset="utf-8">
   <title>Project 2-1</title>
   <style type="text/css">
      .large-font { font-size:1.5em; }
   </style>
   <script src="jquery-1.9.1.min.js" type="text/javascript"></script>
   <script src="size.js" type="text/javascript"></script>
</head>
<body>
<div id="change-size">
This text is important! Click this text to enlarge it if needed!
</div>
</body>
</html>
```

This <div> element will have a class added to it when it is clicked

Next, place the following code into a file and save it as *size.js*:

```
$(document).ready(function() {
    $("#change-size").click(function() {
        $("#change-size").addClass("large-font");
    });
});
```

The click() method calls a function to handle click events on the #change-size element

A class is added to the #change-size element when it is clicked, which in this case will enlarge the font size

Open the *size.html* file in your browser and click the text. It will become larger when clicked, since a class is added to make the font size larger in the function that handles the event. Figure 3-1 shows how the initial page looks in the browser, and Figure 3-2 shows how the page looks after the text is clicked.

While this script works, it isn't very obvious that the font size can be enlarged. The user would need to know to click the text itself to enlarge it. To improve usability, it would be helpful to have the user click a different element that tells the user what it does, such as a button.

Update the Click Script

To update the script, you will need to alter both the HTML code and the jQuery code. First, change the HTML within the <body></body> tags of the *size.html* page to the following code and save the file:

```
<div id="change-size">
This text is important! Click this text to enlarge it if needed!
</div>
<div>
  <form action="size-larger.html">
    <button id="enlarge">Enlarge Text</button>
  </form>
</div>
```

A form button is added so that the user can click it to enlarge the font

Figure 3-1   The initial page

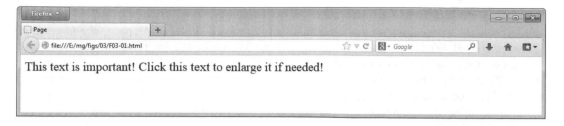

Figure 3-2   The page after the text has been clicked, displaying a larger font size

A form with a button labeled "Enlarge Text" is added, giving the user a clear action to take to enlarge the text.

Notice that it is within a form and that the action attribute of the form is pointed to an alternate HTML page that would have enlarged text. This is a fallback for accessibility in case the user does not have JavaScript enabled: The user will still be able to view the enlarged text since the browser will go to that alternate page.

NOTE
There are a number of ways to make the script accessible; this just demonstrates one option. Other possibilities include the use of a server-side script as the action of the form, hiding the button for those without JavaScript (if the functionality is considered an enhancement rather than a necessity), and other options.

To make the button change the font size, you will need to alter the jQuery script. Change the *size.js* file to use the following code and save it:

> The element that handles the click is changed from the *#change-size* <div> element to the *#enlarge* <button> element

```
$(document).ready(function() {
  $("#enlarge").click(function() {
    $("#change-size").addClass("large-font");
  });
});
```

> The *#change-size* <div> element is still the one that will have the *large-font* class added to it

Notice that the only change is that the *click()* function is now attached to the <button> element (with the id of *enlarge*) rather than the <div> element, which contains the text to enlarge.

Open the *size.html* file in your browser and click the button. The text changes size, but the browser goes to the alternate page (maybe even more quickly than the change occurs)! This is not quite the desired result, and will require a couple of alterations in order to fix it.

Fixing the Updated Click Script

The action attribute specified that the button should go to a second HTML page (*size-larger.html*) when clicked. While this is a good feature for those without JavaScript, it certainly is not what you want it to do for those who have JavaScript enabled.

To fix this, you will need to send the *Event* object to the *click* function as an argument. The *Event* object contains information about the event that occurred, and has a method of its own called *preventDefault()* that can prevent the default action from occurring when the specified event occurs. The *Event* object will be discussed in more detail in Chapter 7, but you can make use of some basics to fix this script.

First, you need to send the *Event* object as an argument to the function that will handle the *click* event. In JavaScript, you simply place arguments within the parentheses () that follow the *function* keyword, and the same is true for jQuery. The following code shows how the function called in the *click* method can be altered to pass along the *Event* object:

```
$("#enlarge").click(function(event) {
```

Notice that *event* is simply placed within the parentheses. Since it is already a defined object, it does not need quote marks around it as a string argument would.

The next thing you will need to do is use the *preventDefault()* method of the *Event* object within the function handling the *click* event. This is shown in this code:

```
$(document).ready(function() {
  $("#enlarge").click(function(event) {
    event.preventDefault();  ◄─────────
    $("#change-size").addClass("large-font");
  });
});
```

This statement prevents the default action from occurring (which would take the user to the alternate HTML page) and allows the user to remain on the current page

Save the updates and then reload the *size.html* file in your browser. With the *event.preventDefault();* statement in place, you will now be able to enlarge the text without leaving the current page.

Figure 3-3 shows the initial page, and Figure 3-4 shows the page after the button is clicked. The text is enlarged and the browser does not redirect you anywhere else.

Now that you know how to handle an event, you can begin learning the other jQuery events.

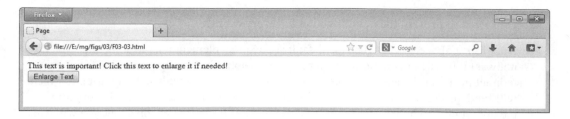

Figure 3-3   The initial page, before the button is clicked

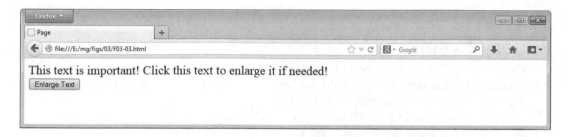

Figure 3-4   The page after the button is clicked

Ask the Expert

Q: Do all events have a shorthand method?

A: Most of them do, but there are a few events that do not. They can be utilized by using the *on()* method, which will be covered later in this chapter. The events that have shorthand methods will be covered in the next section.

Q: Do I need to learn how to do all of this in JavaScript first?

A: No, jQuery handles all of the JavaScript code behind the scenes for you. In the case of handling events, the JavaScript code can get quite long when you want to support the number of browsers that jQuery does. If you are selecting elements using something besides an id, that can add work in JavaScript, as you will need to loop through elements, check for matches, and return the matching elements—all of which the jQuery selectors do for you automatically.

(continued)

Q: **Do I need to prevent the default action for every event?**

A: No, this is only necessary when the default action of an element will do something you do not want it to, such as <button> or <input type= "submit"> (that may submit a form and redirect the user). Another example would be the <a> element with an href attribute, which will send the user to another page or a different location on the same page. These give you the opportunity to provide fallbacks for those without JavaScript enabled, but you will want to prevent the default action for those who are able to run the script.

jQuery Events

The jQuery library offers support for JavaScript events both through shorthand methods and through the use of the *on()* method. As you have seen, the shorthand methods are very handy and make it easy to bind an event to an element.

You can now learn what each event is and when it will occur while a user is interacting with your Web page or application. First, you will learn the events that have shorthand methods available; then you will learn the remaining events and how to use *on()* to bind them to elements.

To begin, Table 3-1 lists the events in jQuery that have shorthand syntax.

These events are discussed in more detail in the following sections.

Mouse Events

Mouse events allow you to react to actions the user can take with the mouse, such as clicking or moving the mouse over a certain element on the page. Many scripts make use of one or more of these events to interact with users.

The click and dblclick Events

You have already been using the *click()* method for *click* events, so it will be no surprise that *dblclick()* does the same thing for double-click events.

A double-click occurs when the mouse button is pressed and released twice within a certain period of time. The time allowed between the two clicks depends on the system, but is typically a short amount of time such as a half-second. Users can override this on most systems to a timing that is more comfortable for them (whether longer or shorter).

An example of the *dblclick()* method is shown in the following code:

```
$("#my-element").dblclick(function() {
  // Code to execute when #my-element is clicked
});
```

The code within the handling function will run when the element is double-clicked.

Name	Syntax	Description
Blur	.blur()	Occurs when an element loses focus
Change	.change()	Occurs when the value of an <input>, <textarea>, or <select> element is changed
Click	.click()	Occurs when the mouse pointer is over an element and the mouse button is clicked and released
Double-click	.dblclick()	Occurs when the mouse pointer is over an element and the mouse button is clicked and released twice
Error	.error()	Occurs when there is an error loading certain types of elements, such as <img>
Focus	.focus()	Occurs when an element receives focus
Focus in	.focusin()	Occurs when an element or any of its child elements receives focus
Focus out	.focusout()	Occurs when an element or any of its child elements loses focus
Key down	.keydown()	Occurs when a key is pressed
Key press	.keypress()	Occurs when a key is pressed and released
Key up	.keyup()	Occurs when a key is released after being pressed
Load	.load()	Occurs when an element and all of its child elements have loaded
Mouse down	.mousedown()	Occurs when the mouse pointer is over an element and the mouse button is pressed
Mouse enter	.mouseenter()	Occurs when the mouse pointer enters an element
Mouse leave	.mouseleave()	Occurs when the mouse pointer leaves an element
Mouse move	.mousemove()	Occurs when the mouse pointer moves inside of an element
Mouse out	.mouseout()	Occurs when the mouse pointer leaves an element
Mouse over	.mouseover()	Occurs when the mouse pointer enters an element
Mouse up	.mouseup()	Occurs when the mouse pointer is over an element and the mouse button is released after being pressed
Resize	.resize()	Occurs when the browser window is resized
Scroll	.scroll()	Occurs when a user scrolls within an element
Select	.select()	Occurs when the user makes a selection within an element
Submit	.submit()	Occurs when the user requests that a form be submitted
Unload	.unload()	Occurs when the user leaves the current page

Table 3-1   Events with Shorthand Methods

The mousedown and mouseup Events

The *mousedown* and *mouseup* events each make up a portion of the *click* event. These events are helpful if you need to capture a particular part of a mouse click. For example, *mousedown* can be used to help determine that the user has begun dragging an item rather than clicking it.

Here is a breakdown of a mouse click:

1. Mouse button is pressed. Triggers the *mousedown* event.

2. Mouse button is released. Triggers the *mouseup* event.

3. Mouse button has been both pressed and released. Triggers the *click* event.

This shows the order in which each event is triggered, which can help you when you need to know what event to react to in various situations.

These shorthand methods are shown in the following code:

```
$("#my-element").mousedown(function() {
  // Code to execute on mousedown
});
$("#my-element").mouseup(function() {
  // Code to execute on mouseup
});
```

The mouseover and mouseout Events

The *mouseover* and *mouseout* events occur when the user moves the mouse into an element or moves the mouse out of an element. Due to the way these events are passed on to other elements that can also handle them, it is usually preferable to use *mouseenter* and *mouseleave*, which are discussed next. The reasoning for this will be discussed in the "Event Capturing and Bubbling" section later in this chapter.

Examples of these shorthand methods are shown in the following code:

```
$("#my-element").mouseover(function() {
  // Code to execute on mouseover
});
$("#my-element").mouseout(function() {
  // Code to execute on mouseout
});
```

The mouseenter and mouseleave Events

The *mouseenter* and *mouseleave* events occur when the user moves the mouse into an element or moves the mouse out of an element. The selected element will always be the one to handle the event, so these methods are recommended over *mouseover* and *mouseout*.

These shorthand methods are shown in the following example code:

```
$("#my-element").mouseenter(function() {
  // Code to execute on mouseenter
});
$("#my-element").mouseleave(function() {
  // Code to execute on mouseleave
});
```

Another shorthand provided by jQuery is the *hover()* method, which can be used to provide event handlers for the *mouseenter* and *mouseleave* events in one single method. An example is shown in the following code:

```
$("#my-element").hover(
  function () {
    // Code to execute on mouseenter
  },
  function () {
    // Code to execute on mouseleave
  }
);
```

This function is executed when the *mouseenter* event occurs

This function is executed when the *mouseleave* event occurs

Notice the comma between the two functions, which separates them as arguments within the *hover()* method.

The mousemove Event

The *mousemove* event occurs when the user has the mouse pointer over an element and moves it. This event will continue to occur as long as the mouse pointer is moving while within the element. Once the mouse pointer leaves the element, the event will stop until the mouse pointer moves back onto the element.

An example of the shorthand method is shown in the following code:

```
$("#my-element").mousemove(function() {
  // Code to execute on mousemove
});
```

Keyboard Events

Keyboard events are triggered when the user presses or releases a key on the keyboard. These will be discussed in more detail in Chapter 7, but here is an overview of each of these events.

The keydown and keyup Events

The *keydown* and *keyup* events occur when the user presses or releases a key on the keyboard. The shorthand methods are shown in the example code that follows.

```
$("#my-element").keydown(function() {
  // Code to execute on keydown
});
$("#my-element").keyup(function() {
  // Code to execute on keyup
});
```

The keypress Event

The *keypress* event occurs after the user has both pressed and released a key on the keyboard. The shorthand method is shown in the following code:

```
$("#my-element").keypress(function() {
  // Code to execute on keypress
});
```

You will learn more about this event and how to capture specific keys in Chapter 7.

Other Events

The remaining events use the same shortcut syntax, and many of them will be covered as example scripts are written throughout the book. A number of them can be used with form elements, while others are related to the window or to other elements in the document.

For now, take a look at how event capturing and bubbling work.

Event Capturing and Bubbling

When an event occurs, there are two phases: capturing and bubbling. These are used when several elements could register the event, and is typically the result of nested elements, such as in the following code (place this code in a file and save it as *bubble.html*):

```
<!DOCTYPE HTML>
<html>
<head>
<title>Example</title>
<style>
#outer { border:1px solid #000; background-color:#00FF33; padding:20px; }
#middle { border:1px solid #000; background-color:#0000FF; padding:10px; }
#inner { border:1px solid #000; background-color:#FFFFFF; padding:5px; }
</style>
<script src="jquery-1.9.1.min.js" type="text/javascript"></script>
<script src="bubble.js" type="text/javascript"></script>
<body>
   <div id="outer">
     <p id="middle">
       <a id="inner" href="page.html">Show Message</a>
     </p>
   </div>
```

Each of these elements can handle an event such as *mouseout*

```
    <div id="text"></div>
</body>
</html>
```

In a case like this, the <a>, <p>, and <div> elements can all register a common event such as *mouseout*. The last <div> element (*#text*) is not affected if an event is added to any of the other elements, since it is outside of that nesting.

In the capturing phase, an event will be sent to the least specific element that can handle it and then passed on to each level until it reaches the most specific element that can handle it (in the case going from <div> to <p> to <a>). In the bubbling phase, an event will be sent to the most specific element that can handle it and then passed on to each level until it reaches the least specific element that can handle it (in this case going from <a> to <p> to <div>).

JavaScript allows you to specify one phase or the other to handle events, but browsers (especially older ones) may not follow this, instead using the default phase of that browser. To help eliminate confusion, jQuery always uses the bubbling phase when registering events, which makes event handling consistent across browsers.

Scripting a mouseout

The only other issue occurs when using methods such as *mouseover()* or *mouseout()*, which do not stop the bubbling from continuing. This means that if you register a *mouseout* event to the <div> element in the example code, the bubbling will cause the event to be registered with the <a> element first, since it is the most specific element that *could* handle the event. It will then register the same event handler to the <p> and then to the <div> element for which it was originally intended.

To see what happens, place the following jQuery code into a file and save it as *bubble.js*:

```
$(document).ready(function() {
  $("#outer").mouseout(function() {
      $("#text").append("Mouseout!<br>");
  });
});
```

Open the *bubble.html* file in your browser and move the mouse in and out of the three elements (which are colored and surrounded by borders to help visualize what is happening). You will notice that each time you move your mouse pointer out of *any* of the elements, a new message is added to the last <div> element (*#text*). This is probably not the functionality you were looking for. Most likely, you would prefer this only to happen when the mouse pointer leaves the originally intended element, which was the top <div> element (*#outer*). Figure 3-5 shows the initial page, while Figure 3-6 shows the page after several *mouseout* events have occurred.

NOTE

The *append()* function in jQuery will add content to an element after any content already in place. You will learn more about this method as you progress.

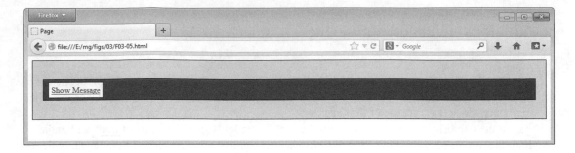

Figure 3-5 The page before any *mouseout* events

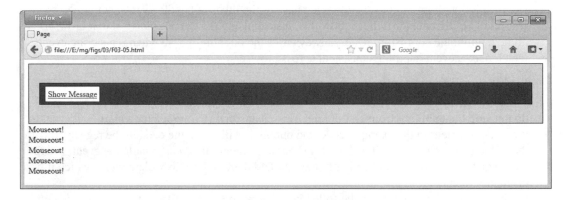

Figure 3-6 The page after several *mouseout* events have been fired

Obtaining the Desired Behavior with mouseleave

Fortunately, jQuery provides the *mouseleave()* method, which does not continue bubbling, but will instead handle the event only on the intended element. For example, update your *bubble.js* file to use the following code and save it:

```
$(document).ready(function() {
  $("#outer").mouseleave(function() {
      $("#text").append("Mouseout!<br>");
  });
});
```

Reload the *bubble.html* page in your browser and try moving the mouse out of the three <div> elements again. This time, the message should only appear when you move the mouse pointer out of the outer <div> element. Figure 3-7 shows the page after one *mouseout* event occurs on the outer <div> element.

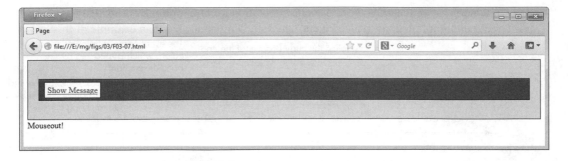

Figure 3-7 Even if you move the mouse pointer over the inner <div> elements, only a single *mouseout* event will occur on the outer <div> element.

Using the on() Method to Handle Events

The *on()* method is relatively new to jQuery. This method was introduced in jQuery 1.7 to supersede other methods of binding event handlers to elements: *bind()*, *delegate()*, and *live()*.

You will very commonly see these used in scripts, especially those written for versions of jQuery before 1.7, so you will need to be familiar with them should you need to update or debug a script that uses them.

The bind() Method

The *bind()* method is used to bind an event handler to an element that currently exists. This means that any element using *bind()* must already exist—this method does not keep track of the possibility of the element being added programmatically later, something *delegate()* can do.

An example of using the *bind()* method is shown in the following code:

```
$("#my-element").bind("click", function() {
  // Code to execute when #my-element is clicked
});
```

While the shorthand *click()* method takes only the handling function as an argument, the *bind()* method takes two arguments: the event name and the function to handle the event.

You can further customize it by having it use the same handler function for two different events, as in the following code:

```
$("#my-element").bind("click keydown", function() {
  // Code to execute when #my-element is clicked or a key is pressed
down
});
```

This code would execute the function when the mouse button is clicked on the element or when the user presses a key while within that element.

In jQuery 1.4 and later, you can use object notation to bind multiple events that use different handling functions to an element. The following code shows an example of this:

Notice the curly bracket at the end of this line, which begins an object

The event name is followed by a colon, which is followed by the handler function

This curly bracket ends the click handler function, followed by a comma indicating another event is to follow

```
$("#my-element").bind({
  click: function() {
    // Code to execute when #my-element is clicked
  },
  keydown: function() {
    // Code to execute when a key is pressed within #my-element
  }
});
```

This provides the function for the *keydown* event

In JavaScript, structures such as functions and objects can be passed as arguments. This structure passes an object using *object literal notation*, which allows you to define a list of properties and values. Here, the properties are event names and the values are handler functions. You will learn more about JavaScript structures that are used within jQuery in Chapter 5.

Finally, if you want to remove an event handler from an element, you can use the *unbind()* method. If you want to unbind *all* events from an element, you can simply call the *unbind()* method on the element, as in the following code:

```
$("#my-element").unbind();
```

If you want to remove one event type but keep others, you can specify the type of event to remove by passing it as an argument, as in the following code:

```
$("#my-element").unbind("click");
```

This will remove all *click* event handlers from the element. If you need to remove specific *click* event handlers, you will need to namespace them. This will be discussed in later in this chapter when you learn the *on()* method.

The delegate() Method

The *delegate()* method allows you to bind an event handler to any element, even if it won't exist until later due to being added through programming. It uses a selector to get any parent elements, and then another selector is passed for the child elements that exist or will be added. Most commonly, this would occur with a table, where you may need to add rows later based on information supplied by the user.

The following code shows an example of the *delegate()* method:

```
$("#my-table").delegate("td", "click", function() {
  // Code to run when a <td> element is clicked
});
```

This will assign the handler function to react to all *click* events on all <td> elements within the table, whether they exist already or get added to the document later.

You can remove handlers defined using *delegate()* by using *undelegate()*. This works much like *unbind()*, as shown in the following code:

```
$("#my-table").undelegate();          ◄──────────  Undelegates all event handlers
$("#my-table").undelegate("click");   ◄──────  Undelegates all click event handlers
```

This method is called *delegate* because it delegates the event handling from the specified element to the selected element using event bubbling. Consider the following code:

```
$("#my-table tr").delegate("td", "click", function() {
    // Code to run when a <td> element is clicked
});
```

Here, the <td> that is passed as the first argument assigns the handling of the *click* event to the <tr> element surrounding it. All <td> elements within the selection (the *#my-table* <tr> elements in this case) will delegate the *click* event to the <tr> element surrounding it.

By delegating the event to its outer element, all of the <td> elements can use the handling function for the *click* event, even if they are added to the document later.

The live() Method

The *live()* method works much like the *delegate()* method, but uses a slower method by attaching events at the document element. The jQuery API documentation recommends using *on()* or *delegate()* in its place.

If you need further information on *live()*, see http://api.jquery.com/live/.

The on() Method

The *on()* method combines the *bind()* and *delegate()* methods, allowing you to use a single method whether you wish to use current and/or future elements. The difference is in whether an argument is present to tell jQuery to delegate the handler to a particular element.

Using on() to Bind an Event Handler   You can use *on()* in the same way as *bind()* by simply calling it, as in the following code:

```
$("#my-element").on("click", function() {
    // Code to execute when #my-element is clicked
});
```

In the same fashion as *bind( )*, you can use it to bind multiple events to elements, as in the following code:

```
$("#my-element").on({
  click: function() {
    // Code to execute when #my-element is clicked
  },
  keydown: function() {
    // Code to execute when a key is pressed within #my-element
  }
});
```

Using on() to Delegate an Event Handler   To use *on( )* for event delegation, you simply add an argument to the *on( )* method, as in the following code:

```
$("#my-table tr").on("click", "td", function() {
  // Code to run when a <td> element is clicked
});
```

Here, you pass an argument after the event name, which determines which elements will delegate the event to the selected element(s). In this case, any <td> element will delegate the *click* event to the <tr> element surrounding it.

Using off() to Unbind or Undelegate an Event Handler   As with *unbind( )* and *undelegate( )*, you can use *off( )* to remove an event handler from an element that added the handler using *on( )*.

To remove all event handlers from an element, you can use the following code:

```
$("#my-element").off();
```

If you want to remove one event type, you can use the following code:

```
$("#my-element").off("click");
```

Finally, if you want to remove a delegated event, you can use the following code:

```
$("#my-table tr").off("click", "td");
```

This example will remove the *click* event delegated from the <td> elements to their surrounding <tr> elements within *#my-table*.

Other Events

In addition to the events with shorthand methods available, there are other events that can be called using *on( )* and the event name. These are listed in Table 3-2.

Event	Description
contextmenu	Occurs when the user activates the context menu
copy	Occurs when the user activates the copy command
cut	Occurs when the user activates the cut command
mousewheel	Occurs when the user rolls the mouse wheel
paste	Occurs when the user activates the paste command
reset	Occurs when the user resets a form

Table 3-2 Other Events

These are JavaScript events for which jQuery has no defined shorthand function. These events tend to be used less often than the others, but can be used in most modern browsers by providing the event name in the *on()* method.

For example, to assign an event handler to the *reset* event, you could use the following code:

```
$("#my-form").on("reset", function() {
  // Code to execute when #my-form is reset
});
```

Since the *reset* event is tied to a <form> element, this example code would execute when the form with an id of *#my-form* is reset by the user.

Try This 3-1   Add Event Handlers

pr03-01.html
pr03-01.js

This project allows you to practice using jQuery event methods by adding an event handler using a shorthand method and another one using the *on()* method.

Step by Step

1. Place the following HTML code into your editor and save the file as *pr03-01.html*:

```
<!DOCTYPE html>
<html>
<head>
  <meta charset="utf-8">
  <title>Project 2-1</title>
  <style type="text/css">
```

(continued)

```
    .bold-font { font-weight:bold; }
  </style>
  <script src="jquery-1.9.1.min.js" type="text/javascript"></script>
  <script src="pr03-01.js" type="text/javascript"></script>
</head>
<body>
<div id="imp-text">
This text is important! Click the button to make it bold if needed!
</div>
<div>
  <form action="bolder.html">
    <button id="make-bold">Make Text Bold</button>
  </form>
</div>
<div id="message"></div>
<div>
  <form action="message.html">
    <button id="show-msg">Show Message</button>
  </form>
</div>
</body>
</html>
```

2. In the *pr03-01.js* file, add jQuery code that will add the *bold-font* class to the first <div> element when the first <button> element is clicked. Use the shorthand *click()* method. Make sure to prevent the default action from occurring.

3. Add jQuery code that will append the text "Hi, hope you liked the important text!" to the *#message* <div> element when the *#show-msg* <button> element is clicked. Use the *on()* method. Make sure to prevent the default action from occurring.

4. Save the file. When complete, it should look like this code:

```
$(document).ready(function() {
  $("#make-bold").click(function(event) {
    event.preventDefault();
    $("#imp-text").addClass("bold-font");
  });
  $("#show-msg").on("click", function(event) {
    event.preventDefault();
    $("#message").append("Hi, hope you liked the important text!");
  });
});
```

5. Open the *pr03-01.html* file in your Web browser. Click the first button and the important text should become bold. Click the second button and the "Hi, hope you liked the important text!" message should be inserted above the clicked button.

Try This Summary

In this project, you practiced adding event handlers to elements by using jQuery shorthand methods and the *on( )* method. Also, you practiced passing the *Event* object to the handling function and preventing the default event from occurring.

Triggering Events

Sometimes it is helpful to be able to simulate an event occurring without the user needing to perform the action.

jQuery provides the *trigger( )* method to allow you to trigger an event without the user performing the actual event. An example of this method is shown in this code:

```
$("#my-element").trigger("click");
```

This will cause the *click* event to fire on the *#my-element* element. Any event handlers for the *click* event that are attached to the element will be executed. For example, consider the following code (save as *trigger.js*):

```
$(document).ready(function() {
  $("#show-msg").click(function(event) {
    event.preventDefault();
    $("#message").append("Hi, here is a message!<br>");
  });
  $("#sim-show-msg").mouseenter(function() {
    $("#show-msg").trigger("click");
  });
});
```

A *click* event handler is applied to the *#show-msg* element, which will append a message to the *#message* element

The *#sim-show-msg* element has a *mouseenter* event attached to it

The *click* event is triggered without the user clicking the *#show-msg* element!

Here, a *click* event handler is assigned to the *#show-msg* element, which will display a message. A *mouseenter* event handler is applied to another element (*#sim-show-msg*), which uses the *trigger( )* method to trigger the *click* event on the *#show-msg* element.

Using the following HTML code with this jQuery code will allow you to see this in action. Save the HTML file as *trigger.html* and the JavaScript file as *trigger.js*.

```
<!DOCTYPE html>
<html>
<head>
  <meta charset="utf-8">
  <title>Example</title>
  <style type="text/css">
    #sim-show-msg { border:1px solid #000; width:50%; }
  </style>
```

```
    <script src="jquery-1.9.1.min.js" type="text/javascript"></script>
    <script src="trigger.js" type="text/javascript"></script>
</head>
<body>
<div id="sim-show-msg">Move the mouse pointer here to avoid
clicking!</div>
<div id="message"></div>
<div>
  <form action="message.html">
    <button id="show-msg">Show Message</button>
  </form>
</div>
</body>
</html>
```

Open the *trigger.html* file in your Web browser. Move the mouse pointer over the bordered
<div> element or click the button to show the message. Each time you perform either action,
the message will be appended to the *#message* element again. Figure 3-8 shows the initial
page, and Figure 3-9 shows the page after one of the actions has been performed.

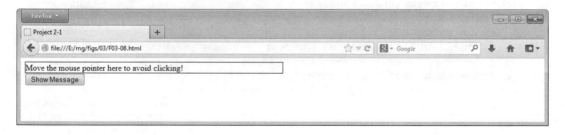

Figure 3-8 The initial page

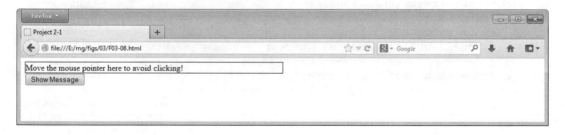

Figure 3-9 The page after the mouse pointer moves over the bordered <div> element or the
button is clicked

Try This 3-2 **Trigger Practice**

pr03-02.html
pr03-02.js

This project allows you to practice firing an event without the user performing that particular event. You will use the *trigger()* method to accomplish this.

Step by Step

1. Insert the following HTML code into your editor and save the file as *pr03-02.html*:

```
<!DOCTYPE html>
<html>
<head>
  <meta charset="utf-8">
  <title>Project 2-1</title>
  <style type="text/css">
    .bold-text { font-weight:bold; }
    #sim-make-bold { border:1px solid #000; width:50%; }
  </style>
  <script src="jquery-1.9.1.min.js" type="text/javascript"></script>
  <script src="pr03-02.js" type="text/javascript"></script>
</head>
<body>
<div id="sim-make-bold">Move the mouse pointer here to avoid
clicking!</div>
<div id="imp-text">This is important! Really it is!</div>
<div>
  <form action="bolder.html">
    <button id="make-bold">Show Message</button>
  </form>
</div>
</body>
</html>
```

2. In the *pr03-02.js* file, add jQuery code that will make the text in the *#imp-text* element bold when the user clicks the *#make-bold* <button> element.

3. Add code to trigger the *click* event of the *#make-bold* <button> element when the user's mouse pointer enters the *#sim-make-bold* element.

4. Save the file. When complete, the code should look like this:

```
$(document).ready(function() {
  $("#make-bold").click(function(event) {
    event.preventDefault();
```

(continued)

```
      $("#imp-text").addClass("bold-text");
   });
   $("#sim-make-bold").mouseenter(function() {
     $("#make-bold").trigger("click");
   });
});
```

5. Open the *pr03-02.html* file in your Web browser. Either moving the mouse pointer over the bordered <div> element or clicking the button will make the text bold. Refresh the page to try the other action if desired.

Try This Summary

In this project, you used your knowledge of the *trigger()* method to trigger an event without the user performing that particular event. This required an event handler for the actual event, which was then triggered using the *trigger()* method.

Chapter 3 Self Test

1. The *ready()* method allows you to begin running your script as soon as all of the elements have been loaded, but it does not wait for _____ or other media to finish loading.

2. When you need to wait for the load event, jQuery provides you its own _____ method, which does the cross-browser work for you.

   A. onload

   B. readyState

   C. load

   D. done

3. In addition to sending the $ argument to *ready()*, jQuery provides the _____ method to ensure that it does not take control of the $ identifier.

   A. doNotControl$

   B. noConflict()

   C. avoidConflict()

   D. no$

4. jQuery provides the shorthand _____ method to handle the *click* event.

    A. onclick()

    B. mouseclick()

    C. squeak()

    D. click()

5. The *Event* object has a method named *preventEvent( )* that can be used to prevent the default event from occurring on an element.

    A. True

    B. False

6. Which of the following properly sends the *Event* object as an argument to the *click( )* method?

    A. $("#my-element").click(function(event) {

    B. $("#my-element").clicked(function(e) {

    C. $("#my-element").mousedown(function(event) {

    D. $("#my-element").click(function[event] {

7. The *blur* event occurs when an element loses focus.

    A. True

    B. False

8. Which of the following events occurs when a key on the keyboard is pressed and released?

    A. keydown

    B. keypress

    C. blur

    D. mousedown

9. The _____ and _____ events occur when the user moves the mouse pointer over and out of an element, and also these events do not bubble.

    A. mouseon, mouseoff

    B. mouseover, mouseout

    C. mousein, mouseexit

    D. mouseenter, mouseleave

10. When using the _____ method to attach an event handler to an element, the element must already exist.

    A. bind()

    B. delegate()

    C. addEvent()

    D. live()

11. The _____ method combines the *bind()* and *delegate()* methods, allowing you to use a single method whether you wish to use current and/or future elements.

    A. bindDelegate()

    B. deleBind()

    C. attach()

    D. on()

12. The _____ method can be used to remove event handlers from elements that used *on()* to add the handlers.

    A. remove()

    B. unbind()

    C. off()

    D. delete()

13. jQuery has shorthand methods for every possible JavaScript event.

    A. True

    B. False

14. The *hover()* method is a shorthand method for combining mouseover and mouseout handlers into one function.

    A. True

    B. False

15. The _____ method allows you to simulate a user event.

    A. trigger()

    B. sim()

    C. fire()

    D. go()

Chapter 4

Working with Styles

Key Skills & Concepts

- CSS Rules
- The *css()* Method
- Class Methods
- Size and Position Methods

Cascading Style Sheets (CSS) plays a major role in Web page design, and jQuery allows you to work with its syntax in numerous ways to meet your scripting goals. You have already seen how the $() function allows you to select elements using CSS selectors. In addition to this, jQuery offers a number of methods that give you the ability to get the values of CSS properties or to alter those properties.

In this chapter, you will learn how to use the *css()* method, class methods, and size and position methods to retrieve or update CSS property values. To begin, you will look at how CSS rules are defined, which will help you understand what the jQuery methods are meant to do.

CSS Rules

As you have seen previously, CSS allows you to select elements by using element names, classes, ids, and other types of selectors. When working with CSS code, you define the selector and then define a rule within a set of curly brackets ({}). A rule consists of one or more property and value pairs, with each pair separated by a semicolon. For example, the following code shows how a typical style sheet definition looks in CSS code:

```
selector { property: value; property: value; }
```

As you can see, you will have a property name, a colon, and a property value. If more than one property is defined, you add a semicolon after each set of property/value pairs and repeat the process.

These properties and values are what jQuery will allow you to retrieve or alter in your scripts. Keep in mind, however, that you can make use of any CSS properties in jQuery, even if they are not specifically defined in CSS code or in a style attribute. As a result, you can obtain or alter any CSS property values as you need to in your script.

The css() Method

The jQuery library offers the *css()* method, which allows you to obtain values or make alterations on the fly. As you will recall, the use of *addClass()* requires that the class to be added already exists in the CSS code. This is not the case with the *css()* method; it allows you to make changes to specific properties without the need to define what the values will be in your CSS code beforehand.

The *css()* method, like the other jQuery CSS methods you will learn, allows you to call it in two different ways. One way will get values and one will set values. In the case of the *css()* method, calling it with one string or array literal argument will get values, and calling it with two string arguments or with an object literal argument will set values.

Getting Values

If you simply want to get one property value, you can call the *css()* method using the property name as the argument, as shown in the following code:

```
var eColor = $("#my-element").css("color");
```

In this example, the method will return the value of the *color* property for the element with an id of *my-element*. In order to make use of the value, the returned result is assigned to a JavaScript variable named *eColor*.

NOTE

When getting property values, you are not able to use shorthand properties. For example, if you need to get the padding on all sides of an element, you will have to use all four padding properties (*padding-top, padding-right, padding-bottom*, and *padding-left*) rather than the shorthand *padding* property.

To use the value, you could append it to an element to display it on the page, as in the following code:

```
var eColor = $("#my-element").css("color");    ◄──── The value of the color property
$("#other-element").append(eColor);  ◄──┐        for #my-element is assigned to a
                                                  variable named eColor
```

The value is written on the page by adding the text to *#other-element*. Notice that since *eColor* is a variable name, it does not need to be within quote marks

This code both assigns a value to a JavaScript variable and uses the variable value. When using the value of a variable, you do not need to enclose it in quote marks.

CAUTION

Different browsers can return different strings for the value of a property. For example, the color value for black could be returned as #000000, rgb(0,0,0), or another string. A plugin such as jQuery Color can help you get a consistent value if you need to compare colors. You will learn about installing and using plugins in Chapter 10.

Should you need to obtain multiple values, you can use an array literal as the argument, as in the following code:

```
var eColor = $("#my-element").css(["color", "background-color"]);
```

This will return an array instead of a string. In this case, *eColor* will be assigned an array, allowing you to access the *color* value using *eColor[0]* and the *background-color* value using *eColor[1]*.

NOTE
If the selection in the $() function matches more than one element, only the property value for the first matched element will be returned.

If you are unfamiliar with JavaScript variables, arrays, and other items, do not fear! They will be explained in more detail in Chapter 5. In the meantime, they will be used in a straightforward fashion as seen in the previous examples.

Setting Values
The *css()* function also allows you to set the values of properties for any selected elements. This can be useful when you don't have access to the CSS code or simply need to quickly change one or more property values on the fly.

Setting a Single Property Value
If you want to set a single property value, you send the *css()* method two arguments: the property name and the value to be set. For example, to set the *color* property to *#FF0000*, you would use the following code:

```
$("#my-element").css("color", "#FF0000");
```

When setting a color, you can use any valid CSS value. In the case of the color red, values such as *#FF0000*, *#F00*, *red*, *rgb(100%, 0%, 0%)*, and *rgb(255,0,0)* are all valid ways of setting a value to red.

Also, hyphenated property names can be written in CSS or JavaScript syntax. For example, the *background-color* property in CSS is represented as *backgroundColor* in JavaScript (the hyphen is removed and the next letter is capitalized). This same pattern holds for all hyphenated properties: *margin-left* to *marginLeft*, *border-right-width* to *borderRightWidth*, and so on.

If you use the JavaScript syntax, quote marks are optional around the property name. As a result, each line of jQuery in the following code would set the background color of the element to red:

```
$("#my-element").css("background-color", "#FF0000");   ◄——  CSS syntax
$("#my-element").css("backgroundColor", "#FF0000");    ◄——  JavaScript syntax with quotes
$("#my-element").css(backgroundColor, "#FF0000");      ◄——  JavaScript syntax without quotes
```

To be consistent, it is best to choose one convention and use it throughout your code. This will make it easier to edit or debug later if needed. In this book, I will use the CSS syntax for property names, but feel free to use one of the others should you feel more comfortable, or if required (a coding convention where you are employed, for example).

NOTE
If the selection in the $() function matches more than one element, the specified property will be set for *all* matched elements in the selection.

Setting Multiple Property Values
If you want to set multiple property values at once, you can send a single argument to the *css()* method in the form of an object literal. An object literal encloses property names and values within curly brackets ({}).

The general format for object literal notation looks like the following code:

```
{ property: value, property: value }
```

Notice that each property/value pair is separated by a comma. Each property and its corresponding value are separated by a colon. The entire set of property/value pairs is enclosed within curly brackets.

To use this with the *css()* method, you simply send an object literal as the argument. Suppose you want to change the *color* property to white and the *background-color* property to black. You could use the following code:

```
$("#my-element").css({"color": "#FFFFFF", "background-color":
"#000000"});
```

For readability (especially when the list becomes long), you may wish to place each property/value pair on its own line, as in the following code:

```
                                    The opening curly bracket        The first property/value pair
                                    is on this line
$("#my-element").css({  ◄─────────┘
  "color": "#FFFFFF",  ◄
  "background-color": "#000000"  ◄─────────  The second property/value pair
});  ◄─────────────────────────────┐
              The ending curly bracket and the
              end of the css() method call
```

In this format, you can quickly scan each property/value entry reading downward, which can be helpful when you need to find something within an extensive list!

Using Relative Values
jQuery 1.6 and higher allows you to use values beginning with += or −= to set relative values (setting the value incrementally higher or lower than its current value) for properties that are based on numeric values, such as *width*, *height*, *font-size*, and so on.

The value that is passed with += or −= will be interpreted by jQuery in pixels. Since you may not always know the current pixel value of *width*, *height,* and other such properties (the element may have its width defined with a percentage or other type of value), this allows you to increment the pixel value rather than guess whether passing a certain pixel value will make a property value larger or smaller.

For example, suppose you have the following HTML code (save it as *expand.html*):

```
<!DOCTYPE html>
<html>
<head>
  <meta charset="utf-8">
  <title>Expand</title>
  <style type="text/css">
    #expandable { width:20%; border:solid 1px #000; }
  </style>
  <script src="jquery-1.9.1.min.js" type="text/javascript"></script>
  <script src="expand.js" type="text/javascript"></script>
</head>
<body>
  <div id="expandable">
  This div can expand! Click the button below to add more width!</div>
  <div>
    <form action="expanded.html">
      <button id="expand">Make Wider</button>
    </form>
  </div>
</body>
</html>
```

As you learned in the last chapter, you can assign a *click* event to the button element and then perform your work. The following code shows how you can use *css()* to widen the *expandable* <div> element by 50 pixels each time the button is clicked (save it as *expand.js*):

```
$(document).ready(function() {
  $("#expand").click(function(event) {
    event.preventDefault();
    $("#expandable").css("width", "+=50em");
  });
});
```

Open the *expand.html* file in your browser and click the button. Each time you click, the width of the <div> element will increase, giving the text more room to expand on the same line.

You can do this with multiple property values as well. As you will recall, you can set multiple property values using object literal notation. So, if you want to set the left padding to expand along with the width, you could edit your JavaScript file to use the following code:

```
$(document).ready(function() {
  $("#expand").click(function(event) {
```

```
      event.preventDefault();
      $("#expandable").css({
          "width": "+=50",
          "padding-left": "+=10"
      });
   });
});
```

Two different properties are incremented using object literal notation

Save the *expand.js* file and reload *expand.html* in your browser. When you click the button, the <div> element will expand and there will be additional padding to the left of the content. Figure 4-1 shows the initial page, and Figure 4-2 shows the page after the button is clicked once.

NOTE
When setting incremental values, you are not able to use shorthand properties. For example, if you need to set the padding on all sides of an element, you will have to use all four padding properties (*padding-top, padding-right, padding-bottom*, and *padding-left*) rather than the shorthand *padding* property.

Figure 4-1 The initial page

Figure 4-2 The page after clicking the button once

Using Functions to Set Values

jQuery versions 1.4 and higher allow you to set the return value of a function as the property value. This can be helpful if you need to perform additional steps or calculations to determine what the value of the property should be.

An example is shown in this code:

The function begins here

```
$("#my-element").css("width", function() {
    var newWidth;                      A variable is defined
    // Perform calculations...         Calculations to alter the value of the
    return newWidth;                   variable can be performed here
});
```

The value of the variable is returned, which will set it as the property value in the *css()* method

Ask the Expert

Q: **Does using *css()* replace the use of *addClass()*?**

A: It can, but whether it needs to depends on your situation. If you don't have access to the CSS code of a page, need to quickly add styles that don't fit an existing class to an element created via scripting, or just need to test something quickly and add a class to the CSS code later, then the *css()* function is a very handy tool to have at your disposal. It is definitely useful for any on-the-fly changes that may need to be made to an element. Your choice of *css()* or *addClass()* will depend on what you need to accomplish at the time.

Q: **What is with all the array and object talk? Do I need to know advanced JavaScript to use jQuery after all?**

A: No, advanced JavaScript knowledge is not required, but a general understanding of some of the basic language elements is useful when using jQuery methods. To assist you, the elements of JavaScript that will help you with jQuery coding (such as variables, functions, arrays, and objects) will be discussed in the next chapter.

Q: **Are there other methods I can use to set property values?**

A: jQuery offers the *width()* and *height()* methods for getting or setting the *width* and *height* properties of an element. The other properties can be set using the *css()* method or by adding, removing, or toggling the classes assigned to an element (class methods will be discussed in the next section).

In this case, a variable named *newWidth* is defined, calculations are performed, and the value of the *newWidth* variable is returned, which will set it as the value of the *width* property for the selected element.

This can be a handy way to calculate or determine a new value for a property. In the next chapter, you will learn some JavaScript tips that will assist you with making calculations or using different values based on certain conditions.

Class Methods

The jQuery library offers four methods that can assist you when you need to work with classes, allowing you to add, remove, and toggle classes, or to see if an element has a particular class. If you have access to the CSS file for a page, you can use the classes you create to make CSS alterations easy by using any of the class methods.

The addClass() and removeClass() Methods

You have been using *addClass()* already to add classes to elements. The *removeClass()* method, in contrast, removes a class from an element.

Suppose you had the following HTML code (save as *remove.html*):

```
<!DOCTYPE html>
<html>
<head>
  <meta charset="utf-8">
  <title>Remove</title>
  <style type="text/css">
    .unread { font-weight:bold; font-style:italic; }
  </style>
  <script src="jquery-1.9.1.min.js" type="text/javascript"></script>
  <script src="remove.js" type="text/javascript"></script>
</head>
<body>
  <div id="imp-msg" class="unread">This message is important!
Really!</div>
  <div>
    <form action="msg-read.html">
      <button id="read">Mark Read</button>
    </form>
  </div>
</body>
</html>
```

You will notice that there is an "important" message being displayed, along with a button that allows you to mark it as read. When the page is loaded, the *imp-msg* <div> will have the class *unread* attached to it, which makes the text bold and italic.

Clicking the button would allow you to mark the message as "read." In this case, removing the *unread* class from the <div> element would take off the bold and italic styles, making the text appear without any additional styling.

To remove the class, you can use the *removeClass()* method, as in the following code (save as *remove.js*):

```
$(document).ready(function() {
  $("#read").click(function(event) {
    event.preventDefault();
    $("#imp-msg").removeClass("unread");
  });
});
```

The *removeClass()* method will remove the *unread* class from the *imp-msg* <div> element

Open the *remove.html* file in your browser. When you click the button, the message should have the bold and italics that were included in the *unread* class removed. Figure 4-3 shows the initial page, and Figure 4-4 shows the page after the button is clicked.

NOTE
While this will remove the class now, refreshing the page will cause the message to be "unread" again. Saving a change like this requires some server-side code in addition to this. These types of coding techniques will be discussed in more detail in Chapter 9.

Remove Multiple Classes
Just like *addClass()*, the *removeClass()* method can be used to remove multiple classes or all classes from selected elements. Separating multiple class names with spaces will remove each

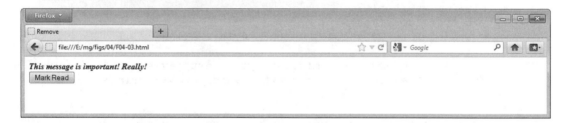

Figure 4-3　The initial page

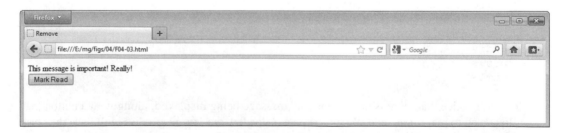

Figure 4-4　The page after the button is clicked

of those classes, while calling the method without an argument will remove all classes. The
following code shows an example of both of these:

Removes *one-class* and *another-*
class from the selected element

```
$("#my-element").removeClass("one-class another-class");  ←─────┘
$("#my-element").removeClass();  ←─────── Removes all classes from the selected element
```

Combine addClass() and removeClass() by Chaining

jQuery supports method *chaining*, which allows you to place methods one after another to
act on selected elements. For example, you could chain the *addClass()* and *removeClass()*
methods to a selection to perform both operations without the need to write the code in two
separate statements.

Consider the following code:

```
$("#my-element").removeClass("one-class");
$("#my-element").addClass("another-class");
```

The first statement will remove *one-class* from *my-element*, and the second statement
will add *another-class* to the same element. These two statements are performed one after
another.

Instead of writing two separate statements and making the same selection twice, you can
chain the two methods together in a single statement, as in the following code:

```
$("#my-element").removeClass("one-class").addClass("another-class");
```

Here, the same effect is achieved with a single statement, and *my-element* does not need to
be selected a second time. Keep in mind, however, that *my-element* will need to be selected
again if you need to do something with it later when the new action won't immediately
follow the current statement.

The toggleClass() Method

The *toggleClass()* method allows you to switch between adding and removing one or more
classes each time the method is applied to a particular selection.

Toggle a Single Class

To toggle a single class, simply send the class name as an argument to *toggleClass()*, as in the
following code:

```
$("#my-element").toggleClass("one-class");
```

In this case, if *my-element* has *one-class*, then it will be removed; if *my-element* does not have
one-class, then it will be added.

You could use this to provide a simple toggle to the user, such as switching the font size of an element back and forth. Suppose you had the following HTML code (save as *toggle.html*):

```
<!DOCTYPE html>
<html>
<head>
  <meta charset="utf-8">
  <title>Toggle</title>
  <style type="text/css">
    .larger { font-size:2em; }
    .imp-text { font-style:italic; }
  </style>
  <script src="jquery-1.9.1.min.js" type="text/javascript"></script>
  <script src="toggle.js" type="text/javascript"></script>
</head>
<body>
  <div id="imp-msg" class="imp-text">This message is important!
Really!</div>
  <div>
    <form action="enlarge.html">
      <button id="tog-font">Toggle Font</button>
    </form>
  </div>
</body>
</html>
```

Here, the *imp-msg* element has a class already applied to it (*imp-text*) to make the text italic. A class named *larger* is available in the CSS code, which can be toggled on the element to allow the user to switch the font to a larger size and back to the original size as needed.

The following code will toggle the *larger* class on the *imp-msg* <div> element when the *tog-font* button is clicked (save as *toggle.js*):

```
$(document).ready(function() {
  $("#tog-font").click(function(event) {
    event.preventDefault();
    $("#imp-msg").toggleClass("larger");
  });
});
```

When the button is clicked the first time, the *larger* class will be added. When it is clicked again, the *larger* class will be removed. Each time the button is clicked, the *larger* class will be added or removed depending on whether the *imp-msg* element has the class or not. Figure 4-5 shows the initial page, and Figure 4-6 shows the page after the first button click.

Toggle Multiple Classes

The *toggleClass()* method can also be used to toggle multiple classes at once (or all classes), much like *addClass()* and *removeClass()*.

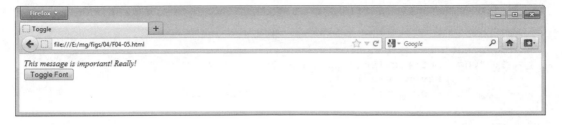

Figure 4-5 The initial page

Figure 4-6 The page after the button is clicked the first time, displaying the text in a larger font

If you call the method with no arguments, *all* classes for the element will be toggled:

```
$("#my-element").toggleClass();
```

To toggle multiple classes by name, simply separate each class name with a space when calling *toggleClass()*, as in the following code:

```
$("#my-element").toggleClass("one-class another-class");
```

In this case, both classes will be added or removed, based on whether the element currently has each class. Keep in mind that this is done separately for each class, so *one-class* could be added while *another-class()* is removed, this could be switched, or both could be in the same state and be added or removed at the same time.

For example, go back to the code for the *toggle.html* page. You will recall that there were two available classes and one was already applied to the <div> element:

```
.larger { font-size:2em; }
.imp-text { font-style:italic; }
```

This class was available, but not applied until added via jQuery code

This class was applied using the class attribute in the <div> element

To see what happens when both classes are toggled at once, open your *toggle.js* file and alter it to use the following code:

```
$(document).ready(function() {
  $("#tog-font").click(function(event) {
    event.preventDefault();
    $("#imp-msg").toggleClass("larger imp-text");
  });
});
```

Save the file and refresh *toggle.html* in your browser. When the button is clicked, *larger* will be added to the *imp-msg* <div> element, while *imp-text* will be removed. Since *imp-msg* did not have the larger class, it was added. Since *imp-msg* already had the *imp-text* class, it was removed. Figure 4-7 shows the initial page, and Figure 4-8 shows the page after the button is clicked.

If you make any changes with jQuery code before the toggle is performed, then it will alter how the toggle works. For instance, change the *toggle.js* code to the following and save the file again:

```
$(document).ready(function() {
  $("#imp-msg").addClass("larger");  ◄──────────  Adding the larger class when the
  $("#tog-font").click(function(event) {           document is ready will change what
    event.preventDefault();                         happens when the button is clicked
    $("#imp-msg").toggleClass("larger imp-text");
  });
});
```

Figure 4-7 The initial page

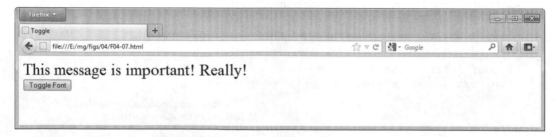

Figure 4-8 The page after the button is clicked. The text loses the italic font but becomes larger.

Figure 4-9   The initial page

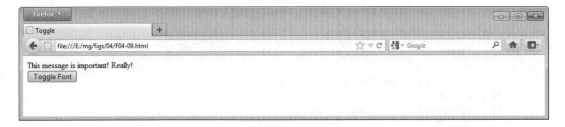

Figure 4-10   The page after the button is clicked

Here, the *larger* class is added when the document is ready, so the text will already be larger and *imp-msg* will already have the *larger* class when the button is clicked to toggle the classes. Thus, both *larger* and *imp-text* will be removed on the first click, both added on the second, and so on. Figure 4-9 shows the initial page, and Figure 4-10 shows the page after the button is clicked.

Specifying an Add or Remove

If you need to be more specific, you can specify whether *toggleClass( )* should add or remove a class by sending a second argument. If the value *true* is sent, then the class will be added; if *false* is sent, then the class will be removed:

This ensures that the class is added

```
$("#my-element").toggleClass("one-class", true);
$("#my-element").toggleClass("one-class", false);
```

This ensures that the class is removed

Using a Function to Determine the Argument

If you need to determine what class name(s) should be sent in the argument through scripting, you can send the return value of a function as the argument to *toggleClass()*, as in the following code:

```
$("#my-element").toggleClass(function(){
  var myClasses;
  // Code to get one or more class names
  return myClasses;
});
```

As with the *css()* method, you can return a value to be used as the argument. In this case, you will want a single class name or a space-separated list of class names to be returned and used as the argument.

The hasClass() Method

The *hasClass()* method determines whether or not the elements in a selection have a specified class. If one or more elements have the class, the method will return a value of *true*; if not, *false* will be returned.

For example, consider the following HTML code snippet:

```
<div id="my-element" class="looking staring">Are you looking at me?</
div>
```

The <div> element has two classes assigned to it: *looking* and *staring*. The following code shows the different values returned by *hasClass()* given several different arguments:

```
$("#my-element").hasClass("looking");  // returns true
$("#my-element").hasClass("staring");  // returns true
$("#my-element").hasClass("gazing");   // returns false
```

If *hasClass()* is run on a collection of elements, then it will return *true* if one or more elements within the selection have the class, and *false* if none of the elements in the selection have the class. Consider this example code:

```
<div class="looking staring">Are you looking at me?</div>
<div class="looking">Are you looking at me?</div>
<div class="staring">Are you looking at me?</div>
```

The following code shows the result of using different class names as the argument to *hasClass()*:

```
$("div").hasClass("looking");  // returns true (1st and 2nd <div>)
$("div").hasClass("staring");  // returns true (1st and 3rd <div>)
$("div").hasClass("gazing");   // returns false (no <div> with the
class)
```

This can be used with a JavaScript *if* statement to selectively perform an action based on whether an element has a given class. The structure of an *if* statement is shown in the following code:

```
if (value) {
  // Code to perform is value is true
}
```

The *value* is typically a statement that evaluates to either *true* or *false*. The code within the curly brackets will only execute if the *value* within the parentheses evaluates to *true* (you will learn more about using the *if* statement in the next chapter).

In the case of *hasClass()*, it will return *true* if one or more of the selected elements has the specified class, so you can use the method in the *if* statement to execute the code inside the curly brackets if it returns true. Consider the following code:

```
<div id="see" class="looking staring">Are you looking at me?</div>
```

Given these <div> elements, you could execute a statement like the one in the following code:

This statement will evaluate to *true* since the element has the *staring* class, so the code inside the curly brackets will be executed

```
if ($("#see").hasClass("staring")) {
  $("#see").css("font-size", "2em");
}
```

This statement executes, making the font size of the element larger

As you can see, *hasClass()* will return *true* in this case, so the statement inside the curly brackets will be executed, and the <div> element will have its font size increased. Had *gazing* been sent as the argument instead, *hasClass()* would have returned *false*, and any code within the curly brackets would have been ignored.

CAUTION

When working with *if*, be careful that you keep its parentheses separate from those of the jQuery methods. Both need to be closed, so be sure to double-check that the outer and inner sets of parentheses are all closed to avoid potential script errors.

Try This 4-1   ## Use toggleClass()

```
pr04-01.html
pr04-01.js
```

This project allows you to practice using the jQuery *css()* and *toggle()* methods to change the value of style properties and to add and remove CSS classes.

Step by Step

1. Place the following HTML code into your editor and save the file as *pr04-01.html*:

```
<!DOCTYPE html>
<html>
<head>
  <meta charset="utf-8">
  <title>Project 4-1</title>
  <style type="text/css">
    .highlight { background-color:#FFFF99; }
  </style>
  <script src="jquery-1.9.1.min.js" type="text/javascript"></script>
```

(continued)

```
        <script src="pr04-01.js" type="text/javascript"></script>
</head>
<body>
<div id="imp-text">
If you need to highlight or remove the highlight from this text,
click the button below!
</div>
<div>
  <form action="highlight.html">
    <button id="highlight">Highlight On/Off</button>
  </form>
</div>
<div id="more-info">Here is some additional information...</div>
<div>
  <form action="more-info.html">
    <button id="make-bold">Make Bold</button>
  </form>
</div>
</body>
</html>
```

2. In the *pr04-01.js* file, add jQuery code that will toggle the *highlight* class on the *imp-text* <div> element when the *highlight* button is clicked.

3. Add jQuery code that will make the text in the *more-info* <div> element bold when the *make-bold* button is clicked (use the *css()* method).

4. Save the file. When complete, the code should look like this:

```
$(document).ready(function() {
  $("#highlight").click(function(event) {
    event.preventDefault();
    $("#imp-text").toggleClass("highlight");
  });
  $("#make-bold").click(function(event) {
    event.preventDefault();
    $("#more-info").css("font-weight", "bold");
  });
});
```

5. Open the *pr04-01.html* file in your Web browser. Click the first button, and the important text should become highlighted. Click the second button, and the additional text should become bold (clicking this button again will have no further effects).

Try This Summary

In this project, you practiced using both the *toggleClass()* and *css()* jQuery methods to add/remove a class as needed and to change the value of a CSS property on an element.

Size and Position Methods

Sometimes it is helpful to be able to get positional CSS property values, since they may be useful when positioning an element on the screen or giving an element a particular width, height, border, padding, and so on.

The jQuery library has a number of methods for obtaining different values that can help you in your scripts. Some of the methods only retrieve information, but others also serve as shorthand methods for setting property values.

NOTE

When using these methods to get or set values, the selection process works like that of the *css()* method. The first matched element is selected when getting values, while *all* matched elements are changed when setting values.

The width() and height() Methods

The *width()* and *height()* methods can get or set the width or height of an element. When getting a value, you simply call one of the methods with no arguments, as in the following code:

```
var eWidth = $("#my-element").width();
```

This gets the width of *my-element* and assigns it to a variable named *eWidth*. The value it gets will be the width in pixels, without the string "px" attached to the end of it. This can make it easier to perform calculations on the returned value, as opposed to the value returned by *css("width")*, which would need to have the "px" string removed from the end to perform any numerical calculations.

The width and height values for an element are the width and height of the element *before* any padding, borders, or margins are added. You will see as you progress that there are other methods for determining the width and height based on different rules.

To set a value, you send the methods an argument with the new value. This can be any string such as "40", "20px", "2em", "50%", and so on. If you use a number without providing the unit behind it, then jQuery will assume it is a pixel value. Some examples are shown here:

```
$("#my-element").width("45"); //Sets the width to 45px
$("#my-element").width("22px"); //Sets the width to 22px
$("#my-element").width("40%"); //Sets the width to 40%
$("#my-element").width("5em"); //Sets the width to 45em
```

Each of these is valid and will set the width accordingly. The *height()* method works the same way as *width()* but sets the height of the element instead.

The innerWidth() and innerHeight() Methods

The *innerWidth()* and *innerHeight()* methods get the width or height of an element plus its padding, in pixels. The borders and margins are not included in this value. For example, suppose you had the following CSS code:

```
#my-element { width:20; height:100; padding:10px; }
```

The examples in the following code show what is returned by both methods when they are called for *my-element*:

```
var eIWidth = $("#my-element").innerWidth(); // eIWidth = 40
var eIHeight = $("#my-element").innerWidth(); // eIHeight = 120
```

Notice that when the shorthand *padding* property is used, it adds the specified padding value to all sides of the element, so calling *innerWidth()*, for example, will include the width (20), plus the left padding (10), plus the right padding (10), for a total of 40. The call to *innerHeight()* works the same way (100 + 10 + 10 = 120).

The outerWidth() and outerHeight() Methods

The *outerWidth()* and *outerHeight()* properties get the width or height of an element plus its padding and border, in pixels. The margins are not included in this value. For example, suppose you had the following CSS code:

```
#my-element { width:20; height:100; padding:10px; border:1px; }
```

The examples in this code show what is returned by both methods when they are called for *my-element*:

```
var eOWidth = $("#my-element").outerWidth(); // eOWidth = 42
var eOHeight = $("#my-element").outerWidth(); // eOHeight = 122
```

These methods also provide an option for you to include the margin along with the padding and border. This is done by sending the value of *true* as an argument to *innerWidth()* or *innerHeight()*.

Suppose you had the following CSS code:

```
#my-element { width:20; height:100; padding:10px; border:1px;
margin:5px; }
```

The examples in the following code show what is returned by both methods when they are called for *my-element* using the optional argument to include the margin values:

```
var eOWidth = $("#my-element").outerWidth(true); // eOWidth = 52
var eOHeight = $("#my-element").outerWidth(true); // eOHeight = 132
```

This can be helpful when you need to know how much space an element will use on the screen.

The offset() Method

The *offset()* method allows you to get or set the left and top coordinates of an element on the page relative to the *document* element. This means that the coordinates are defined where (0,0) is at the top-left of the page.

Getting the Offset

To get the offset of an element, you can call the offset method without any arguments, as in the following code:

```
var oSet = $("#my-element").offset();
```

The method returns two values, the width and the height, which can be accessed by including *.left* or *.top* after the variable name that is assigned the result (it returns an object with the properties *left* and *top*). Assuming *#my-element* was positioned at (20, 30), the following code shows examples of the results of calling *offset()* on the element:

```
var oSet = $("#my-element").offset();
$("#another-element").append(oSet.left); // oSet.left = 20
$("#another-element").append(oSet.top); // oSet.top = 30
```

Setting the Offset

To set the offset of an element, you send the *left* and *top* values as an argument using object literal notation, as in the following code:

```
$("#my-element").offset({left: 40, top: 50});
```

This will move the element to the coordinates (40, 50) on the page.

NOTE

If the element has a *position* value set to anything other than *relative*, then this method will reset it to *relative* in order to perform the repositioning of the element.

The position() Method

The *position()* method works like the *offset()* method, but gets or sets the position of an element based on its parent element. This keeps you from needing to find the position of the parent element and then set the position of the element. Instead, you can simply use the *position()* method.

For example, the code here shows examples of getting or setting an element's coordinates using the *position()* method:

```
var pos = $("#my-element").position();
$("#another-element").append(pos.left);
$("#another-element").append(pos.top);
$("#my-element").position({left: 10, top: 10});
```

NOTE

If the element has a *position* value set to anything other than *relative*, then this method will reset it to *relative* in order to perform the repositioning of the element.

The scrollLeft() and scrollTop() Methods

The *scrollLeft()* and *scrollTop()* methods get or set the position of the horizontal and vertical scroll bars, in pixels. For example, to get the position of the horizontal scroll bar, you could use the following code:

```
var scrollPosHz = $("#my-element").scrollLeft();
```

If you want to set the position, you simply send the pixel value as the argument, as in the following code:

```
$("#my-element").scrollLeft(20);
```

This would cause the scroll bar to be positioned 20 pixels from the left edge of the element.

To see how you could use one of the scroll methods, suppose you had the following HTML code (save as *scroll.html*):

```
<!DOCTYPE html>
<html>
<head>
  <meta charset="utf-8">
  <title>Scroll</title>
  <style type="text/css">
  #text-box { border:1px solid #000; width:50px; height:100px;
  overflow:scroll; }
  </style>
  <script src="jquery-1.9.1.min.js" type="text/javascript"></script>
  <script src="scroll.js" type="text/javascript"></script>
</head>
<body>
  <div id="text-box">
  <p>This is a story that I have been meaning to write for some
  time.</p>
  <p>It all started long ago, when I decided to try writing HTML for the
     first time. I thought I would never get my Web site to work, but
     then...</p>
  </div>
  <div>
    <form action="scrolled.html">
      <button id="scroll-box">Scroll down to 270px</button>
    </form>
  </div>
</body>
</html>
```

This will create a bordered text box with a vertical scroll bar to scroll through the remaining text. You can move the position of the scroll bar using *scrollTop()*, as in the following code (save as *scroll.js*):

```
$(document).ready(function() {
  $("#scroll-box").click(function(event) {
    event.preventDefault();
    $("#text-box").scrollTop(270);
  });
});
```

This will move the vertical scroll bar position down 270 pixels from the top of the *text-box* element. In this case, that will be somewhere near the beginning of the second paragraph (the exact position will depend on your default font size, and so on). Figure 4-11 shows the initial page, and Figure 4-12 shows the page after the button is clicked.

As you can see, the scroll bar is repositioned and the text is scrolled down to the new position.

Figure 4-11   The initial page

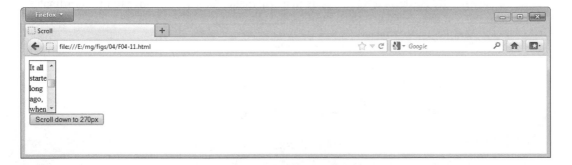

Figure 4-12   The page after the button is clicked

Try This 4-2 Use offset()

pr04-02.html
pr04-02.js

This project allows you to practice using CSS position methods by setting the coordinates of an element using the *offset()* method.

Step by Step

1. Insert the following HTML code into your editor and save the file as *pr04-02.html*:

```
<!DOCTYPE html>
<html>
<head>
  <meta charset="utf-8">
  <title>Project 4-2</title>
  <style type="text/css">
    #my-box { border:1px solid #000; width:30%; }
  </style>
  <script src="jquery-1.9.1.min.js" type="text/javascript"></script>
  <script src="pr04-02.js" type="text/javascript"></script>
</head>
<body>
<div id="my-box">
This box has some information in it and can be moved!
</div>
<div>
  <form action="moved.html">
    <button id="move-box">Move Box</button>
  </form>
</div>
</body>
</html>
```

2. In the *pr04-02.js* file, add jQuery code that will make the text box move to the coordinates (100, 50) on the page when the button is clicked.

3. Save the file. When complete, the code should look like this:

```
$(document).ready(function() {
  $("#move-box").click(function(event) {
    event.preventDefault();
    $("#my-box").offset({left:100, top:50});
  });
});
```

4. Open the *pr04-02.html* file in your Web browser. Click the button to move the text box to the new location in the document.

Try This Summary

In this project, you used your knowledge of the *offset()* method to move an element to a new position on the page based on the coordinates you sent as an argument.

Chapter 4 Self Test

1. When working with CSS code, you define the selector and then define a rule within a set of
_____.

2. The jQuery library has the _____ method, which allows you to obtain property values or make alterations on the fly.

    A. style()

    B. css()

    C. getPropVals()

    D. docStyles()

3. Which of the following will properly get the value of the *color* property for an element with an id of *code* and assign it to a variable named *eColor*?

    A. var eColor = $("#main").css("color");

    B. var eColor = $("#code").css("background-color");

    C. var eColor = $("#code").style("color");

    D. var eColor = $("#code").css("color");

4. When getting property values with the *css()* method, you are not able to use _____ properties.

    A. any

    B. position

    C. color

    D. shorthand

5. If the selection in the $() function matches more than one element when using the *css()* method, only the property value for the last matched element will be returned.

    A. True

    B. False

6. Which of the following properly sets the value of the *background-color* property to *#FFFFFF* for an element with an id of *text-box*?

   A. $("#text-box").css("background-color", "#FFFFFF");

   B. $("#text-box").style("background-color", "#FFFFFF");

   C. $("#text-box ").css("color", "#FF0000");

   D. $("#box-text").css("color", "#FFFFFF");

7. The *css()* method can be used to set more than one property value at a time.

   A. True

   B. False

8. jQuery 1.6 and higher allows you to use values beginning with _____ or _____ to set relative values (setting the value incrementally higher or lower than its current value) for properties that are based on numeric values, such as *width*, *height*, *font-size*, and so on.

   A. ++, −−

   B. =+, =−

   C. +=, −=

   D. plus, minus

9. jQuery versions 1.4 and higher allow you to set the return value of a _____ as the property value.

   A. mouseover

   B. variable

   C. constant

   D. function

10. The _____ method removes a class from an element.

   A. removeClass()

   B. deleteClass()

   C. closeClass()

   D. clearClass()

11. jQuery supports method _____, which allows you to place methods one after another to act on selected elements.

    A. opening

    B. listing

    C. chaining

    D. talking

12. The _____ method allows you to switch between adding and removing one or more classes each time the method is applied to a particular selection.

    A. removeClass()

    B. toggleClass()

    C. switchClass()

    D. swapClass()

13. jQuery has shorthand methods for getting and setting the *width* and *height* properties of an element.

    A. True

    B. False

14. The _____ method allows you to get or set the coordinates of an element based on the document element.

    A. position()

    B. offset()

    C. coords()

    D. placement()

15. The _____ method allows you to get or set the position of the vertical scroll bar within an element.

    A. scrollLeft()

    B. top()

    C. left()

    D. scrollTop()

Chapter 5

JavaScript and the Document Object Model

Key Skills & Concepts

- Basic JavaScript
- The Document Object Model (DOM)
- The DOM and jQuery

Since jQuery is a JavaScript library, you will sometimes find it helpful to know some of the basics of the JavaScript language. This knowledge can help you better understand jQuery syntax, and can also help you when you need to do things such as use variables, make comparisons, write custom functions, and so on.

In this chapter, you will learn some of the basic constructs in JavaScript. This won't go into as much detail on these topics as a book specifically for JavaScript, but will give you an overview of these basic constructs so that you can apply them in jQuery.

You will also learn about the Document Object Model (DOM) and how to use jQuery to add, move, or remove elements from the DOM tree.

Basic JavaScript

There are a number of things used in JavaScript that are helpful to know when coding jQuery, since the library returns particular types of values from its methods, uses syntax from JavaScript, and allows you to provide your own function code.

In this section, you will learn about JavaScript comments, variables, data types, operators, flow control statements, functions, arrays, and objects. Understanding the basic concepts behind these features of the JavaScript language will prove helpful when you need to use them with your jQuery code.

NOTE
This will be a high-level overview of these concepts for you to better understand them when they are used with jQuery. If you want to learn JavaScript in more detail, refer to one of the resources provided in Chapter 1.

If you are already familiar with the basics of JavaScript, feel free to proceed to the section entitled "The Document Object Model (DOM)" as you will likely know the information that follows already.

Comments

Comments allow you to place characters into your JavaScript code that are ignored by the JavaScript interpreter. These are often descriptive comments about the code, but they can also be used to disable pieces of code when needed.

JavaScript allows for both single-line and multiple-line comments. A single-line comment begins with two forward slashes (//) and ends at the end of the line. For example, the following code shows a single-line comment:

```
// This is a comment!
```

The comment can begin anywhere on the line, so you may see code like the following as well:

```
var guitars = 2; // Stores the number of guitars on hand
```

In this case, the code at the beginning of the line will still run, but the text after the // is ignored.

A multiple-line comment begins with /* and does not end until */ is found in the code. For example, the following code shows a comment that runs over several lines, all of which are ignored by the JavaScript interpreter:

```
/*
This is ignored
var y = 2; this is also ignored and not run
nothing to see here...
*/
```

The comment only ends when the ending */ characters appear in the code.

Variables and Data Types

In the last chapter, you saw values being assigned to variables. A variable simply stores a value in memory. This value can be used or changed in your code as needed.

Declaring Variables

JavaScript uses the *var* keyword to declare a variable. The only requirements for declaring a variable are to use the *var* keyword and to provide a valid variable name. For example, the following code would declare a variable named *guitars*:

```
var guitars;
```

If you want to declare multiple variables in a single statement, you can separate the variable names with commas, as in the following code:

```
var guitars, pianos, trumpets;
```

When doing this, remember to use a semicolon after the last variable name in the list to end the statement.

When declaring a variable in this manner, you are not explicitly assigning it a value. In such cases, variables are assigned an initial value of *undefined* by JavaScript. If you want to give the variable a different initial value, you can assign it by adding an equal sign (=) followed by the desired value, as in the following code:

```
var guitars = 2;
```

This assigns a value of *2* to the variable *guitars*.

As with the basic variable declaration, you can declare and assign values to multiple variables by separating each with a comma. The following code shows an example of this:

```
var guitars = 2, pianos = 1, trumpets = 3;
```

Here, all three variables are given initial values. If the list becomes longer, it is often coded with each variable assignment on its own line to make it easier to scan, as shown in the following example code:

```
var guitars = 2,
    pianos = 1,
    trumpets = 3;  ←——————— Remember to include the semicolon at the end of the list!
```

Here, all three variable assignments appear on their own line in the code, and you can quickly scan down vertically if you need to find one of the variable assignments at a later time.

Using Variables

To use a variable, you need only place the variable name in your code to use its value. For example, the following code sends a pop-up alert to the user with the value of the *guitars* variable:

```
var guitars = 2;
alert(guitars);  ←——————— Notice that the variable name does not use quote marks around it
```

This uses the JavaScript *alert()* method, which sends the user a pop-up dialog with the content contained in the argument (the value of the *guitars* variable in this case, which is *2*). You will notice that when a JavaScript variable is used, quote marks are not used around the variable name.

Naming Variables

Variables must begin with a letter, underscore (_), or dollar symbol ($), and each character after that must be a letter, number, underscore, or dollar symbol. The following code shows some examples:

```
var cool; // Valid
var _cool$beans2; // Valid
var $cool; // Valid
var 2cool; // Invalid - cannot begin with a number
var cool beans; Invalid - cannot contain a space
var %cool; // Invalid - % character not allowed
```

Another thing you need to know is that JavaScript keywords and reserved words such as *if, var, function,* and so on should not be used as variable names, as they could potentially cause a script to malfunction. For a complete list, see www.scripttheweb.com/js/ref/javascript-reserved-words/.

JavaScript Data Types

JavaScript has five basic data types, outlined in Table 5-1.

JavaScript does not differentiate between integers, floats, doubles, and so on. Instead, any number simply falls under the *number* data type. Boolean values are either *true* or *false*, making them effective values for comparison operations (discussed later in this chapter). The undefined and null types describe undefined variables and empty objects (objects are discussed later in this chapter). This leaves string values, which can be a bit tricky at times.

Working with Strings   As you have seen previously, string values are placed in quotes. For example, to assign a string value to a variable, you could use the following code:

```
var name = "Frank";
```

This assigns the string "Frank" to the *name* variable.

A string can be placed in single or double quotes without any differences, so the following code would also be perfectly valid:

```
var name = 'Frank';
```

If you need quote marks within other quote marks, you will need to either switch between single and double or to escape the additional quotes with backslashes (\). For example, any of the examples in the following code would be valid:

```
var text = "Frank said, 'Great!'";
var text2 = 'Frank said, "Great!"';
var text3 = "Don't do that!";
```

Type	Description
Number	Any numeric value. Includes integer, float, and so on. Some examples: 5, -2, 3.5, 123.32345677, 5.65e21 (exponential notation).
String	A string of text, such as "Hi", "Bye", "This is a sentence.", and so on.
Boolean	*true or false*—These values are literal values and do not need quote marks around them as string values would.
Undefined	A value that has not yet been defined. For example, declaring a variable without assigning it an initial value and using it will result in a value of *undefined*.
Null	The value of an empty object. Similar to *undefined,* but for objects.

Table 5-1   JavaScript Data Types

Each of these contains one type of quote mark to enclose the string and uses the other within the string. Problems arise, however, if the same type of quote used to enclose the string is used within the string, as in the following code examples:

```
var text = "Frank said, "Great!"";
var text2 = 'Frank said, 'Great!'';
var text3 = 'Don't do that!';
```

Both of these end the string before the G in *Great* due to the matching enclosing quote appearing there

This string is ended before the *t* in *Don't* due to the matching enclosing quote there

The strings will produce a JavaScript error when you try to run the code.

If you decide you would rather escape the inner quote marks rather than alternate, the strings could be fixed using the following code:

```
var text = "Frank said, \"Great!\"";
var text2 = 'Frank said, \'Great!\'';
var text3 = 'Don\'t do that!';
```

Notice that any quote marks that match the enclosing quote marks are preceded by a backslash. This will keep them from ending the string and producing errors. In some situations, this will be required since alternating has already been done. Consider the following example:

```
var text = 'Frank said, "Don\'t do that!"';
```

By the time you get to the single quote in the word *Don't*, you have already alternated quote marks, and single quotes are being used to enclose the string. Here, the backslash before the *t* is required for the string to be valid.

Operators

JavaScript includes a number of operators that allow you to perform calculations, assign values, compare values, and more. These are helpful to know in jQuery, since you will often need to perform one or more of these operations in your scripts.

Arithmetic

The JavaScript arithmetic operators are shown in Table 5-2.

Most operations will work as expected, as seen in the following code examples:

```
var num = 2 + 3;       // num = 5
var num2 = 4 - 2;      // num2 = 2
var num3 = ++num2;     // num3 = 3
var num4 = 1 * 0;      // num4 = 0
```

Operator	Symbol	Description
Addition	+	Adds two values
Subtraction	-	Subtracts one value from another
Multiplication	*	Multiplies two values
Division	/	Divides one value by another
Modulus	%	Returns the remainder of dividing one value by another
Increment	++	Adds one to a number
Decrement	--	Subtracts one from a number
Unary Plus	+	Attempts to convert non-numeric values into numbers
Unary Negation	-	Alters the sign of a number

Table 5-2 Arithmetic Operators

When using the addition operator, you have to watch out for numbers and strings being combined. Since the + operator is also used to combine (concatenate) strings, unexpected results can occur. For example, consider the following code:

```
var num = 2,
    num2 =  "4",
    num3 = num + num2;  ◄——————— The value of num3 is "24"!
```

Here, a number and a string are added together and the result is assigned to the *num3* variable. You may think adding these two values would cause an error, but that is not the case. When JavaScript sees this, it attempts to perform *type coercion*, which means it will attempt to make one of the values match the data type of the other.

In the case of numbers and strings being added, JavaScript will coerce the number into a string value (*"2"* in this case) before performing the operation. If you know that the string value consists of only numbers, you can correct this by using the unary plus operator (+). This will attempt to coerce a string to a number *first*, and then the data types will both be numbers *before* the addition operation is attempted. The following code would give *num3* a value of *6*:

```
var num = 2,
    num2 =  "4",
    num3 = num + +num2;  ◄——————
```

Notice the + immediately preceding the *num2* variable value here, which will attempt to coerce the value to a number before it is added to the *num* value.

If the string value did not consist of only numeric characters, then *num2* is given the special value of *NaN*, which means "Not a Number." When this is added to another value, the result will be *NaN*. Thus, if "4" is changed to *"4something,"* this workaround will simply cause a result of *NaN*.

If you know that the string at least *begins* with numeric characters, you can use the *parseInt()* or *parseFloat()* JavaScript methods to get the numeric characters from the beginning of the screen (*parseFloat()* allows the first period (.) it encounters to be treated as a decimal point). So, the following code would also allow you to have a value of *6* for the *num3* variable:

```
var num = 2,
    num2 =  "4something",
    num3 = num + parseInt(num2);
```

The *num2* variable is sent as an argument to *parseInt()*, which removes the non-numeric characters after the numerical *4* at the beginning of the string

NOTE
This type of issue can often occur when the user fills in a number in an HTML form field, which is sent to JavaScript code as a string value. Depending on the situation, using the unary plus or *parseInt()* method should allow you to validate that a number has been entered and to convert the value to a number for calculations.

Assignment
The assignment operators are listed in Table 5-3.

The equal sign (=) simply assigns a value to a variable, as in the following code:

```
var num = 4;
num = 5;  // num = 5  ◄──────── The variable is assigned a new value of 5
```

Operator	Symbol	Description
Assignment	=	Assigns a value to a variable
Add and Assign	+=	Adds the value on the right to the current value of the variable and assigns the variable the new value
Subtract and Assign	-=	Subtracts the value on the right from the current value of the variable and assigns the variable the new value
Multiply and Assign	*=	Multiplies the value on the right by the current value of the variable and assigns the variable the new value
Divide and Assign	/=	Divides the current value of the variable by the value on the right and assigns the variable the new value
Modulus and Assign	%=	Divides the current value of the variable by the value on the right and assigns the variable the value of the remainder

Table 5-3   Assignment Operators

The others perform an operation on the current value of the variable and assign the result as the new value of the variable. For example, the Add and Assign operator will add the value on the right side of it to the value of the variable on the left side, then assign the result as the new value of the variable, as in the following code:

```
var num = 4;
num += 5;  // num = 9 (4+5)
```

These assignment operators are typically used as shorthand for writing out the equivalent calculation (in this case, *num = num + 5)*.

Comparison

Comparison operators are used to compare two values and return a Boolean value of *true* or *false*. This is often used with the *if* statement (and other flow control statements) to determine whether or not to run particular sections of code. The comparison operators are shown in Table 5-4.

In the case of an *if* statement, you can compare two values to determine if the block of code within the curly brackets should be run, as in the following code:

```
var num = 2;
if (num === 3) {        The comparison returns false, so the code
  // Code to execute...  within the curly brackets is ignored
}
```

Operator	Symbol	Description
Is equal to	==	Returns true if the values on both sides are equal
Strict is equal to	===	Returns true if the values on both sides are equal and of the same data type
Is not equal to	!=	Returns true if the values on both sides are not equal
Strict is not equal to	!==	Returns true if the values on both sides are not equal or not of the same data type
Is greater than	>	Returns true if the value on the left is greater than the value on the right
Is greater than or equal to	>=	Returns true if the value on the left is greater than or equal to the value on the right
Is less than	<	Returns true if the value on the left is less than the value on the right
Is less than or equal to	<=	Returns true if the value on the left is less than or equal to the value on the right

Table 5-4   Comparison Operators

Here, the code will only execute if the value of *num* is equal to *3*. Since the value of *num* is *2*, the comparison returns false and the code within the curly brackets is not executed. The others work in much the same way and will return *true* or *false* once the comparison is made.

NOTE

The strict equal to operator is used here, as this has become a best practice when making an equality comparison. The == operator allows for type coercion, which can yield unexpected results.

Logical

Logical operators allow you to combine comparisons to form a more complex statement that will, in the end, return *true* or *false*. The logical operators are listed in Table 5-5.

As an example, if you want to make sure two comparisons are both true before executing a block of code, you could use the *&&* operator, as in the following code:

```
var num = 2;
if ( (num > 0) && (num < 5) ) {
  // Code to execute...
}
```

Since both *num > 0* and *num < 5* return *true*, the whole operation returns *true* and the code within the curly brackets is executed.

The *!* operator will simply negate the result of a comparison, making it *true* if it returned *false* and *false* if it returned true. For example, consider the following code:

```
var num = 2;
if ( !(num < 1) ) {
  // Code to execute...
}
```

The comparison *num < 1* returns *false*, but placing the *!* operator in front of it will now cause the result to be *true*. It is essentially saying "If it is not the case, then the value of *num* is less than *1*," which is true, since 2 is not less than *1*.

Operator	Symbol	Description
AND	&&	Returns true if the comparisons on both sides return true
OR	||	Returns true if either one or both of the comparisons returns true
NOT	!	Returns true if a comparison returns false, and vice versa

Table 5-5 Logical Operators

Flow Control Statements

Flow control statements allow you to execute code based on certain conditions being met. You have already used the *if* statement, but there are a few more basic statements that you may want to learn as well.

The if/else Statement

You have used the *if* statement already to execute code only when a condition returns *true*, but you can optionally add an *else* statement directly afterward that will execute when the condition returns *false*. For example, consider the following code:

```
var num = 2;
if (num === 3) {  ◄─────── This comparison will return false, since 2 is not equal to 3
  // Code to execute if true...
}
else {  ─────────────────────────
  // Code to execute if false...        The code within these curly brackets
                                        will be executed since the comparison
}  ──────────────────────────          returned false
```

The *else* statement allows you to provide an alternate set of statements to execute when the condition in an *if* statement does not return *true*. This allows you to customize your code even further when needed.

The for Loop

A *loop* is a block of code that is executed a particular number of times based on information provided in the statement. The *for* loop allows you to provide an initial value for a counting variable, a condition to test on that variable, and an expression that will increase or decrease the value of that count variable.

For example, take a look at the following code:

```
for (var num = 0; num < 10; num++) {
  Code to execute as long as the value of num is less than 9...
}
```

Each of the three statements is separated by a semicolon. Notice that a variable can be initialized in the first statement within the parentheses. Typically, the variable is initialized to a value of *0* because loops often cycle through arrays, which begin with an index of zero (you will see more about this later in the chapter).

The next statement determines when the loop will end. In this case, as long as the value of *num* is less than 10, the code within the curly brackets will execute again.

The last statement changes the value of the variable after each execution of the loop. In this case, *1* is added to the value of *num* each time the loop is run. Thus, the first time through the loop, *num* will be *0*, the second time *num* will be *1*, and so on. When *num* finally reaches *10*, the loop will no longer be executed and the script will proceed to the next line of code following the loop.

Functions

Functions provide a way for you to reuse code that is created for a particular purpose. You have been using functions in your jQuery code already—from executing a function when the document is ready to running one when an event occurs.

Expression and Declaration

To this point, you have been using what is known as a function *expression* in JavaScript, which is also often called an *anonymous* function. The following shows the basic syntax of a function expression:

```
var ref = function() {
  // Code to execute when run...
};
```

Notice that the function is assigned to some type of reference, which in this case is a variable name. This function could later be called using *ref()*, though *ref* is a reference to the function rather than a function name, which can only occur when using a function *declaration*. This is why it is often called an *anonymous* function.

A better example is to look at how you have been using function expressions up to this point—to handle events, as in the following code:

```
$("#my-element").click(function(event) {
  event.preventDefault();
  $("#other-element").addClass("myClass");
});
```

Here, the function expression is not assigned to a reference name, but to handle an event. The only time this function is executed is when the event occurs, rather than having the ability to be called from elsewhere in the script.

A function *declaration* allows you to name the function and call it anywhere in the script. The following code shows the basic syntax of a function declaration:

```
function funcName() {
  // Code to execute...
}
```

When declaring a function, you begin with the *function* keyword, followed by the function name. The code to execute is placed inside the curly brackets, just as with a function expression.

Using a declaration, you can call a declared function directly at any time by simply using the function name followed by parentheses, as in the following code:

```
function sendAlert() {
```

```
  alert("Hi!");
}
sendAlert();
```

If you want to assign the function to handle an event, you leave off the parentheses when assigning it, so that the function itself is assigned to handle the event (otherwise, it is assumed you want to run the function and/or return the result of it). The following code shows an example of this:

```
function sendAlert() {
  alert("Hi!");
}
$("#my-element").click(sendAlert);
```

Here, the *sendAlert()* function is assigned to handle the click event on *#my-element*, and will pop up the alert message when the event occurs. The only issue here is that you cannot send any arguments, so any values needed have to be gathered within the function itself. The function can, however, be reused as many times as needed by simply calling or assigning it again.

Function expressions are often used to handle events in jQuery, since event reactions are not typically reused by other elements and since you can easily add any needed arguments.

Arguments and Return Values

You have been using arguments already. These are simply values that are passed on to a function, which can then be used within the function. Each argument is separated by a comma and enclosed in the parentheses following the *function* keyword (for expressions) or the function name (for declarations).

You have been passing the *Event* object as an argument to allow you to use the *preventDefault()* method, but any value can be used as an argument. Numbers, strings, Boolean values, variables, arrays, objects, and more can be sent as arguments to a function. Consider the following code:

A variable named *num* is assigned a value of 5

```
var num = 5;
$("#my-element").click(function(event, num) {
  event.preventDefault();
  if (num < 5) {
    $("#other-element").addClass("myClass");
  }
  else {
    alert("Sorry, the number is too large to add the class!");
  }
});
```

Both *event* and *num* are sent as arguments to the function that handles the *click* event

This code is executed if the value of *num* is less than 5

This code is executed if the value of *num* is not less than 5

Here, the value of the *num* variable is sent as an argument and then used to determine which statements to execute using an *if/else* statement.

Functions can also return values. For example, you saw an example of this in Chapter 4 when using a function as an argument to the *css()* method, as in the following code:

```
$("#my-element").css("width", function() {
  var curWidth = parseInt($("#my-element").css("width")),
      newWidth = curWidth * 3;
  return newWidth;
});
```

The value returned from the function is used as the new value for the *width* property. In this case, the function assigns the current width of the element to a variable named *curWidth*, then multiplies it by *3* and assigns the result to a variable named *newWidth*. The value of *newWidth* is then returned from the function to be set as the new value of the CSS *width* property.

Notice that *parseInt()* was used to get the numeric value from the pixel width (otherwise, it would be "100px," which cannot be multiplied). It returns the new width as a number, which jQuery implements as a pixel value.

Arrays

An array allows you to store a list of data. This data can be accessed by using an index number, starting from 0. In jQuery, array literal notation is typically used when defining arrays.

Defining Arrays

In JavaScript, you can define an array in array literal notation as shown in the following code:

```
var arrayName = [item0, item1, item2];
```

It starts out looking like a typical variable, but the square brackets define the value as an array. Each array item is separated by a comma, but the last item in the array does not have a comma after it. Here, an array named *arrayName* is defined with three items.

An array can be defined with no items (empty) and added to later, or you can add as many items as you need by including them in the list. The following code defines one empty array and one array with four items:

```
var myMoney = [];
var randomStuff = [2, true, "hi", -3.457 ];
```

As you can see, JavaScript does not require data in an array to be all of the same data type, so you can have numbers, strings, Boolean values, objects, and even other arrays within an array.

Accessing Items in Arrays

To access items in an array, you simply use the array name followed by brackets, which include the index of the item you need. Arrays begin counting at zero, so the first item in an array will be at index 0, the second at index 1, and so on.

The following code shows examples of accessing items in an array:

```
var randomStuff = [2, true, "hi", -3.457 ];
var num = randomStuff[0]; // num = 2
var result = randomStuff[1]; // result = true
var greet = randomStuff[2]; // greet = "Hi"
var negNum = randomStuff[3]; // negNum = -3.457
```

As you can see, this allows for easy access to any item in the list; you need only remember to begin counting at zero rather than one.

Array Length

It can be useful to know the length of an array, and JavaScript provides the *length* property for arrays to provide you with that information. The *length* property contains the number of items in an array. For example, consider the following code:

```
var randomStuff = [2, true, "hi", -3.457 ];
var numItems = randomStuff.length; // numItems = 4
```

Since the array contains four items, the value of its *length* property is *4*.

This information is often used to loop through each item in an array and execute code based on the value of each item. For example, the following code will alert the value of each item in the array to the user:

```
var randomStuff = [2, true, "hi", -3.457 ];
for (var i = 0; i < randomStuff.length; i++) {
  alert(randomStuff[i]);
}
```

The value of the *length* property is used here to have the loop stop running after the last item in the array has been cycled through

Notice how the counting variable (*i*) is initialized to *0*, which is the first item of an array. The loop then runs until *i* is no longer less than the length of the array. Here, the loop will go from item 0 through item 3 (the fourth item) and then stop. In this way, you can easily cycle through any array, regardless of its length.

Objects

Objects are similar to arrays, in that they provide a list—but rather than using an index, an object is a list of name/value pairs. They can be used for many things, such as encapsulating code and building patterns with constructors and prototypes, but for the purposes of this book, we will simply look at object literal notation at this time.

Defining Objects

To define an object using object literal notation, the syntax looks like the following code:

```
var objectName = { property: value, property: value }
```

You can have as many property/value pairs as needed, each separated by a comma. The property and value in each pair are separated by a colon (:).

As with arrays, the values can be of any type, but the property names must be unquoted string values, as in the following code:

```
var myCar = { type: "Sedan", engine: "V4", seats: "Cloth" }
```

You may recall that when using the jQuery *css()* method, property names could be within quotes. This is because jQuery converts these to the proper value for you. This allows you to use an object while also using the more familiar CSS syntax for property names, as in the following code:

```
$("#my-element").css({
  "color": "#FFFFFF",
  "background-color": "#000000"
});
```

The jQuery library does support the use of CSS properties in their JavaScript form, so if you prefer it, you can use that form instead, as in the following code:

```
$("#my-element").css({
  color: "#FFFFFF",
  backgroundColor: "#000000"
});
```

Working with Objects

When you need to get the value of a property in JavaScript, you can simply follow the object name with a dot (.) followed by the property name, as in the following code:

```
var myCar = { type: "Sedan", engine: "V4", seats: "Cloth" }
var carType = myCar.type;        // carType = "Sedan"
var carEngine = myCar.engine;    // carEngine = "V4"
var carSeats = myCar.seats;      // carSeats = "Cloth"
```

This syntax makes it easy to access any properties within the object by name when needed.

Ask the Expert

Q: **That sure is a lot of JavaScript! Do I really need to know all of that?**

A: While you won't necessarily use a lot of JavaScript when coding in jQuery, it is still good to understand the basic syntax used since jQuery makes use of this syntax in many cases as well. Other times, you may decide you need an *if* statement, a variable, an array, or something else, and it is good to have that knowledge when you need to make use of one or more of these features.

Q: **Doesn't jQuery iterate over objects on its own? Do I need to know the for loop?**

A: In most cases, jQuery takes care of looping for you, such as when the $() function selects elements. Recall that if the selection returns more than one element, then many jQuery methods will act on *all* of the elements in the selection when executed by running a loop behind the scenes for you. jQuery also has an *each()* method that loops through items, so for the most part you won't need to use a JavaScript *for* loop, but it is good to understand how it works in case you should need it.

Q: **You can't possibly sum up all of JavaScript in such a short section, right?**

A: No, there are many more details on these concepts that can be covered, plus many additional features. Since the focus of this book is primarily on using jQuery, detailed analyses of HTML, CSS, and JavaScript are not possible. The resources listed in Chapter 1 can help you if you find you would like to learn any of these languages in more detail.

Try This 5-1   Use JavaScript with jQuery

pr05-01.html
pr05-01.js

This project allows you to practice using the jQuery *css()* combined with some JavaScript to react to an event and change the width of a <div> element.

Step by Step

1. Place the following HTML code into your editor and save the file as *pr05-01.html*:

```
<!DOCTYPE html>
<html>
<head>
  <meta charset="utf-8">
  <title>Project 5-1</title>
```

(continued)

```
<style type="text/css">
  #box { width:100px; border:solid 1px #000; }
</style>
<script src="jquery-1.9.1.min.js" type="text/javascript"></script>
<script src="pr05-01.js" type="text/javascript"></script>
</head>
<body>
<div id="box">
The width of this box can be changed! Click the button below!
</div>
<div>
  <form action="change-size.html">
    <button id="change-size">Change Size</button>
  </form>
</div>
</body>
</html>
```

2. In the *pr05-01.js* file, add jQuery/JavaScript code that will change the size of the *box* <div> element to four times its current width when the *#change-size* button is clicked. Hint: Remember to use the JavaScript *parseInt()* method!

3. Save the file. When complete, the code should look like this:

```
$(document).ready(function() {
  $("#change-size").click(function(event) {
    event.preventDefault();
    $("#box").css("width", function() {
      var curWidth = parseInt($("#box").css("width")),
          newWidth = curWidth * 4;
      return newWidth;
    });
  });
});
```

4. Open the *pr05-01.html* file in your Web browser. Click the button and the size of the box should change. If you continue clicking the button, the width of the box will keep growing.

Try This Summary

In this project, you practiced using jQuery methods along with a native JavaScript method. With the basic JavaScript knowledge you now have, you can effectively use the JavaScript features you have learned when needed.

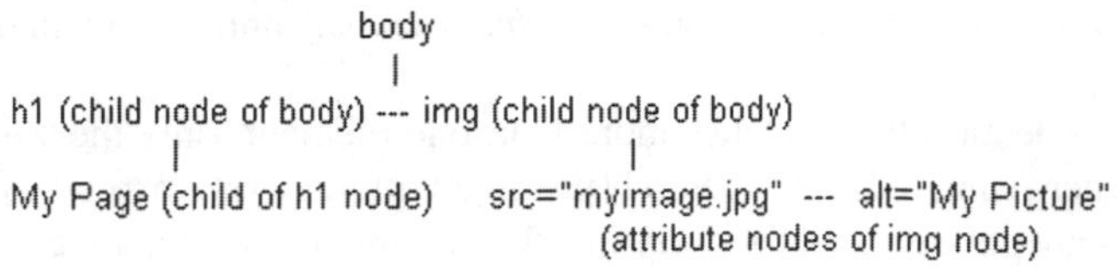

```
                              body
                               |
        h1 (child node of body) --- img (child node of body)
                  |                        |
        My Page (child of h1 node)    src="myimage.jpg" --- alt="My Picture"
                                       (attribute nodes of img node)
```

Figure 5-1   Example document node structure

The Document Object Model (DOM)

The Document Object Model (DOM) gives languages access to the structure of a document. A document is made up of a series of *nodes*. For example, consider the following piece of HTML code:

```
<body>
<h1>My Page</h1>
<img src="myimage.jpg" alt="My Picture">
</body>
```

Each element is an element node and can contain child nodes. For instance, the <body> element in this code example is a node with two child nodes: <h1> and <img>. In addition to elements, text within elements and attributes create text and attribute nodes, respectively.

Figure 5-1 shows an example of the node structure of this document. Notice how each node is represented.

This is the structure used by jQuery to access the elements that you select with the $() function. It goes through and finds each matching node, then returns a jQuery object that contains each of those nodes to allow you to perform any needed actions.

The DOM and jQuery

The jQuery library includes a number of methods to make DOM traversal and manipulation easier for you than it would be in JavaScript. jQuery gives you methods to create, remove, move, wrap, or copy elements as needed.

Attributes

jQuery allows you to set, add, or remove attributes and to get or set values for those attributes using the *attr()* method. Like *css()*, it can contain one argument to get the value of an attribute, can set values one at a time with two arguments, or can send an object literal to set multiple attribute values at once.

Getting Attribute Values

To get an attribute value, you simply invoke the *attr()* method with a single argument: the name of the attribute. This will get the value of that attribute for the first matched element, as in the following code:

```
var attrValue = $("#my-element").attr("title");
```

This would get the value of the title attribute for *#my-element* and assign that value to the *attrValue* variable.

When you have a selection that matches more than one element, only the value of the first element is returned when using the *attr()* method (just like with the *css()* method). In cases where a jQuery method does not get executed for every matched element, you can use the jQuery *each()* method, which will tell jQuery to explicitly run a function on all of the matches for a selection.

Suppose you have the following HTML code (save as *get-attrs.html*):

```
<!DOCTYPE html>
<html>
<head>
  <meta charset="utf-8">
  <title>Get Attributes</title>
  <style type="text/css">
    #desc { width:40%; border:solid 1px #000; }
  </style>
  <script src="jquery-1.9.1.min.js" type="text/javascript"></script>
  <script src="get-attrs.js" type="text/javascript"></script>
</head>
<body>
  <p title="Intro">To whom it may concern:</p>
  <p title="Body">I am very pleased with your product and would buy it
again!</p>
  <p title="Conclusion">Thanks!</p>
  <div id="desc"></div>
</body>
</html>
```

Notice that there are three <p> elements, so a selection of $("p") will match all three of the elements. Using *$("p").attr("title")* will only return the value of the title attribute for the first <p> element, which is *Intro*.

Suppose you would like to get the value of the title attribute for all of the <p> elements rather than just the first and then display these values within the *#desc* <div> element that follows them. Calling the *each()* method will allow you to iterate over each of the matched <p> elements and execute a function for each of them. The following code shows an example of this:

```
$("p").each(function() {
    // Code to get attribute values
});
```

This code essentially says, "Execute the following function for each element that matches the selection." You can now add the code to get the value of the title attribute of each matched element.

With this in place, you will still need to be able to select the right element each time the function is executed. Since *$("p").attr("title")* would only get the first value, you will want to change the selection to one that will get the title attribute value of the <p> element that is currently having the *each()* method run on it.

To do this, you can make use of a special selection in jQuery: *$(this)*. Using *$(this)* will always refer to the current element in the iteration. In this case, the first time *each( )* is executed, *$(this)* will be the first <p> element. The second time *each()* is executed, *$(this)* will be the second <p> element, and so on. With this information, you know that you can always get the value of the title attribute of the current matched <p> element within the *each( )* method by using the following code:

```
$(this).attr("title")
```

Having this at hand, you can now append the value of each of the title attributes to the *#desc* element by selecting the *#desc* element, calling the *append()* method, and sending it the value of the current title attribute, as shown in the following code (save as *get-attrs.js*):

```
$(document).ready(function() {
  $("p").each(function() {
    $("#desc").append($(this).attr("title") + "<br>");
  });
});
```

Notice that the argument to the *append()* method is the value of the title attribute for the currently matched element followed by an HTML line break (the JavaScript + operator is used to add the "<br>" string after the attribute value). Open the *get-attrs.html* file in your browser and you should see the *#desc* <div> element below the paragraphs displaying the value of the title attributes for all three <p> elements. Figure 5-2 shows how this page would appear in a browser.

Setting Attribute Values

The *attr()* method can also be used to set values. To set the value for a single attribute, you can simply provide the attribute name as the first argument and the value as the second argument, as in the following code:

```
$("#my-element").attr("title", "Descriptive Title");
```

This will set the value of the title attribute to *Descriptive Title*.

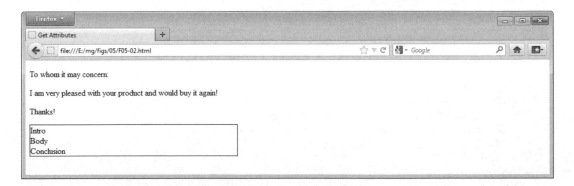

Figure 5-2   The result of using *each()* to get the title attribute for all of the <p> elements

NOTE

When an attribute that is not already present in an element is set using *attr()*, the specified attribute will be added to the element and given the specified value.
If the selection contains more than one matched element, *attr()* will set the specified attribute and value for *all* of the matched elements.

If you want to set more than one attribute value at a time, you can use an object literal as the argument to the *attr()* method, as in the following code:

```
$("#my-element").attr({
  "title": "Descriptive Title",
  "rel": "section"
});
```

This would set both the title and rel attributes for the element. With the *attr()* method, only the class attribute must be enclosed within quotes when using an object literal. Other attribute names allow you the option to leave off the quote marks if desired, as in the following code:

```
$("#my-element").attr({
  title: "Descriptive Title",
  rel: "section"
});
```

Keep in mind, however, that the values will still need to be enclosed within quote marks.

As with other methods, when *attr()* is executed to set attribute values on a selection that has more than one match, the attribute will be set for *all* matches. For example, suppose you had the following HTML code (save as *set-attrs.html*):

```
<!DOCTYPE html>
<html>
<head>
  <meta charset="utf-8">
  <title>Set Attributes</title>
  <style type="text/css">
    #navbox { width:40%; border:solid 1px #000; }
  </style>
  <script src="jquery-1.9.1.min.js" type="text/javascript"></script>
  <script src="set-attrs.js" type="text/javascript"></script>
</head>
<body>
  <div id="navbox">
    <a href="about.html">About</a><br>
    <a href="services.html">Services</a><br>
    <a href="contact.html">Contact</a>
  </div>
</body>
</html>
```

Suppose you want all of the <a> elements in the *#navbox* element to have a title attribute with a value of "Visit page" and a rel attribute with a value of "section." This is easily done by using the *attr()* method, as in the following code:

```
$("#navbox a").attr({
  title: "Visit page",
  rel: "section"
});
```

This will do as expected, and each one of the links will have both attributes set to the specified values.

The only issue here is that each <a> element has the exact same title attribute. It would be better if each title uniquely described each link. To fix this, you can define a function as the value for title within the object literal. Since *attr()* will execute on all matched elements in the selection, you can use a function in combination with *$(this)* to create a unique title for each of the <a> elements, as shown in the following code (save as *set-attrs.js*):

```
$("#navbox a").attr({
  title: function() {
    return "Visit our " + $(this).text() + "page.";
  },
  rel: "section"
});
```

The function returns a value for each matched element in the selection.

As you can see, the function returns a string value based on the text within the element.

The *text()* function in jQuery is used to get (or set) the text within an element without any of the HTML code. In this case, no HTML is present within the <a></a> tags, but this just ensures you do not get unwanted HTML code with the text should any ever get within the tags (if you *do* want the HTML code, you can use *html()* instead).

NOTE
If the *text()* method is called on a selection that contains more than one matched element, it will combine the text from *all* matched elements and return that value.

Open the *set-attrs.html* file in your browser and move your mouse over each link to reveal the title. Each element now has its own title ("Visit our About page" for the first link, "Visit our Services page" for the second link, and "Visit our Contact page" for the last link).

Creating New Elements
The jQuery library makes it easy to create and insert new elements into the document. Using a combination of the $() function and several available methods, you can add elements anywhere you need to in your documents.

In fact, one of the available methods is one you have used already: *append()*. As you will recall, *append()* allows you to insert content at the end of each matched element in a selection, as in the following code:

```
$(".my-elements").append("<p>Thanks!</p>");
```

This appends the paragraph with text to the end of each matched element. Each insertion is added to the DOM tree, allowing you to access the added elements for further scripting. For example, the <p> elements added in the code could now be accessed using *$(".my-elements p")*.

In addition to this, you can use the *appendTo()* method, which allows you to insert content within the $() function and append it to the end of each matched element of a selection that is sent as an argument in the *appendTo()* method. The following code shows an example of this:

```
$("<p>Thanks!</p>").appendTo(".my-elements");
```

As you can see, both *append()* and *appendTo()* perform the same task, but having both gives you the flexibility to specify the selection and then the content or to specify the content and then the selection.

Insertion Methods

There are several other methods for inserting content within, before, or after matched elements. These are listed in Table 5-6.

All of these work the same way as *append()/appendTo()*, but place the specified content in different places. For example, *before()/insertBefore()* will place the specified content outside the matched elements right before each element's opening tag, while *prepend()/prependTo()* will place the content within the matched elements immediately after each element's opening tag.

Some examples of this will be shown based on the following HTML code snippet:

```
<div class="bio">
John is a writer.
</div>
```

Methods	Description
append() appendTo()	Inserts content within each matched element immediately before the element's closing tag
prepend() prependTo()	Inserts content within each matched element immediately after the element's opening tag
after() insertAfter()	Inserts content immediately after the closing tag of each matched element (outside of the matched element)
before() insertBefore()	Inserts content immediately before the opening tag of each matched element (outside of the matched element)

Table 5-6   Methods That Insert Content

```
<div class="bio">
Marty is a black belt in Kung Foo.
</div>
```

Using *$(".bio").before("<p>Some random text</p>");* will result in the following HTML after being executed:

```
<p>Some random text</p>
<div class="bio">
John is a writer.
</div>
<p>Some random text</p>
<div class="bio">
Marty is a black belt in Kung Foo.
</div>
```

Using *$(".bio").prepend("<p>Some random text</p>");* will result in the following:

```
<div class="bio">
<p>Some random text</p>
John is a writer.
</div>
<div class="bio">
<p>Some random text</p>
Marty is a black belt in Kung Foo.
</div>
```

Using *$(".bio").after("<p>Some random text</p>");* will result in the following:

```
<div class="bio">
John is a writer.
</div>
<p>Some random text</p>
<div class="bio">
Marty is a black belt in Kung Foo.
</div>
<p>Some random text</p>
```

As you can see, you can make any selection you need and combine it with one of these methods to place content into the document wherever you need it.

Moving Elements

Elements in the DOM tree can be moved using the same methods. You simply select the elements to move and insert them into a specified new location. For example, suppose you had the following HTML code (save as *move-els.html*):

```
<!DOCTYPE html>
<html>
<head>
```

```
  <meta charset="utf-8">
  <title>Move Elements</title>
  <style type="text/css">
    #navbox { width:40%; border:solid 1px #000; }
  </style>
  <script src="jquery-1.9.1.min.js" type="text/javascript"></script>
  <script src="move-els.js" type="text/javascript"></script>
</head>
<body>
  <div>
    <form action="moved-box.html">
      <button id="move-box">Move Navigation Box</button>
    </form>
  </div>
  <div id="navbox">
    <a href="about.html">About</a><br>
    <a href="services.html">Services</a><br>
    <a href="contact.html">Contact</a>
  </div>
  <p id="mystuff">
  I like to talk about stuff. I think most stuff is cool, so it
probably is no surprise to you that I keep talking about stuff!
  </p>
</body>
</html>
```

Here, you have a navigation box (*#navbox*) and a paragraph (*#mystuff*). There is also a button (*#move-box*) that will allow you to move the navigation box. Suppose you wanted to move the navigation box below the paragraph. jQuery allows you to easily do this using the following code (save as *move-els.js*):

```
$(document).ready(function() {
  $("#move-box").click(function(event) {
    event.preventDefault();
    $("#navbox").insertAfter("#mystuff");
  });
});
```

As you can see, *#navbox* is selected, then inserted after *#mystuff* using *insertAfter()*. Figure 5-3 shows the initial page, and Figure 5-4 shows the page after the button has been clicked.

Inserting Wrapper Elements

There may be times when you want to wrap an element around each matched element (multiple wrapper elements) or wrap all of the matched elements within a single wrapper element. These adjustments can be made using *wrap()* and *wrapAll()*.

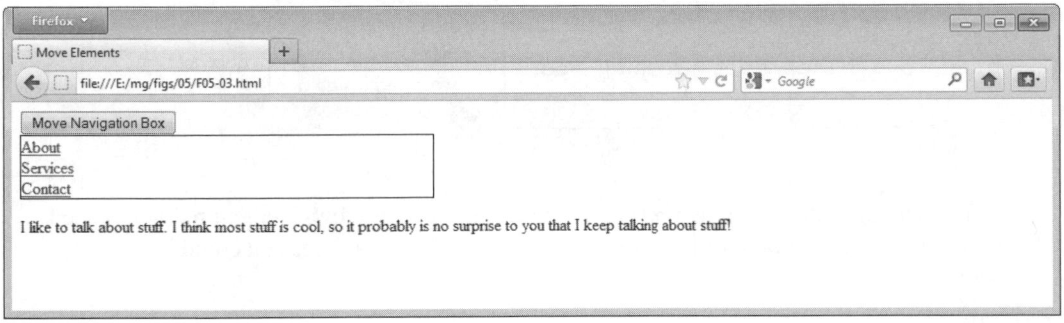

Figure 5-3 The initial page

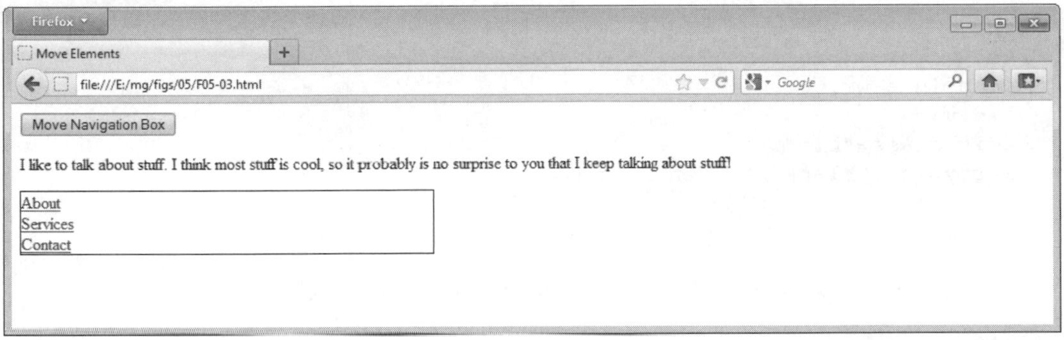

Figure 5-4 The page after the button is clicked

Suppose you had the following HTML code snippet:

```
<div class="bio">
John is a writer.
</div>
<div class="bio">
Marty is a black belt in Kung Foo.
</div>
```

You can use *wrap( )* to wrap an element around each one of the <div> elements individually, as in the following code:

```
$(".bio").wrap("<div></div>");
```

This will result in the following HTML code:

```
<div>
<div class="bio">
John is a writer.
</div>
</div>
```

The first <div> element is wrapped inside a <div> element

```
<div>
<div class="bio">
Marty is a black belt in Kung Foo.
</div>
</div>
```

The last <div> element also gets wrapped inside a <div> element

In contrast to this, using *wrapAll( )* will result in a single <div> element being wrapped around the outside of both of the *.bio* <div> elements. For example, you could use the following code:

```
$(".bio").wrap("<div></div>");
```

This will result in the following HTML code:

```
<div>
<div class="bio">
John is a writer.
</div>
<div class="bio">
Marty is a black belt in Kung Foo.
</div>
</div>
```

Here, there is only a single <div> wrapped around the *.bio* <div> elements.

Copying Elements

The *clone( )* method allows you to copy selected elements and then place the copy into the document where you need it using one of the content insertion methods. For example, suppose you had the following HTML code (save as *clone.html*):

```
<!DOCTYPE html>
<html>
<head>
  <meta charset="utf-8">
  <title>Clone Elements</title>
  <style type="text/css">
    #navbox { width:40%; border:solid 1px #000; }
  </style>
  <script src="jquery-1.9.1.min.js" type="text/javascript"></script>
  <script src="clone.js" type="text/javascript"></script>
</head>
<body>
  <div>
    <form action="clone-box.html">
      <button id="clone-box">Clone Navigation Box</button>
```

```
    </form>
  </div>
  <div id="navbox">
    <a href="about.html">About</a><br>
    <a href="services.html">Services</a><br>
    <a href="contact.html">Contact</a>
  </div>
  <p id="mystuff">
  I like to talk about stuff. I think most stuff is cool, so it
  probably is no surprise to you that I keep talking about stuff!
  </p>
</body>
</html>
```

You could use *clone()* to copy the *#nav-box* element, then chain the *appendTo()* method to insert the copied navigation box just before the closing </body> tag when the button is clicked, as shown in this code:

```
$(document).ready(function() {
  $("#clone-box").click(function(event) {
    event.preventDefault();
    $("#navbox").clone().appendTo("body");
  });
});
```

This will make a copy of the navigation box after the other content on the page. Figure 5-5 shows the initial page, and Figure 5-6 shows the page after the button is clicked.

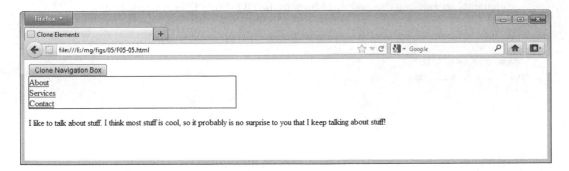

Figure 5-5 The initial page

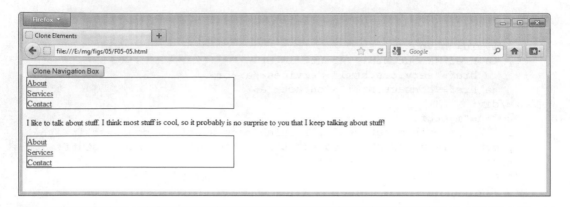

Figure 5-6 The page after the button is clicked, with the additional navigation box

Removing Elements

When you need to remove elements, you can choose between *empty()*, *remove()*, and *detach()*.

- The *empty()* method removes all elements and their children that are inside of the matched elements (including text).

- The *remove()* method removes the matched elements themselves in addition to all children of the matched elements (including text).

- The *detach()* method works just like *remove()*, except that it keeps a record of the detached elements so that you can add them back to the DOM tree later if needed.

For example, suppose you had the following HTML code snippet:

```
<div class="bio">
John is a writer.
</div>
<div class="bio">
Marty is a black belt in Kung Foo.
</div>
```

Using *$(".bio").empty();* would result in the following HTML code when complete:

```
<div class="bio"></div>
<div class="bio"></div>
```

Using *$(".bio").remove();* or *$(".bio").detach();* would result in the <div> elements being removed entirely from the document, but when using *detach()*, they can be restored using an insertion method, as in the following code:

```
$(".bio").appendTo("body");
```

All of these can be helpful to remove elements from the document when needed.

Try This 5-2   Add Elements

pr05-02.html
pr05-02.js

This project allows you to practice using DOM insertion methods in jQuery to add elements to a document.

Step by Step

1. Insert the following HTML code into your editor and save the file as *pr05-02.html*:

```
<!DOCTYPE html>
<html>
<head>
  <meta charset="utf-8">
  <title>Project 5-2</title>
  <style type="text/css">
    .summary { border:1px solid #000; width:30%; margin:1em;
padding:10px; }
  </style>
  <script src="jquery-1.9.1.min.js" type="text/javascript"></script>
  <script src="pr05-02.js" type="text/javascript"></script>
</head>
<body>
<div class="summary">
This article is very interesting!
</div>
<div class="summary">
This article is also very interesting!
</div>
<div>
  <form action="added.html">
    <button id="add">Add Elements</button>
  </form>
</div>
</body>
</html>
```

2. In the *pr05-02.js* file, add jQuery code that will add a paragraph with the text "Article by Me!" at the end of each element with a class of *summary*.

3. Save the file. When complete, the code should look like this:

```
$(document).ready(function() {
  $("#add").click(function(event) {
    event.preventDefault();
```

(continued)

```
        $(".summary").append("<p>Article by Me!</p>");
    });
});
```

4. Open the *pr05-02.html* file in your Web browser. Click the button to add the paragraph to the end of both <div> elements.

Try This Summary

In this project, you used your knowledge of DOM insertion methods to add elements to a document.

Chapter 5 Self Test

1. A single-line comment begins with two _____ and ends at the end of the line.

2. A multiple-line comment begins with _____ and does not end until _____ is found in the code.

   A. //, //

   B. \\, //

   C. /*, */

   D. #, #

3. JavaScript _____ and _____ should not be used as variable names.

   A. keywords, reserved words

   B. names, ids

   C. keys, known words

   D. ids, names

4. JavaScript has five basic data types: number, string, Boolean, undefined, and _____.

   A. float

   B. double

   C. char

   D. null

5. A Boolean value is either *true* or *false*.

  A. True

  B. False

6. If you need quote marks within other quote marks, you will need to either switch between single and double quotes or to escape the additional quotes with _____.

  A. forward slashes (/)

  B. number symbol (#)

  C. backslashes (\)

  D. percent symbol (%)

7. The ++ operator adds 2 to a number.

  A. True

  B. False

8. The === operator returns *true* if the values on both sides of it are both _____ and of the same _____ _____.

  A. equal, data type

  B. not equal, data type

  C. integers, original origin

  D. strings, array name

9. The _____ statement allows you to provide an alternate set of statements to execute when the condition in an *if* statement does not return *true*.

  A. otherwise

  B. else

  C. in lieu of

  D. instead

10. A function _____ allows you to name the function and call it anywhere in the script.

  A. constant

  B. definer

  C. declaration

  D. creator

11. The _____ property contains the number of items in an array.

    A. count

    B. length

    C. num

    D. total

12. The Document Object Model (DOM) gives languages access to the structure of a document, which is made up of a series of _____.

    A. nodes

    B. points

    C. spots

    D. spaces

13. jQuery allows you to set, add, or remove attributes and to get or set values for those attributes using the *attribute()* method.

    A. True

    B. False

14. You can use the _____ or the _____ method to insert content immediately before the opening tag of each matched element.

    A. priorTo(), insertPriorTo()

    B. inFront(), insertInFront()

    C. before(), insertBefore()

    D. prepend(), prependTo()

15. When you need to remove elements, you can choose between *empty()*, *remove()*, and _____.

    A. erase()

    B. detach()

    C. delete()

    D. pop()

Chapter 6

Animations and Effects

Key Skills & Concepts

- Show and Hide Animation Methods
- Callback Functions
- Creating Custom Animations
- Stopping Animations

The jQuery library gives you a number of options for animating elements in the document. These include showing, hiding, sliding, fading, and even creating your own custom animations. Since jQuery deals with any cross-browser issues, you can simply call the jQuery methods you need to use and the library will handle the animation work across the various browsers.

In this chapter, you will learn how to use the different animation methods available in the jQuery library, how to create custom animations, and how to stop animations that are currently running.

Show and Hide Animation Methods

The jQuery library provides a set of methods for common animations. These are listed in Table 6-1.

The options range from simply showing and hiding elements to sliding and fading. To begin, you will look at the *show()* and *hide()* methods.

Method	Description
show()	Displays an element
hide()	Hides an element
toggle()	Alternates between *show()* and *hide()*
slideDown()	Displays an element by gradually moving it down into the display area
slideUp()	Hides an element by gradually moving it up from the display area
slideToggle()	Alternates between *slideDown()* and *slideUp()*
fadeIn()	Displays an element by gradually increasing its opacity
fadeOut()	Hides an element by gradually decreasing its opacity
fadeToggle()	Alternates between *fadeIn()* and *fadeOut()*

Table 6-1   Common Animation Methods

The show() and hide() Methods

The *show()* and *hide()* methods allow you to show and hide elements in the document: *show()* will display hidden elements, and *hide()* will hide elements that are already displayed. The showing and hiding is done through the CSS *display* property—*hide()* works like *display:none*, while *show()* returns the *display* property to its original state (*block*, *inline*, and so on).

It is typically a good idea to display all content by default for accessibility (for those who don't have JavaScript to uncover a hidden element, for instance). With that in mind, you will likely want to do any initial hiding via your jQuery/JavaScript code. In jQuery, this can be done using the *hide()* method.

As an example, suppose you had an element you wanted to be hidden initially, but it could be uncovered by clicking a link. You might, for instance, have something similar to the following HTML code snippet:

The link on this line should cause the
<div> element below it to display

```
<div id="question">
   What is the answer? <a href="answer.html" id="ans-link">Get Answer</a>
</div>
<div id="answer">
   The answer is 42!
</div>
```

This <div> element needs to be hidden initially and displayed when the link is clicked

You want to hide the *answer* <div> element until the link is clicked to uncover it. Since you don't want to hide it from those without JavaScript enabled, it is best not to hide it via CSS (Cascading Style Sheets). Instead, you can use jQuery code to hide it as soon as the document is ready to be manipulated, as in the following code:

```
$(document).ready(function() {
   $("#answer").hide();
});
```

The *hide()* method is used to hide the *answer* <div> element

This will simply hide the element immediately, which works well in this case (since you want it to appear hidden without any delay).

As you can see, calling *hide()* without an argument will just hide any selected elements instantly. If you want to hide an element with a gradual animation, you can supply an argument to determine the speed at which the element will be hidden. Table 6-2 lists the valid types of values for the speed argument.

The three string values are presets that will animate over 600, 400, or 200 milliseconds. In addition, you can supply your own number of milliseconds to have the animation operate at a

Example	Description
hide("slow")	Hides the element in 600 milliseconds
hide("normal")	Hides the element in 400 milliseconds
hide("fast")	Hides the element in 200 milliseconds
hide(*number*)	Hides the element in the specified number of milliseconds

Table 6-2 Possible Speed Values

custom speed. For example, *hide(2000)* will hide the element in 2000 milliseconds (2 seconds).

The *show()* method will show a hidden element, restoring its original *display* property. In the case of the example, the default display for a <div> element *(block)* would be used since it was not specified in the CSS or changed before being hidden in the jQuery code.

For example, to display the hidden *answer* element when the link is clicked, you could use the following code:

```
$(document).ready(function() {
  $("#answer").hide();
  $("#ans-link").click(function(event) {
    $("#answer").show();
  });
});
```

When the link is clicked, the *answer* element will be displayed immediately, and will move any elements following it to fit back into its space in the document.

This will simply show the element once. If you want to alternate between *show()* and *hide()* each time the button is clicked, you can use *toggle()* as in the following code:

```
$(document).ready(function() {
  $("#answer").hide();
  $("#ans-link").click(function(event) {
    $("#answer").toggle();
  });
});
```

The answer will now be shown on the first click, hidden on the second click, and so on.

The *show()* and *toggle()* methods can take the same speed argument that *hide()* does, so they, too, can be animated if desired. When using the speed argument to animate a show/hide, the element's height, width, and opacity will all be changed during the animation [*show()* causes the element to become larger and more visible, while *hide()* causes the element to become smaller and less visible]. If this is not the desired animation effect, you can use one of the other predefined methods or create your own custom animation (all of which will be discussed as you proceed through this chapter).

Building a FAQ Page

For the examples in this chapter, it will be helpful to have a document that you can build on in order to see the different effects in action. To begin, use the following HTML code (save as *animate.html*):

```
<!DOCTYPE html>
<html>
<head>
  <meta charset="utf-8">
  <title>Animations</title>
  <style type="text/css">
    header { float:left; background-color:#000; color:#FFF; width:90%;
             padding:1% 5%; text-align:center; }
    #main { clear:both; float:left; width:76%; font-family:Arial;
margin:2%; }
    #sidebar { float:left; width:16%; margin:2% 0%; text-align:center; }
    footer { clear:both; float:left; background-color:#000; color:#FFF;
             width:90%; padding:1% 5%; text-align:center; }
    .question { font-weight:bold; font-size:1.3em; width:80%; margin-
top:1em; }
    .answer { font-style:italic; width:80%; }
  </style>
  <script src="jquery-1.9.1.min.js" type="text/javascript"></script>
  <script src="animate.js" type="text/javascript"></script>
</head>
<body>
<header>
<h1>Frequently Asked Questions</h1>
</header>
<article id="main">
  <div class="question">
    What does this site do?
    <form action="answers.html">
      <button id="ans-00">Show Answer</button>
    </form>
  </div>
  <div class="answer">
    We answer questions. We try to think of every possible set of
questions that could be asked and then create a FAQ for each set of
questions we can group together. We put it on this site and then you
find one of the FAQ pages from our main page or by searching. Once you
find a page, you get answers.
  </div>
  <div class="question">
    Do you charge for this exemplary service?
    <form action="answers.html">
      <button id="ans-01">Show Answer</button>
```

```
      </form>
    </div>
    <div class="answer">
      Not at this time. Until we decide to do so, you can sign up for a
free account to view any FAQ page you choose. If you sign up before we
begin charging, the site will always remain free for you to use, while
the others must pay large amounts of money to access all of these
extraordinary FAQ pages!
    </div>
  </article>
  <aside id="sidebar">
    <div>
      <form action="answers.html">
        <button id="book-show">Show Book Info!</button>
      </form>
    </div>
    <div id="book-info">
      Yes, I wrote a book called <cite>How to Write FAQs: The Rules</cite>!
      Buy it today!
    </div>
  </aside>
  <footer>
    This page copyright &copy; this year by me!
  </footer>
</body>
</html>
```

This creates a very basic page with a header, main content, sidebar, and footer. Figure 6-1 shows the page before any scripting is done. Notice that all of the elements are currently displayed.

Within the page, you will be reacting to clicks on the various buttons to show or hide elements as needed. The first thing you will want to do is hide all of the elements that have the *answer* class. This is done easily by using the class as the selector and calling the *hide()* method, as in the following code (save as *animate.js*):

```
$(document).ready(function() {
  $(".answer").hide();
});
```

Next, you will want to hide the *book-info* element. This is another easy task to perform by selecting its id and using *hide()*. This is added in the following code:

```
$(document).ready(function() {
  $(".answer").hide();
  $("#book-info").hide();
});
```

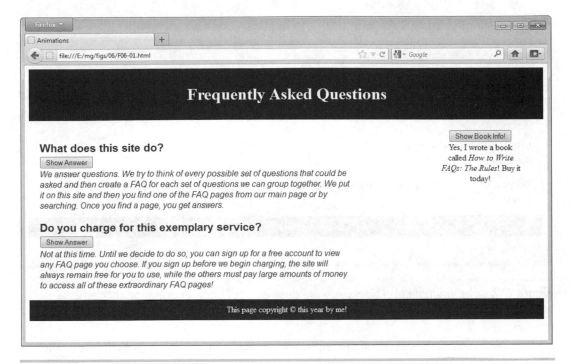

Figure 6-1 The static *animate.html* page

At this point, everything you need to hide has been hidden. When you load the *animate* *.html* page in a browser now, it should display as shown in Figure 6-2.

In this section, you will write the code to toggle the first answer in the list between show and hide (the others will be dealt with as you proceed through the sections that follow). To select the first answer, you can use *:eq()* to get the element when selecting the *answers* class. This can be done as in Chapter 2, shown in the following code:

```
$(".answer:eq(0)")
```

Recall that *:eq()* uses a zero-based index, so the first item will be at index 0, the second item at index 1, and so on.

Alternatively, jQuery provides a separate *eq()* method. This allows you to make a selection first, then apply the *eq()* method to it in order to get any element using a zero-based index. Using this, you can make the selection of the first *answer* <div> element with the following code:

```
$(".answer").eq(0)
```

In either case, you can chain further jQuery methods to the selection, such as the one you need here, which is *toggle()*. To complete the code, you will need to select the show/hide button for the first answer (id *ans-00*), register the *click* event, and add the toggle to the

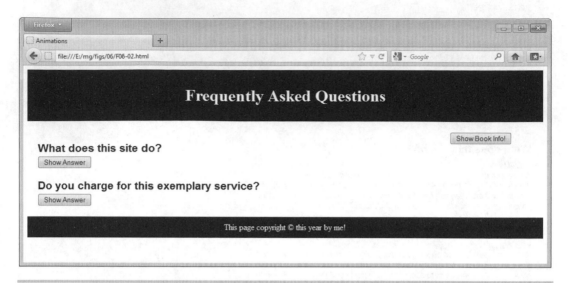

Figure 6-2 The *animate.html* page with the answers and book information hidden

<div> element containing the first answer. For practice, you will use *1000* as the argument to *toggle()*, which will animate the showing and hiding of the element over one second. The following code adds this functionality:

```
$(document).ready(function() {
  $(".answer").hide();
  $("#book-info").hide();
  $("#ans-00").click(function(event) {
    event.preventDefault();              ◄──────────── Prevents the default action
    $(".answer").eq(0).toggle(1000);  ◄─────────────┐
  });                                                │
});            Selects the first element from the selection (which got all of the elements with the answer
              class) and toggles between showing and hiding the element over one second each time
              that the button is clicked
```

Refresh the *answers.html* page in your browser and click the button. Figure 6-3 shows the result once the button is clicked and the show animation completes.

There is one final issue to deal with here. You will notice that the button is labeled "Show Answer" when the toggle is showing the element *and* when the element is being hidden. It would be better for the user to see which type of action will take place when the button is clicked each time.

The good news is that you can fix this by simply alternating the text of the button using the *text()* method you learned in the last chapter. Since it is set to "Show Answer" in the

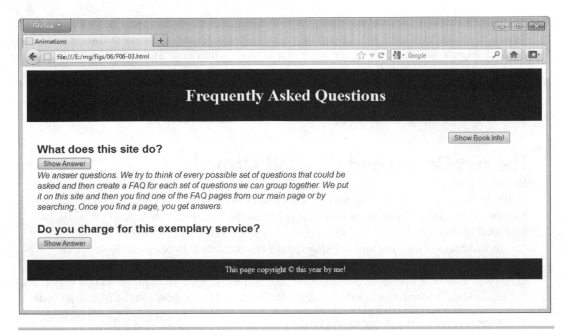

Figure 6-3 The first answer is displayed after the button is clicked.

HTML code, you can use that value to alternate the text between "Show Answer" and "Hide Answer" each time the button is clicked with an *if/else* statement. This is shown in the following code:

```
$(document).ready(function() {
  $(".answer").hide();
  $("#book-info").hide();
  $("#ans-00").click(function(event) {
    event.preventDefault();
    $(".answer").eq(0).toggle(1000);
    if ($("#ans-00").text() === "Show Answer") {
      $("#ans-00").text("Hide Answer");
    }
    else {
      $("#ans-00").text("Show Answer");
    }
  });
});
```

Begins an *if* statement that checks the value of the text in the <button> element

If the text is equal to "Show Answer," this statement is executed, which changes the text to "Hide Answer"

If the text is not equal to "Show Answer," this statement is executed, which changes the text to "Show Answer"

Reload the *animate.html* page in your browser and click the button. Each time the button is clicked, its label will change to reflect what will happen the next time it is clicked. Figure 6-4 shows the page when the answer is hidden ("Show Answer" label for the button), and Figure 6-5 shows the page when the answer is displayed ("Hide Answer" label for the button).

You now have the setup complete for the first answer. To tackle the display of the second answer, you will use the methods jQuery provides for sliding elements.

The slideDown() and slideUp() Methods

In contrast to *show()* and *hide()*, the *slideDown()* and *slideUp()* methods show and hide elements by animating only the height. This makes the elements appear to "slide" in and out of the page. If you want to toggle between the two, the *slideToggle()* method is provided to do so.

To make use of this, you will use *slideToggle()* to alternate between *slideDown()* and *slideUp()* each time the button for the second answer is clicked. This will be nearly identical to the code to handle the previous answer <div>, but will register the event to the second button and display/hide the second answer <div> using *slideToggle()*. This is shown in the following code:

```
$("#ans-01").click(function(event) {          Notice the id for the second <button>
    event.preventDefault();                   element is used to register a new click event
    $(".answer").eq(1).slideToggle("slow");
});
```

The second element in the selection of elements with the *answer* class is selected and the *slideToggle()* method is applied using "slow" as the argument

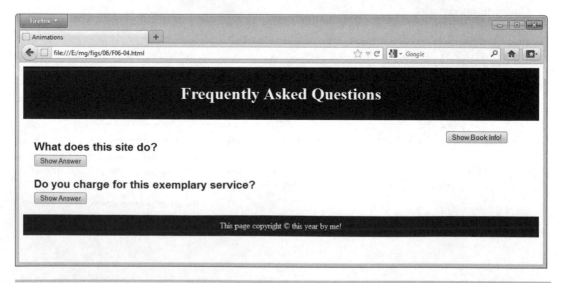

Figure 6-4 The page when the answer is hidden

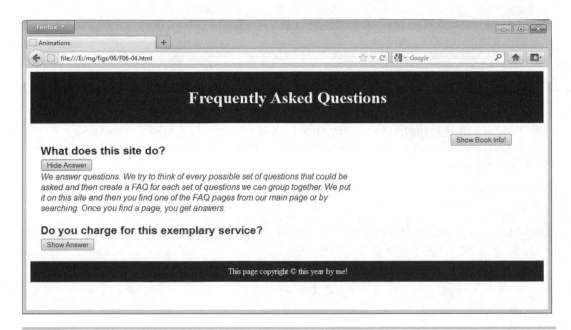

Figure 6-5 The page when the answer is shown

Notice here that the second <button> element (id ans-01) gets a *click* event registered to it. The second *answer* element is selected by providing 1 as the index in *eq()*. Finally, *slideToggle()* is applied with the "slow" argument, which will animate the slide animation over 600 milliseconds (a little faster than your previous element's animation, which was set to 1000 milliseconds).

This can now be added to the code in place to animate both of the *answer* <div> elements when the corresponding buttons are clicked. This is shown in the following code:

```
$(document).ready(function() {
  $(".answer").hide();
  $("#book-info").hide();
  $("#ans-00").click(function(event) {
    event.preventDefault();
    $(".answer").eq(0).toggle(1000);
    if ($("#ans-00").text() === "Show Answer") {
      $("#ans-00").text("Hide Answer");
    }
    else {
      $("#ans-00").text("Show Answer");
    }
  });
```

The first *click* event for the first button is handled

```
$("#ans-01").click(function(event) {
    event.preventDefault();
    $(".answer").eq(1).slideToggle("slow");
});
});
```

The *click* event for the second button is handled—but it isn't alternating the button text yet!

This will slide the text in and out when the second button is clicked, but that pesky button text is at it again! One solution would be to rewrite the *if/else* statement here, as in the following code:

```
$("#ans-01").click(function(event) {
    event.preventDefault();
    $(".answer").eq(1).slideToggle("slow");
    if ($("#ans-01").text() === "Show Answer") {
        $("#ans-01").text("Hide Answer");
    }
    else {
        $("#ans-01").text("Show Answer");
    }
});
```

The *if/else* statement is added to change the button label text

Notice that this is the same *if/else* statement you used for the previous button (*#ans-00*), with the only change being the selection of *#ans-01* instead of *#ans-00*. It would be nice if you did not need to duplicate this code each time you want to change button label text. Instead, you could write this *if/else* statement into a separate JavaScript function and send it the selected element as an argument. The following code shows how this could be written as a function:

The function is declared with a single argument, a jQuery object (an element selection in this case)

```
function labelChange($jqObject) {
    if ($jqObject.text() === "Show Answer") {
        $jqObject.text("Hide Answer");
    }
    else {
        $jqObject.text("Show Answer");
    }
}
```

Since the *$jqObject* argument is already a jQuery object, the $() function is not required to reselect the necessary element(s); all jQuery methods are available to it, and *text()* is used here

The function performs the same task, but is sent an argument to determine which <button> element is to be changed when it is called. If you go back to the *click()* event handler for the *#ans-00* element, you could use the following code to call the function:

```
$("#ans-00").click(function(event) {
  event.preventDefault();
  $(".answer").eq(0).toggle(1000);
  labelChange($(this));
});
```

The *labelChange()* function is called using *$(this)*, which refers to the *#ans-00* button here (since it is the object that invoked the *click()* method)

Here, the value of *$(this)* is sent as the argument to the *labelChange()* function. You could send it *$(ans-00)* specifically if preferred, but using *$(this)* allows the function call to remain more consistent when used in other event handlers (you won't have to use *#ans-00*, *#ans-01*, and so on for the argument each time).

To put this all together, edit your *animate.js* file so that you have the following code (adds the function and both function calls):

```
$(document).ready(function() {
  function labelChange($jqObject) {
    if ($jqObject.text() === "Show Answer") {
      $jqObject.text("Hide Answer");
    }
    else {
      $jqObject.text("Show Answer");
    }
  }
  $(".answer").hide();
  $("#book-info").hide();
  $("#ans-00").click(function(event) {
    event.preventDefault();
    $(".answer").eq(0).toggle(1000);
    labelChange($(this));
  });
  $("#ans-01").click(function(event) {
    event.preventDefault();
    $(".answer").eq(1).slideToggle("slow");
    labelChange($(this));
  });
});
```

The function is added

The function is called in both cases using *$(this)* as the argument, which will be *#ans-00* for the first button and *#ans-01* for the second button

Reload the *animate.html* file in your browser. Both buttons should now have the label text change when clicked. The use of the function saves some duplicate coding, and each animation still works as expected. Figure 6-6 shows the page after the second button is clicked and the label text is changed.

The fadeIn() and fadeOut() Methods

The *fadeIn()* and *fadeOut()* methods alter the opacity of the element, increasing it for *fadeIn()* and decreasing it for *fadeOut()*. To toggle between them, you can use *toggleFade()*.

The last element to animate in your *animate.html* file is in the sidebar. In this case, you will use *toggleFade()* to fade the element in or out when the "Show Book Info!" button is clicked.

The only difference here is that this element is not part of the *answers* class, but has its own id (*#book-info*). The button element has an id of *#book-show*. The following code can be used to toggle the fade effect when the button is clicked:

```
$("#book-show").click(function(event) {
  event.preventDefault();
  $("#book-info").fadeToggle("slow");
});
```

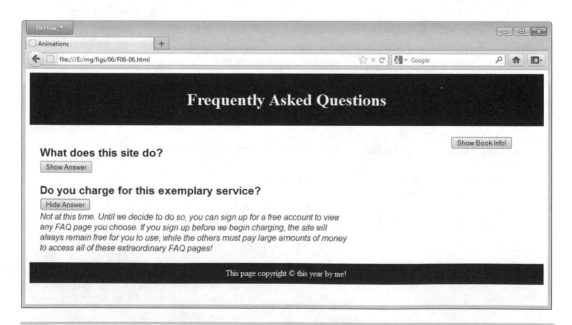

Figure 6-6 The label text for the button now changes as expected when the second button is clicked.

While this is easily added, it is not altering the label text for the <button> element yet. Not only that, but you can't simply plug in the handy function you already created as it is, because rather than "Show Answer" and "Hide Answer," you now want to use "Show Book Info!" and "Hide Book Info!" for the label text.

Looking at the label text more closely, however, shows that there is one thing in common: Both types of label text start with either "Show" or "Hide." If the remainder of the text can be sent as a second argument, then you just need a way to figure out whether the first word is "Show" or "Hide" and adjust that as needed.

The indexOf() Method in JavaScript

JavaScript offers a handy method for finding the starting position of any set of characters within a string: *indexOf()*. This method takes a string as an argument and searches for it within another string. If it is found, then the starting position of the string (zero-based) is returned. Otherwise, the value of *-1* is returned.

An example of this is shown in the following code:

```
var myText = "Is Bob here?";  ←——————— A string value is assigned to the variable myText
var whereIsBob = myText.indexOf("Bob");  // whereIsBob = 3 ←
var isThereAnI = myText.indexOf("I");  // isThereAnI = 0 ←
var whereisJoe = myText.indexOf("Joe");  // whereIsJoe = -1 ←
```

The string "Joe" is not found, so *-1* is returned ———

The string "I" is found at position 0 ———

The string "Bob" is located at position 3 (counting begins at zero) ———

Notice that you append the *indexOf()* method to a string by adding a dot and then the method, just as you would use a jQuery method. It returns the position at which the string argument is found, beginning with zero.

Altering the labelChange() Function

Using *indexOf()*, you can now alter the *labelChange()* function to work for all three buttons on the page. You will need to add a second argument, which will be the text for the label that will follow "Show" or "Hide" in each case.

The following code shows the altered *labelChange()* function:

A new argument is added, *labelText*

```
function labelChange($jqObject, labelText) {  ←——————
  if ($jqObject.text().indexOf("Show") === 0) {  ←——————
```

The *indexOf()* method determines if the string "Show" is at the beginning of the label text for the current <button> element

```
    $jqObject.text("Hide " + labelText);  ◄─────────────────┐
  }                                                          │
  else {                                                     │
    $jqObject.text("Show " + labelText);  ◄──────┐           │
    }                                            │           │
  }                                              │           │
```

If "Show" is not at the beginning of the label text, the label text is changed to "Show" plus the value sent as the second argument

If "Show" is at the beginning of the label text, the label text is changed to "Hide" plus the value sent as the second argument (which could be "Answer" or "Book Info!" in this case)

Notice that the function now looks for "Show" at the beginning of the label text for the <button> element that is sent to the function. It will then append the value of the second argument after the word "Hide" or "Show," depending on the result. So, if the function were called from the event handler for *#ans-00*, using *$(this)* and *"Answer"* as the arguments, the result of the first click would be to change the label text to *"Hide Answer"*. Calling the function from the *#book-show* event handler using *$(this)* and *"Book Info!"* as arguments would result in the first click changing the button text to *"Hide Book Info!"*.

You can now alter your *animate.js* file to alter the function and update the function calls. Edit the file to use the following code and save it:

```
$(document).ready(function() {
  function labelChange($jqObject, labelText) { ───────┐
    if ($jqObject.text().indexOf("Show") === 0) {     │
      $jqObject.text("Hide " + labelText);            │
    }                                                 │
    else {                                            │
      $jqObject.text("Show " + labelText);            │
    }                                                 │
  } ──────────────────────────────────────────────────┘
  $(".answer").hide(); ─────────────┐
  $("#book-info").hide(); ──────────┴── Hiding elements
  $("#ans-00").click(function(event) { ───┐
    event.preventDefault();                │
    $(".answer").eq(0).toggle(1000);       │
    labelChange($(this), "Answer");        │
  }); ─────────────────────────────────────┘
  $("#ans-01").click(function(event) { ───┐
    event.preventDefault();                │
    $(".answer").eq(1).slideToggle('slow');│
    labelChange($(this), "Answer");        │
  }); ─────────────────────────────────────┘
```

The *labelChange()* function now using *indexOf()*

Handles a click on the first button

Handles a click on the second button

```
$("#book-show").click(function(event) {
    event.preventDefault();
    $("#book-info").fadeToggle("slow");
    labelChange($(this), "Book Info!");
});
});
```

Handles a click on the third button

Notice that the first argument each time the function is called is *$(this)*, since *$(this)* will be the <button> element that is being handled at the time in each case. The second argument is *"Answer"* for the first two buttons, but is *"Book Info!"* for the third, allowing the single function to update the button labels for all of the buttons on the page.

Reload the *animate.html* file in your Web browser. Clicking the buttons will now show and hide each piece of content with the specified animation and will alter the button text to assist the user. Figure 6-7 shows the page after the "Show Book Info!" button is clicked once, which fades in the additional information and changes the button label text to "Hide Book Info!".

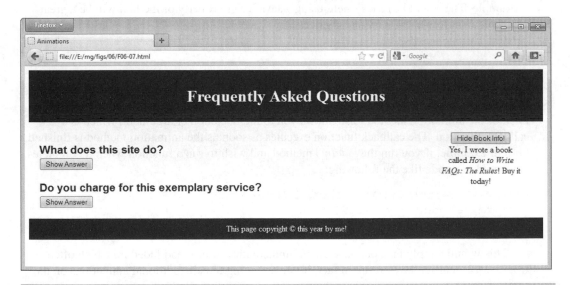

Figure 6-7   The page after the first click of the "Show Book Info!" button

Ask the Expert

Q: Those are some nice animations, but I would like to customize them more. Is there a way to place several animations in sequence or to create a custom animation?

A: Yes, both can be done! As you progress through this chapter, you will learn to use callback functions, which will allow you to call a function once the current animation is complete, giving you the option to string several animations together. You will also learn the *animate()* method, which gives you the opportunity to determine which CSS properties are animated and create a custom animation.

Q: Why use a JavaScript function when I could just replicate the *if/else* statement?

A: Referring to the example, you can use either method. Keep in mind, however, that once more buttons are added, you will need to continue replicating the *if/else* statement for every single button. The function gives you the freedom to simply call it rather than duplicating the entire statement and changing the button id each time.

Q: Do I really need another JavaScript method like *indexOf()*?

A: Often, this won't be necessary; but it is handy in some situations, such as the one in the example. There will be times where using a JavaScript property or method will be a great complement to what jQuery already does.

Callback Functions

Each of the animation methods also allows you to include another argument, which is a callback function. The callback function executes as soon as the animation method is finished.

For example, if you run the *fadeIn()* method and wish to run a function when it completes, you could use code like the following:

```
$("#my-element").fadeIn("slow", function() {
  $("#my-element").fadeOut("slow");
});
```

This would simply fade out the element immediately after it had faded in, which often would not be particularly useful. In fact, if you are going to call additional animations on the same element, you can simply chain them together, as in the following code:

```
$("#my-element").fadeIn("slow").fadeOut("slow");
```

In such a case, the chain would be quicker and easier to write. However, you can also use the callback function to animate other elements, which will give it further use.

Going back to your *animate.html* file, suppose you wanted to add another <div> element below the *#book-info* <div>, have it hidden, and have it slide down only after the "Show Book Info!" button is clicked and the animation for the *#book-info* <div> is complete. This will create what appears to be an extended animation sequence, and can be done using the callback function to do the work.

First, open your *animate.html* file and update it to use the following code for the <aside> element and save it:

```
<aside id="sidebar">
  <div>
    <form action="answers.html">
      <button id="book-show">Show Book Info!</button>
    </form>
  </div>
  <div id="book-info">
    Yes, I wrote a book called <cite>How to Write FAQs: The Rules</cite>!
    Buy it today!
  </div>
  <div id="more-book-info">
  Special! Buy the book now and save 50%! This is a limited time offer
so don't delay! Buy it today!
  </div>
</aside>
```

This <div> element is added and will be shown using a callback method

Next, alter the *animate.js* file to use the following code and save it:

```
$(document).ready(function() {
  function labelChange($jqObject, labelText) {
    if ($jqObject.text().indexOf("Show") === 0) {
      $jqObject.text("Hide " + labelText);
    }
    else {
      $jqObject.text("Show " + labelText);
    }
  }
  $(".answer").hide();
  $("#book-info").hide();
  $("#more-book-info").css({"color": "#FFF", "background-color":
"#333"}).hide();
  $("#ans-00").click(function(event) {
    event.preventDefault();
    $(".answer").eq(0).toggle(1000);
    labelChange($(this), "Answer");
  });
  $("#ans-01").click(function(event) {
    event.preventDefault();
```

Giving the *#more-book-info* element some additional CSS to highlight it and hiding it by chaining the *css()* and *hide()* methods

```
    $(".answer").eq(1).slideToggle('slow');
    labelChange($(this), "Answer");
  });
  $("#book-show").click(function(event) {
    event.preventDefault();
    $("#book-info").fadeToggle("slow", function() {
      $("#more-book-info").slideToggle("slow");
    });
    labelChange($(this), "Book Info!");
  });
});
```

Adds the callback function to slide the *#more-book-info* element down or up once the fade animation is complete

As you can see, the new element is first hidden along with the others. Within the *fadeToggle()* method for the *#book-info* element, a callback function is added as an argument, which then uses *slideToggle()* on the *#more-book-info* element once the fade is complete on the *#book-info* element.

Reload the *animate.html* file in your browser and click the "Show Book Info!" button. The first element will fade in, and the second element will slide down. Figure 6-8 shows the page once both animations have completed.

When you click a second time to hide the elements, you will notice that the fade occurs first, then the slide. While this order is great for showing the elements, it provides a bit of a jolt

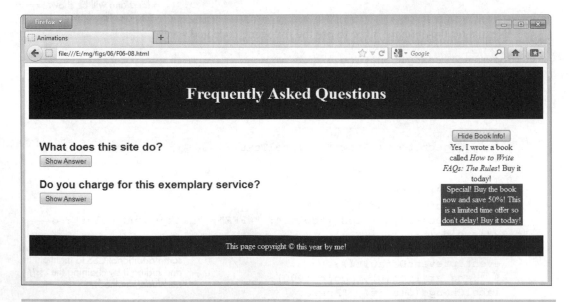

Figure 6-8 The page after the "Show Book Info!" button is clicked and the animations are complete

when hiding the elements since the fade out will "jump" the second <div> up the screen once the first one has faded out. It will then perform the slide up.

Instead of the current toggle, you may wish to perform the hiding of the elements in the reverse order of their showing. A slide up followed by a fade out would look like a much smoother transition. To do this, recall that when you hide an element, the CSS *display* property is changed to the value of *none*. This could be used with an *if/else* statement to allow you to perform the animations one way when showing and the other way when hiding. Consider the following code:

```
if ($("#book-info").css("display") === "none") {
  // Fade in #book-info and then slide down #more-book-info
}
else {
  // Slide up #more-book-info and then fade out # book-info
}
```

Here, the *if* statement uses the *css* method to determine the value of the *display* property for the *#book-info* element (since these are being shown and hidden together, testing one of them should be sufficient in this case, but be careful to adjust as needed if different tasks are performed). If *display* is *none*, then the elements will be shown by fading in the first <div> and sliding down the second. If they are currently visible, then the order will be reversed to hide them.

To complete this, you will need to fill in the additional code. Since toggling does not produce the desired effect here, you will need to specifically use *fadeIn( )*, *slideDown( )*, *slideUp( )*, and *fadeOut( )*. This would produce the following code for the *click( )* method for the "Show Book Info!" button:

```
$("#book-show").click(function(event) {
  event.preventDefault();
  if ($("#book-info").css("display") === "none") {
    $("#book-info").fadeIn("slow", function() {
      $("#more-book-info").slideDown(1500);
    });
  }
  else {
    $("#more-book-info").slideUp(1500, function() {
      $("#book-info").fadeOut("slow");
    });
  }
  labelChange($(this), "Book Info!");
});
```

If the *#book-info* element is currently hidden, then it is displayed using *fadeIn( )*, which uses a callback function to slide down the *#more-book-info* element when complete

If *#book-info* is already displayed, then the *#more-book-info* element is hidden first using *slideUp( )*, which uses a callback function to fade out the *#book-info* element when complete

This works, but the repeated use of the same two selections of *$("#book-info")* and *$("#more-book-info")* require that the elements be located in the DOM (Document Object Model) for each use (which, over time and with enough calls, will cause the script to run more slowly than it otherwise could). To keep this from being necessary, you can cache the selections in a JavaScript variable. Consider the following code:

```
var $bookInfo = $("#book-info"),
    $moreBookInfo = $("#more-book-info");
```

This places both selections into JavaScript variables. When this is done, the script will already know what element(s) to alter when it sees the variable, rather than needing to search the DOM for the element(s) again.

Since the variables represent jQuery objects (selections in this case), the variables use a $ symbol as the first character. This is not required, but can be a helpful convention to use in your code so that you can quickly recognize that the variable represents a jQuery object rather than a simple string or one of the other possible data types in JavaScript.

In this case, the variables can be defined at the beginning of the function that handles the *click()* method for the button, and can be used anywhere within that function. Thus, you could update the function to use the following code:

```
$("#book-show").click(function(event) {
  var $bookInfo = $("#book-info"),                    ─── The selections that will be
      $moreBookInfo = $("#more-book-info");           ─── reused are assigned to
  event.preventDefault();                                 variables
  if ($bookInfo.css("display") === "none") {
    $bookInfo.fadeIn("slow", function() {
      $moreBookInfo.slideDown(1500);
    });
  }
  else {
    $moreBookInfo.slideUp(1500, function() {
      $bookInfo.fadeOut("slow");
    });
  }
  labelChange($(this), "Book Info!");
});
```

The variables are used in place of the selection syntax to perform the necessary operations

With the variables in place, you can now use them in place of the usual selection syntax. The selections are now cached and used as needed, and the animations still run in the desired order.

Try This 6-1	Practice with slideDown()

pr06-01.html
pr06-01.js

This project allows you to practice using the jQuery *slideDown()* method to show a hidden <div> element on the page.

Step by Step

1. Place the following HTML code into your editor and save the file as *pr06-01.html*:

```
<!DOCTYPE html>
<html>
<head>
  <meta charset="utf-8">
  <title>Project 6-1</title>
  <style type="text/css">
    #box, #more { font-family:Verdana, sans-serif; }
  </style>
  <script src="jquery-1.9.1.min.js" type="text/javascript"></script>
  <script src="pr06-01.js" type="text/javascript"></script>
</head>
<body>
<div id="box">
  We have something new!<br>
  <a href="more.html" id="show-more">Show More</a>
</div>
<div id="more">
  We have a new product out and you really
  must see it to believe it!
</div>
</body>
</html>
```

2. In the *pr06-01.js* file, add jQuery code that will hide the *#more* element, then slide down the *#more* element slowly when the *#show-more* element is clicked ("Show More" link).

3. Save the file. When complete, the code should look like this:

```
$(document).ready(function() {
  $("#more").hide();
  $("#show-more").click(function(event) {
    event.preventDefault();
```

(continued)

```
        $("#more").slideDown("slow");
    });
});
```

4. Open the *pr06-01.html* file in your Web browser. You should see the first <div> element and the link. Clicking the link should slide down the *#more* <div> into view.

Try This Summary

In this project, you used your knowledge of one of the preset *slideDown()* animation methods to show an element using a "slide down" animation when a link was clicked.

Creating Custom Animations

The jQuery library provides the *animate()* method, which allows you to customize what CSS properties are animated, specify the speed, specify the easing, and provide a callback function when it is run. This gives you the ability to create a custom animation to fit your needs.

The *animate()* method has the following basic syntax:

```
$("#my-element").animate({ property: value, property: value },
                         duration, easing, callback);
```

The last three arguments are optional and will simply use default values if one or more of them is not specified.

The arguments and their possible values are listed in Table 6-3.

Argument	Description
{ property: value, property: value }	Lists CSS properties that are to be animated and the value of each property at the completion of the animation
duration	The time it will take to complete the animation (in milliseconds) or one of the preset values *slow*, *normal*, or *fast*
easing	The type of easing to use for the animation: either *swing* or *linear*
callback	The callback function to execute when the animation completes

Table 6-3 Arguments for the *animate()* Method

Property/Value Map

The first argument is a property/value map, which is simply a list of properties and values in object literal notation. The properties are the CSS properties to be animated, and the values are the target values for each property when the animation is complete.

You can animate one property or as many as you need using this method. The limitation is that only properties with numeric values can be animated, such as width, height, top, left, font-size, margin, padding, border, and so on. The values can be a target number or a relative target number using += or -= followed by the value. They can also be one of the preset values of *show*, *hide*, and *toggle*. Some examples of this are shown in the following code:

```
$("#my-element").animate({"height":"20px"});
    // increases or decreases the height to 20px
$("#my-element").animate({"height":"+=20px"});
    // increases the current height by 20px
$("#my-element").animate({"height":"toggle"});
    // increases the height from 0 to its original value, or decreases
it to zero
$("#my-element").animate({"height":"+=20px", "font-size": "-=0.3em"});
    // increases the height by 20px and decreased the font by 0.3em
```

As you can see, you can come up with any number of combinations within the map. This can be used to customize the properties and values that are animated according to your specific needs.

Duration Values

Just like the other animation methods, the *animate()* method itself can use the preset values of *slow*, *normal*, and *fast*, as well as define a specific number of milliseconds that the animation should last.

Some examples of providing the duration argument are shown here:

```
$("#my-element").animate({"height":"20px"}, 1000);
    // Animates for 1000 milliseconds (one second)
$("#my-element").animate({"height":"20px"}, "fast");
    // Animates "fast" (200 milliseconds)
```

As with the other animation methods, specifying this argument is fairly straightforward.

Easing Values

There are only two values for the easing argument: *swing* and *linear*. The *swing* value is used by default if the argument is not specified. Other values are possible, however, using jQuery plugins, which will be discussed in Chapter 10.

The easing defines the speed of the animation at different points in the animation sequence. For example, the *linear* setting keeps the speed constant throughout the animation, while *swing* will start, speed up a bit, and then slow down a bit as the animation progresses.

Some examples are shown in the following code:

```
$("#my-element").animate({"height":"20px"}, 1000, "swing");
    // Animates using swing easing
$("#my-element").animate({"height":"20px"}, 1000, "linear");
    // Animates using linear easing
```

Callback Function

As with the other animation methods, you can provide a callback function to be executed when the animation completes. An example of this is shown next:

```
$("#my-element").animate({"height":"20px"}, 1000, "swing", function()
{
  // Code to run when animation completes
});
```

The Second Form of animate()

In addition to the standard form with four arguments, you can call *animate()* using a second form, which uses the first argument (the property/value map), then moves the other arguments to a map to provide the second argument. The map for the second argument adds the ability to provide special easing for specific properties, specify whether the animation should run in queue or at the same time as the previous animation, and provide a *step* function that is called for each animated property and element.

The following code shows the general syntax for this form of the *animate()* method:

```
$("#my-element").animate({
    property: value,
    property: value
  }, {
    duration: value,
    easing: value,
    specialEasing: {
      property: value,
      property: value
    },
    complete: function() {
      // Code to run when animation completes
    },
```

```
    queue: value,
    step: function() {
      // Code to run for each animated property and element
    }
});
```

The key new elements here are the *specialEasing* map within the second map, the *queue* property, and the *step* function.

Special Easing

The *specialEasing* map allows you to define the easing for each animated property individually, rather than having all of the properties use the same easing. So, if you want to animate both the height and border width of an element but use *swing* for the height and *linear* for the border width, you could write the *specialEasing* map as in the following code:

```
specialEasing: {
    "height": "swing",
    "border-width": "linear"
    },
```

Queue

The *queue* property can be set to *true* or *false*. If set to *true*, the animation will run in its normal position in the queue (after all previous animations). If set to *false*, then the animation will run at the same time as the animation prior to it in the normal queue, and the normal queue will then resume again afterward.

Step Function

The last new option is a step function, which allows you to execute code at each step of the animation for each animated element. This can be useful if you wish to alter the animation at each step or need to make additional customizations.

Updating the FAQ Page

Now that you have seen how the *animate()* method works, you can use it to update your *animate.html* and *animate.js* files. Suppose you want to provide a custom animation when the page loads that will hide the <h1> element, add a border around it, and then show it by animating both the border width and height of the element.

This can all be done in your jQuery code, so no updates are needed to the HTML file. The first part of this is straightforward. The element can be hidden by simply calling the *hide()* method, as in the following code:

```
$("header h1").hide();
```

Next, you can chain together the *css()* method (to add the border) and the *animate()* method to create the animation:

```
$("header h1").css({ "border-style": "solid",
                     "border-color": "#FFF",
                     "border-width": "10px" })
      .animate({ "border-width": "show", "height": "show" }, 5000);
```

Here, the CSS is altered to add a 10px border around the <h1> element while it is hidden. The *animate()* method then uses *show* as the value for the *border-width* and *height* properties, which allows the element to show the animation.

CAUTION

Unless an element is already visible, the *animate()* method will run while the element is hidden and be invisible to the user unless either *show()* is called on the element before *animate()* or the properties are animated using the value *show,* as in this example.

You can now add this to your JavaScript file. Update *animate.js* to use the following code and save it:

```
$(document).ready(function() {
  function labelChange($jqObject, labelText) {
    if ($jqObject.text().indexOf("Show") === 0) {
      $jqObject.text("Hide " + labelText);
    }
    else {
      $jqObject.text("Show " + labelText);
    }
  }
  $(".answer").hide();                                          The new code is
  $("#book-info").hide();                                       inserted here
  $("#more-book-info").css({"color": "#FFF", "background-color":
"#333"}).hide();
  $("header h1").hide();
  $("header h1").css({ "border-style": "solid",
                       "border-color": "#FFF",
                       "border-width": "10px" })
          .animate({ "border-width": "show", "height": "show" }, 5000);
  $("#ans-00").click(function(event) {
    event.preventDefault();
    $(".answer").eq(0).toggle(1000);
      labelChange($(this), "Answer");
  });
  $("#ans-01").click(function(event) {
    event.preventDefault();
    $(".answer").eq(1).slideToggle('slow');
```

```
      labelChange($(this), "Answer");
   });
   $("#book-show").click(function(event) {
      var $bookInfo = $("#book-info"),
          $moreBookInfo = $("#more-book-info");
      event.preventDefault();
      if ($bookInfo.css("display") === "none") {
        $bookInfo.fadeIn("slow", function() {
          $moreBookInfo.slideDown(1500);
        });
      }
      else {
        $moreBookInfo.slideUp(1500, function() {
          $bookInfo.fadeOut("slow");
        });
      }
      labelChange($(this), "Book Info!");
   });
});
```

Reload the *animate.js* file in your Web browser. When the page loads, the heading will animate itself into the page. Figure 6-9 shows the page once the animation is complete.

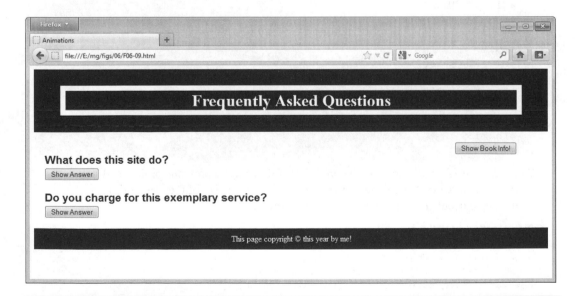

Figure 6-9 The completed animation, which showed the heading by animating its height and border width

Try This 6-2 Chain on a Custom Animation

pr06-02.html
pr02-02.js

This project allows you to practice adding a custom animation by chaining on to the end of the preset animation from Try This 6-1.

Step by Step

1. Insert the following HTML code into your editor and save the file as *pr06-02.html* (this is the same code used in Try This 6-1):

```
<!DOCTYPE html>
<html>
<head>
  <meta charset="utf-8">
  <title>Project 6-2</title>
  <style type="text/css">
    #box, #more { font-family:Verdana, sans-serif; }
  </style>
  <script src="jquery-1.9.1.min.js" type="text/javascript"></script>
  <script src="pr06-02.js" type="text/javascript"></script>
</head>
<body>
<div id="box">
  We have something new!<br>
  <a href="more.html" id="show-more">Show More</a>
</div>
<div id="more">
  We have a new product out and you really
  must see it to believe it!
</div>
</body>
</html>
```

2. Copy your jQuery code from the *pr06-01.js* file from the previous project and save it as *pr06-02.js*. Add jQuery code that will animate the font size of the element to 2em larger than its current size once the slide down is complete.

3. Save the file. When complete, the code should look like this:

```
$(document).ready(function() {
  $("#more").hide();
  $("#show-more").click(function(event) {
    event.preventDefault();
    $("#more").slideDown("slow").animate({"font-size":"+=2em"});
  });
});
```

4. Open the *pr06-02.html* file in your Web browser. Click the link and the <div> will slide down, and then the font size will grow very large!

Try This Summary

In this project, you used your knowledge of *animate()* to create a custom animation that was placed in the queue after a preset animation was complete. This added another effect to the animated element.

Stopping Animations

There are times where stopping an animation can be helpful, such as when many animations could end up in the queue, all happening one after another while the user is trying to do other things.

This is most common with mouse hover effects, where an animation often lasts longer than the amount of time the mouse is over the element. Often, the user will have moved the mouse over another element, and if it has an animation, this is also placed in the queue but not run until the first one completes. With enough of these in place, the page could become quite jumpy for the user.

To avoid this type of behavior, jQuery provides the *stop()* method, which stops an animation in its tracks. When used without any arguments, it will stop the animation "in-place" immediately. For example, an element being shown will still show the portion of the element that made it into view before *stop()* was called.

To provide additional stopping options, jQuery gives you two arguments you can send to the *stop()* method: The first one specifies whether to clear the animation queue for the selected element(s), and the second specifies whether or not to jump to the end of the animation before stopping it [which will completely show an element animated using *show()* or completely hide an element animated using *hide()*].

The following code shows some examples of the *stop()* method at work:

```
$("#my-element").stop();
  // Stops the current animation in place, any queued animations for
the element
  // will now run.
$("#my-element").stop(true, false);
  // Stops the current animation in place, any queued animations for
the element
  // will not be run.
$("#my-element").stop(false, true);
  // Stops the current animation by jumping to the end values, any queued
  // animations for the element will now run.
$("#my-element").stop(true, true);
  // Stops the current animation by jumping to the end values, any queued
  // animations for the element will not be run.
```

As you can see, the optional arguments provide you with the ability to customize the way in which the animation is stopped.

A common use for this is to stop any animations occurring on mouseenter/mouseleave on an element before queuing another animation on it. For example, if you were animating the height of an element when the mouse moves over it, then back when the mouse moves away, you might use the *hover()* method to provide a custom animation for these events, as in the following code:

```
$("footer").hover(function() {
    $(this).animate({"height": "+=20px"}, 1000);
}, function() {
    $(this).animate({"height": "-=20px"}, 1000);
});
```

This looks perfectly normal on the surface. If the user moves the mouse over the footer element, it will expand by 20px in height, then returns when the mouse moves away. However, an unexpected result occurs when the mouse moves back over the element before the animation completes.

To see what happens, update the code to your *animate.js* file as shown here and save it:

```
$(document).ready(function() {
  function labelChange($jqObject, labelText) {
    if ($jqObject.text().indexOf("Show") === 0) {
      $jqObject.text("Hide " + labelText);
    }
    else {
      $jqObject.text("Show " + labelText);
    }
  }
  $(".answer").hide();
  $("#book-info").hide();
  $("#more-book-info").css({"color": "#FFF", "background-color":
"#333"}).hide();
  $("header h1").hide();
  $("header h1").css({ "border-style": "solid",
                       "border-color": "#FFF",
                       "border-width": "10px" })
            .animate({ "border-width": "show", "height": "show" }, 5000);
  $("#ans-00").click(function(event) {
    event.preventDefault();
    $(".answer").eq(0).toggle(1000);
      labelChange($(this), "Answer");
  });
  $("#ans-01").click(function(event) {
    event.preventDefault();
    $(".answer").eq(1).slideToggle('slow');
```

```
        labelChange($(this), "Answer");
    });
    $("#book-show").click(function(event) {
        var $bookInfo = $("#book-info"),
            $moreBookInfo = $("#more-book-info");
        event.preventDefault();
        if ($bookInfo.css("display") === "none") {
          $bookInfo.fadeIn("slow", function() {
            $moreBookInfo.slideDown(1500);
          });
        }
        else {
          $moreBookInfo.slideUp(1500, function() {
            $bookInfo.fadeOut("slow");
          });
        }
        labelChange($(this), "Book Info!");
    });
    $("footer").hover(function() {
      $(this).animate({"height": "+=20px"}, 1000);
    }, function() {
      $(this).animate({"height": "-=20px"}, 1000);
    });
});
```

— The code is inserted here

Reload the *animate.html* file in your browser and move your mouse in and out of the footer element several times. The animation gets queued again each time you do this, causing it to run the animation for each of the mouse hovers in sequence before stopping, which is likely to be a good while after you have stopped!

To keep this from happening, you can cause the animation to stop, be removed from the queue, and then start again when the mouse moves in or out of the affected area. To do this, simply alter the *hover()* method in *animate.js* as shown here and save the file again:

```
$("footer").hover(function() {
  $(this).stop(true, true).animate({"height": "+=20px"}, 1000);
}, function() {
  $(this).stop(true, true).animate({"height": "-=20px"}, 1000);
});
```

Reload the *animate.html* file in your browser and move the mouse in and out of the footer element several times again. It may be a little jumpy if you do so rapidly, but once you have left the element for good, the animation will simply complete and stop, rather than running over and over again until it reaches the number of times it would have otherwise been queued.

Chapter 6 Self Test

1. The _____ method displays an element by increasing its width, height, and opacity.

2. What method is used to alternate between *show()* and *hide()* when called?

    A. alternate()

    B. switch()

    C. toggle()

    D. showOrHide()

3. Which method hides an element by gradually moving it up from the display area?

    A. slideDown()

    B. fadeout()

    C. hide()

    D. slideUp()

4. The *fadeIn()* method displays an element by gradually increasing its _____.

    A. opacity

    B. width

    C. height

    D. width and height

5. To alternate between *fadeIn()* and *fadeOut()*, you can use *fadeToggle()*.

    A. True

    B. False

6. The keyword _____ can be used to show or hide an element in 200 milliseconds.

    A. slow

    B. normal

    C. fast

    D. ultraFast

7. If you want to customize how long an animation runs, you can supply the duration argument using the number of seconds it should take.

    A. True

    B. False

8. Which method allows you to select an element based on its index in a selection?

    A. eq()

    B. atIndex()

    C. indexOf()

    D. location()

9. A _____ allows you to reuse similar code by placing it in one location and sending it arguments.

    A. code saver

    B. function

    C. block

    D. if statement

10. JavaScript has the _____ method for finding the starting position of any set of characters within a string.

    A. indexAt()

    B. indexOf()

    C. startPos()

    D. where()

11. Each animation method allows you to use a _____ _____, which executes when the animation is complete.

    A. completion function

    B. done function

    C. next method

    D. callback function

12. You can create custom animations using the _____ method.

   A. animate()

   B. custom()

   C. animation()

   D. customAn()

13. You can specify the easing method to use when using animate().

   A. True

   B. False

14. You cannot specify the speed of an animation using animate().

   A. True

   B. False

15. The _____ method ends an animation.

   A. stop()

   B. end()

   C. quit()

   D. theEnd()

Chapter 7

The Event Object

Key Skills & Concepts

- The Event Object in jQuery
- Event Properties
- Event Methods

In Chapter 3, you learned about handling events in jQuery. One of the pieces of this topic that was touched on was the *Event* object, which has properties and methods that can be used for any event that occurs.

You have been passing the *Event* object as an argument to many of your event handlers using *event* (lowercase) as a convenient name. Technically, you could use any name you like, such as *ev*, *evt*, *myEvent*, and so on, but you will typically see either *event* or *e* used in jQuery scripts. In this book, I use *event*, since it makes it as clear as possible what type of object is being passed around.

This chapter will cover the jQuery *Event* object in more detail by looking at how it works in jQuery, its properties, and its methods.

The Event Object in jQuery

The jQuery *Event* object is designed to work like the JavaScript *Event* object, but helps you to avoid many of the issues of using it cross-browser by working behind the scenes to ensure that the *Event* object is available and that properties and methods work in a consistent fashion.

Browser Inconsistencies

If you have worked with the *Event* object in JavaScript, you will likely have run across browser differences. When registering events using the DOM 0 method (which is often done as a fallback when *addEventListener()* is not available), Internet Explorer versions prior to version 9 required you to use *window.event* to access the *Event* object, while others used *event*. This caused the need to write an additional statement in the code to handle this so that the *Event* object could be used, as shown in the following code:

```
document.getElementById("my-Element").onclick = function(event) {
  var e = event || window.event;
  alert(e.type);

}
```

This causes the variable *e* to hold the *Event* object whether the browser uses *event* or *window.event* to access it

As mentioned, the latest versions of the major browsers all have the *addEventListener()* method available and allow you to access the *Event* object using *event*. However, if you need the script to work in older browsers, your JavaScript will need to adjust for the additional possibilities for obtaining the *Event* object and for handling events.

With jQuery, you can simply use the *Event* object while this other work is done by the library in the background. The event-handling methods and the *Event* object are designed to work cross-browser so that you do not need to worry about creating your own custom functions to handle all of the browser differences.

About the Event Object

The *Event* object itself is actually a straightforward JavaScript object containing properties and methods that are helpful to you when certain events are triggered. The properties contain information about the event, such as the type of event that was triggered, the target of the event, and other information, while the methods allow you to perform actions such as stopping the bubbling process or preventing the default event action.

One useful tool jQuery offers in versions 1.6 and higher is the ability to use the *Event* constructor to trigger an event that contains customized information in the *Event* object. For example, consider the following code:

```
var customEvent = jQuery.Event("keydown", { keyCode: 80 });
$("#my-element").trigger(customEvent);
```

Here, a *keydown* event is triggered, which uses *80* as the *keycode*. This allows it to simulate the user pressing the P key while within *#my-element*.

As you move through the chapter, you will learn the various properties and methods of the *Event* object, which will make it a useful tool when you need to perform additional customizations for events that occur on the page.

Ask the Expert

Q: If it is just one difference with *event* vs. *window.event*, why not just use the JavaScript *Event* object?

A: When coupled with the need to edit JavaScript code to handle events for older browsers, this becomes more significant, and jQuery can save you a lot of time creating any necessary code adjustments. However, there is certainly nothing wrong with using the JavaScript event system if you prefer it or don't need the jQuery library for other things (such as element selection). For example, a short script that handles a small number of events could be coded in JavaScript to avoid the need to load the jQuery library into the document.

(continued)

Q: I'd like to use JavaScript for events instead. Any helpful tips?

A: In addition to getting the *Event* object itself, you will need to be able to select elements using JavaScript and to use it to handle events for each of the different browsers. A helpful function for event handling can be found at http://dean.edwards.name/weblog/2005/10/add-event2/.

Q: So, does jQuery make all of the properties and methods of the *Event* object work consistently?

A: The jQuery library has a number of properties and methods that it normalizes to work consistently cross-browser, while others are made available as-is. This is discussed in more detail in the sections that follow.

Event Properties

The *Event* object has numerous properties that store information about the event. The jQuery library supports a number of these that work well cross-browser naturally or through the help of jQuery.

Table 7-1 lists the properties of the *Event* object that are available cross-browser in jQuery (some are specific to jQuery itself).

Property	Description
currentTarget	The element that is currently handling the event
data	An object of data that can be passed to an event handler
delegateTarget	The element to which the event was delegated
metaKey	Whether or not the meta key was pressed at the time of the event (this key may be different on different platforms and keyboards)
namespace	The namespace that was used for the event
pageX	The position of the mouse from the left of the page
pageY	The position of the mouse from the top of the page
relatedTarget	The related DOM element involved in the event
result	The last value returned by the event handler, unless the value is *undefined*
target	The element that is the target of (initiated) the event
timeStamp	The time difference between January 1, 1970, and the time the event occurred
type	The event type (for example, click, mouseover, and so on)
which	The key code for a pressed key or the code for which mouse button was clicked

Table 7-1 jQuery Event Properties

You will learn about how to use selected properties from this list as you move through this section of the chapter. You can go to http://api.jquery.com/category/events/event-object/ to learn more about any of these properties if needed.

Other event properties are available in JavaScript, though they are not necessarily supported in jQuery. They also tend not to work cross-browser, though some can work in tandem with others as a workaround. These additional properties are listed in Table 7-2.

Property	Description
altKey	Whether or not the ALT key was pressed when the event occurred
bubbles	Whether or not the event bubbles
button	The mouse button that created the event
cancelable	Whether or not the default action of the event can be canceled
cancelBubble	Cancels event bubbling when set to *false*
charCode	The Unicode value of a pressed key
clientX	The left position of the mouse in the client area (not the page)
clientY	The top position of the mouse in the client area (not the page)
ctrlKey	Whether or not the CTRL key was pressed when the event occurred
defaultPrevented	Whether or not *preventDefault()* has been called
detail	Additional information about the event
eventPhase	The phase in which the event handler was called: 1 = capturing, 2 = at target, 3 = bubbling
keyCode	The key code of a pressed key
offsetX	The left position of the mouse relative to the element that triggered the event
offsetY	The top position of the mouse relative to the element that triggered the event
originalTarget	The original target of the event
prevValue	The previous value of an *attribute* that was modified
returnValue	The return value for the event *(true or false)*
screenX	The left position of the mouse relative to the entire screen
screenY	The top position of the mouse relative to the entire screen
shiftKey	Whether or not the SHIFT key was pressed
srcElement	The element that is the target of the event
trusted	Whether or not the event was initiated by the browser or the programmer
view	The window object where the event occurred

Table 7-2 Other Event Properties

While they may prove useful in some circumstances, these properties will not be covered in further detail here. Instead, you will learn how to use some of the properties from Table 7-1, which are fully supported in jQuery.

The type Property

The *type* property simply returns the type of event that occurred. For example, if the event was a click, *click* is returned; if the event was a mouseover, *mouseover* is returned; and so on.

As an example, the following code would show the event type to the user when it occurs:

```
$("#my-element").click(function(event) {
  alert("The event was a " + event.type + "!");
});
```

This simply sends a pop-up alert that displays the type of event that occurred to the user.

This information can be used for other things as well. Suppose you had an element that could react to two different types of events: a click and a keypress. Save the following HTML code as *event-type.html*:

```
<!DOCTYPE html>
<html>
<head>
  <meta charset="utf-8">
  <title>Event Type</title>
  <style type="text/css">
    #more { font-family:Verdana, sans-serif; width:30%; }
  </style>
  <script src="jquery-1.9.1.min.js" type="text/javascript"></script>
  <script src="event-type.js" type="text/javascript"></script>
</head>
<body>
<form action="clicked.html">
  <button id="more-button">Click for More</button>
</form>
<div id="more">
  This is more text. It can go on and on as long as needed. Sometimes
  things like this go on for way too long, huh?
</div>
</body>
</html>
```

This creates a simple button to show more text, which, when clicked, or when a key is pressed while over the element, should display the text in the *#more* element, which will be hidden. This can easily be done by creating a function to handle both events and assigning it to each event handler. However, you want to perform a slightly different animation when the user presses a key than when the user clicks the button.

While you could simply write the different animations into the individual event handlers rather than calling the single function, a program with longer code would be better suited to the single function to avoid needing to repeat all of the additional lines of code. Thus, a single function will be used, but the *type* property will be used to determine the type of event that occurred and react with the appropriate event.

In this case, you will use *fadeIn()* if the button is clicked and *slideDown()* if a key is pressed while over the button element. Save the following code as *event-type.js*:

The selected elements are stored as jQuery objects available for later use (since they will be used repetitively)

```
$(document).ready(function(event) {
  var $moreButton = $("#more-button"),
      $more = $("#more");
  function showMore($jObj, event) {
    event.preventDefault();
    if (event.type === "click") {
      $jObj.fadeIn(2000);
    }
    if (event.type === "keypress") {
      $jObj.slideDown(2000);
    }
  }
  $more.hide();
  $moreButton.click(function(event) {
    showMore($more, event);
  });
  $moreButton.keypress(function(event) {
    showMore($more, event);
  });
});
```

Begins a function named *showMore()*, which will show the element sent to it as the first argument (*$jObj*)

If the event type is a click, the element is faded in over 2 seconds

If the event type is a keypress, the element slides down over 2 seconds

The *#more* element is hidden

When the *#more-button* element is clicked, *showMore()* is called, and the element and the *Event* object are sent as arguments

When the *#more-button* element has a keypress, *showMore()* is called and the element and the *Event* object are sent as arguments

First, the selection of both elements is made, and these are assigned as jQuery objects in variables for later use, since they will be used more than once in the code. Next, the *showMore()* function is defined, which takes a specified jQuery object and specified *Event* object as arguments. Here, the jQuery object will be *$more* each time, which is the selection containing the *#more* element. This and the *Event* object are passed to the function when the event handlers are registered later in the script. The default action is prevented, and then the script checks the event type. If the event is a click, a fade-in occurs; if it is a keypress, a slide-down occurs. If neither is the case, then nothing happens.

The remainder of the code hides the *#more* element initially, then registers the event handlers for the *click* and *keypress* events, which both call the *showMore()* function and send it *$more* and the current *Event* object as arguments.

To try this out, open *event-type.html* in your browser and click the button. This will cause the element to fade in. Refresh the page and press the TAB key to reach the button and then press any other key. This will cause the element to slide down instead. Figure 7-1 shows the result of clicking the button while the fade-in is in progress, and Figure 7-2 shows the result of pressing a key while the slide-down is in progress.

To make the script more interesting, you can use the "toggle" versions of each effect. When this is done, it will toggle each time the button is clicked or a key is pressed while over the button—and the effect will be the one specified for the event that occurs. Change the code in *event-type.js* to the following and save the file:

```
$(document).ready(function(event) {
  var $moreButton = $("#more-button"),
      $more = $("#more");
  function showMore($jObj, event) {
   event.preventDefault();
    if (event.type === "click") {
```

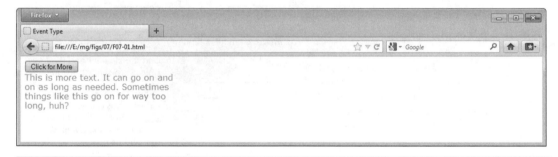

Figure 7-1   Clicking the button causes a fade-in.

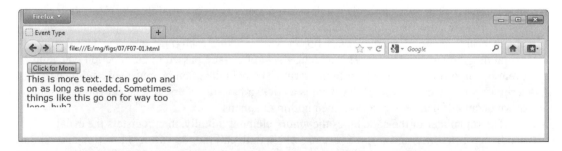

Figure 7-2   Pressing a key while over the button causes a slide-down.

```
        $jObj.fadeToggle(2000);
    }
    if (event.type === "keypress") {
        $jObj.slideToggle(2000);
    }
}
$more.hide();
$moreButton.click(function(event) {
    showMore($more, event);
});
$moreButton.keypress(function(event) {
    showMore($more, event);
});
});
```

The effects are changed to use *fadeToggle()* and *slideToggle()*

Refresh the *event-type.html* file in your Web browser and either click the button or press the TAB key to access it and press a key. When you click, a fade occurs, and when you press a key, a slide animation is performed.

The timeStamp Property

The *timeStamp* property contains the number of milliseconds that elapsed from January 1, 1970, to the time the event occurred. While this may not be of particular interest on its own, it can be used to find out the time difference between two events, which can be useful for testing where a slowdown is occurring.

The time difference between two events can also be useful if you want to create a simple game. Suppose you wanted to create a game where the user clicks a "Start" button that, when clicked, displays another button in a random position on the page for the user to click. When the user clicks the second button, the time between the two clicks is determined and displayed to the user to see how fast the second button was clicked.

You already know enough to perform most of the tasks, but there is a little extra to learn in order to get two random numbers. To do this, you can access the JavaScript *Math* object, which offers a *random()* method that will allow you to generate a random number between 0 and 1. This can be multiplied by another number to allow for additional numbers. The *floor()* method allows you to take off additional decimal points so that you obtain an integer as the final number. For example, this code will get a random number from 0 to 4 (the counting begins at zero, so for a range of five random numbers, you will multiply by 5 to get numbers from 0 to 4):

```
var rand = Math.floor(Math.random() * 5);
```

Here, *Math.random() * 5* generates a random float between 0 and 5, which then has anything after the decimal point taken off by *Math.floor()* so that the number ends up being an integer from 0 to 4.

With this in mind, you can now combine this with the *timeStamp* property, some jQuery animations, and a little math to create the game. First, save the following HTML code as *time-game.html*:

```html
<!DOCTYPE html>
<html>
<head>
  <meta charset="utf-8">
  <title>Time Game</title>
  <script src="jquery-1.9.1.min.js" type="text/javascript"></script>
  <script src="time-game.js" type="text/javascript"></script>
</head>
<body>
<form action="clicked-start.html">
  <button id="start-button">Start</button>
</form>
<div id="msg"></div>
<form action="clicked-click.html">
  <button id="clicked-button">Click!</button>
</form>
</body>
</html>
```

The "Start" button that the user will click to begin

This <div> will display the user's time when the second button is clicked

The "Click!" button that the user will need to find and click as quickly as possible

Here, you have two buttons: one to start the game and one that must be found and clicked to get a time. The *#msg* <div> will display the amount of time between the click on the "Start" button and the click on the "Click!" button.

With this in place, you can begin building your script. First, start a JavaScript file and save it as *time-game.js*. Then you will set up some variables that will be used within the script and do an initial hiding of the "Click!" button. Place the following code into the file:

```javascript
$(document).ready(function() {
  var $sButton = $("#start-button"),
      $cButton = $("#clicked-button"),
      $msg = $("#msg");
      sTime = 0,
      cTime = 0;
  $cButton.hide();
});
```

Each element is stored for later use

A start time (*sTime*) and a click time (*cTime*) are created with initial values of zero

The "Click!" button is hidden so that it does not display on the page when it loads

Now that the initial work is done, you need to handle the first event: a click on the "Start!" button. Add this code to your *time-game.js* file:

```javascript
$sButton.click(function(event) {
  var posX = Math.floor(Math.random() * 300),
      posY = Math.floor(Math.random() * 300);
```

Two variables are created (*posX* and *posY*), which will be assigned random numbers between 0 and 299 and used for the *left* and *top* CSS property values for the "Click!" button

```
      event.preventDefault();
      sTime = event.timeStamp;
      $msg.text('');
      $cButton.css({
          position: 'relative',
          left: 0,
          top: 0
      }).animate({left: posX, top: posY }, 0).show(0);
  });
```

The *sTime* variable is updated to contain the starting time stamp (time stamp when the "Start" button was clicked)

This effectively does nothing the first time the event occurs, but clears the message text after each subsequent click so that the user does not create additional messages

The "Click!" button (currently hidden) is given a relative position of 0,0 with the *css()* method, then moved with the *animate()* method to the new random position and then is shown to the user

Notice that a random integer is set for the variables *posX* and *posY*. These values will be used later to set the left and top position of the button to these random values. Next, the default action is prevented. The time stamp for when the "Start" button was clicked is retrieved using *event .timeStamp* and stored in the *sTime* variable. This will be used in the event handler for the "Click!" button later. After that, the message (which will display the user's time to click the second button) is set to be an empty string. It will be updated each time the user clicks the "Click!" button. Finally, the "Click!" button is repositioned (it needs to be *relative* for the *animate()* method) and then animated to the new position instantly (0 is used for the duration) and then shown (again using 0 for the duration). The user can now click the "Click!" button.

With this set up, you can now code the event handler for the "Click!" button, which will calculate the time between the two clicks, display the time to the user, and then hide the button until the user clicks the "Start!" button again. Add this code to your *time-game.js* file:

```
$cButton.click(function(event) {
  var timeDiff = 0;
  event.preventDefault();
  cTime = event.timeStamp;
  timeDiff = (cTime - sTime) / 1000;
  $msg.text('It took you ' + timeDiff + ' second(s) to click the
  button!');
  $cButton.hide(0);
});
```

The *timeDiff* variable is defined and given an initial value of 0

The *cTime* variable is updated to the value of the time stamp for when the button was clicked

The *#msg* <div> element has its text updated to show the user how many seconds it took to click the "Click!" button

The "Click!" button is hidden until the "Start" button is clicked again

The time difference between the two clicks (in milliseconds) is calculated, then divided by 1000 to provide the number of seconds, then stored in the *timeDiff* variable

Here, you again get the time stamp, which this time will be for the "Click!" button. The time difference between the two clicks is calculated, made more user-friendly (using seconds instead of milliseconds), and then displayed in the *#msg* <div> for the user. Once complete, the button is again hidden until "Start" is clicked again. The full *time-game.js* file is shown in the following code:

```
$(document).ready(function() {
  var $sButton = $("#start-button"),
      $cButton = $("#clicked-button"),
      $msg = $("#msg");
      sTime = 0,
      cTime = 0;
  $cButton.hide();
  $sButton.click(function(event) {
    var posX = Math.floor(Math.random() * 300),
        posY = Math.floor(Math.random() * 300);
    event.preventDefault();
    sTime = event.timeStamp;
    $msg.text('');
    $cButton.css({
        position: 'relative',
        left: 0,
        top: 0
    }).animate({left: posX, top: posY }, 0).show(0);
  });
  $cButton.click(function(event) {
    var timeDiff = 0;
    event.preventDefault();
    cTime = event.timeStamp;
    timeDiff = (cTime - sTime) / 1000;
    $msg.text('It took you ' + timeDiff + ' second(s) to click the
    button!');
    $cButton.hide(0);
  });
});
```

Save the *time-game.js* file and open the *time-game.html* file in your browser. Click the "Start" button to begin, and try to click the "Click!" button as fast as you can! The result will be displayed once the "Click!" button is clicked. Figure 7-3 shows the initial page, and Figure 7-4 shows one possible result after the "Click!" button is clicked.

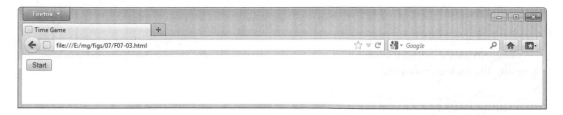

Figure 7-3   The initial page

Figure 7-4   The message is displayed.

The which Property

The *which* property contains the code of a pressed key or the code for the mouse button that was pressed. In jQuery, it makes these codes consistent across browsers so that you can more easily write code based on the information returned.

Mouse Clicks

When used with mouse events, the *which* property will return *1* if the left mouse button was pressed, *2* for the middle button, and *3* for the right button. This allows you to write different code depending on which mouse button was clicked.

For example, you could alert the value of the *which* property when a mouse button is pressed over an element. Save the following code as *mouse-button.html*:

```
<!DOCTYPE html>
<html>
<head>
  <meta charset="utf-8">
  <title>Mouse Button</title>
  <script src="jquery-1.9.1.min.js" type="text/javascript"></script>
  <script src="mouse-button.js" type="text/javascript"></script>
</head>
<body>
<form action="clicked.html">
  <button id="mouse-button">Click</button>
</form>
```

```
</body>
</html>
```

This provides a button where you can determine which mouse button was pressed while over it using the *mousedown* event. Save the following code as *mouse-button.js*:

```
$(document).ready(function() {
  $("#mouse-button").mousedown(function(event) {
    alert(event.which);
  });
});
```

Open the *mouse-button.html* file in your browser and try pressing any of the three mouse buttons while over the "Click" button. You should receive a different number (*1*, *2*, or *3*) depending on which mouse button was pressed.

Key Presses

When used with keyboard events, the *which* property will return the key code of the pressed key. For example, if the J key is pressed, it will return 74. Other keys have their codes as well, so you can find out which key was pressed and write code to be run when specific keys are pressed.

For example, suppose you want to show/hide different <div> elements depending on which keys are pressed. By using the value of *which*, you can provide different results for different key presses.

To begin, save the following HTML code as *keydown.html*:

```
<!DOCTYPE html>
<html>
<head>
  <meta charset="utf-8">
  <title>KeyDown</title>
  <script src="jquery-1.9.1.min.js" type="text/javascript"></script>
  <script src="keydown.js" type="text/javascript"></script>
</head>
<body>
<h1>Widget 147 Version 43.02</h1>
<div id="main">
Press "U" for current updates or "W" to view our latest Widget tweets.
</div>
<div id="news">
  <h2>News (Press "U" again to hide)</h2>
  <h3>Version 43.02 Released</h3>
  <p>
    We have released <a href="v43-02.php">version 43.02</a>,
    which fixes a few bugs that were brought to our attention.
    Thanks for letting us know about them!
  </p>
```

```
</div>
<div id="tweets">
  <h2>Tweets (Press "W" again to hide)</h2>
  <p>
    <strong>Widget 147:</strong> Just released version 43.02!
    <a href="http://widget147.com/v43-02.php">http://widget147.com/
v43-02.php</a>
  </p>
</div>
</body>
</html>
```

This provides the *#main* <div>, which gives the instructions, followed by two <div> elements
that will be hidden when the page loads. These will be revealed when the user presses the
specified key on the keyboard.

To do this, you can use the *which* property to determine which key was pressed and take
the appropriate action. Save the following code as *keydown.js*:

```
$(document).ready(function() {
  var $news = $("#news"),
      $tweets = $("#tweets");
  $news.hide();
  $tweets.hide();
  $(document).keydown(function(event) {
    event.preventDefault();
    if (event.which === 85) {  // "U" pressed  ◄——— The code for the U key is 85
      $news.slideToggle(1000);
    }
    if (event.which === 87) {  // "W" pressed  ◄——— The code for the W key is 87
      $tweets.slideToggle(1000);
    }
  });
});
```

Load the *keydown.html* page in your browser and press either key to toggle the appropriate
<div> element in and out of view. Pressing other keys that do not otherwise have functionality
(for example, F3 or CTRL-F will open the Find dialog in Firefox) will simply do nothing.
Figure 7-5 shows the initial page, and Figure 7-6 shows how the page would look after the
W key is pressed the first time.

With that in mind, you have to be careful when using key presses that you use keys that
are not used for essential purposes and could override important functionality. Also, if you use
the accesskey attribute for site navigation, you will want to be careful not to use any of those
specified keys either.

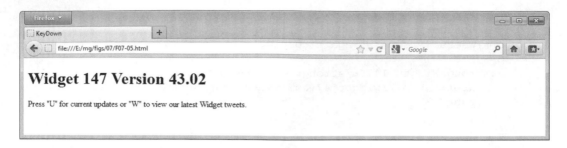

Figure 7-5 The initial page

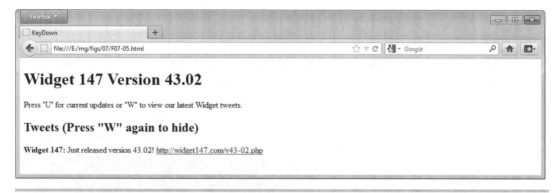

Figure 7-6 The page after the w key is pressed.

The *keydown* event is used in order to keep other possible codes from being used (sometimes the code for *keypress* or *keyup* is different from the target key due to the use of SHIFT or other modifiers). If you need to look up a code or want to see these differences, you can use the JavaScript and jQuery Key Code Checker tool found at www.west-wind.com/WestwindWebToolkit/samples/Ajax/html5andCss3/keycodechecker.aspx to get the codes you need.

Try This 7-1   Practice Using which

pr07-01.html
pr07-01.js

This project allows you to practice using the *which* property to perform different actions for different mouse buttons.

Step by Step

1. Place the following HTML code into your editor and save the file as *pr07-01.html*:

```
<!DOCTYPE html>
<html>
<head>
```

```
    <meta charset="utf-8">
    <title>Project 7-1</title>
    <style type="text/css">
      #mouse-div { width:200px; border:solid 1px #000; padding:5px; }
    </style>
    <script src="jquery-1.9.1.min.js" type="text/javascript"></script>
    <script src="pr07-01.js" type="text/javascript"></script>
  </head>
  <body>
  <div id="mouse-div">
    Left/Middle Click for More
  </div>
  <div id="content">
    Hi! We offer many Widgets you can use with your Web site! Try one
  today!
  </div>
  <div id="menu">
    <a href="home.html">Home</a>
    <a href="about.html">About</a>
    <a href="contact.html">Contact</a>
  </div>
  </body>
  </html>
```

2. In the *pr07-01.js* file, add jQuery code that will hide the *#content* and *#menu* elements, then toggle a slide animation for each one when the appropriate mouse button is clicked (slide the *#content* element for a left click and the *#menu* element for a middle click).

3. Save the file. When complete, the code should look like this:

```
$(document).ready(function() {
  $("#content").hide();
  $("#menu").hide();
  $("#mouse-div").mousedown(function(event) {
    event.preventDefault();
    if (event.which === 1) {
      $("#content").slideToggle();
    }
    if (event.which === 2) {
      $("#menu").slideToggle();
    }
  });
});
```

4. Open the *pr07-01.html* file in your Web browser. If you left-click the <div> element, the content will be toggled. Middle-clicking the <div> element will toggle the menu.

(continued)

Try This Summary

In this project, you used your knowledge of the codes returned by the *which* property to perform different actions based on which mouse button was clicked while over a <div> element.

Event Methods

In addition to its properties, the *Event* object has several useful methods that can be used with jQuery. These are listed in Table 7-3.

You have already used the *preventDefault( )* method, so the following sections will cover the use of *stopPropagation( )* and *stopImmediatePropagation( )*.

The stopPropagation() Method

The *stopPropagation( )* method stops the event from bubbling up to any further parent elements that could handle the event. One way this bubbling can happen is with nested elements of the same type. For example, consider the following code (save as *stop-prop.html*):

```
<!DOCTYPE html>
<html>
<head>
  <meta charset="utf-8">
  <title>Stop Propagation</title>
  <style type="text/css">
    .outer { border:solid 1px #000; padding:15px; width:400px; }
    .inner { border:solid 1px #000; padding:5px; width:300px; }
  </style>
  <script src="jquery-1.9.1.min.js" type="text/javascript"></script>
  <script src="stop-prop.js" type="text/javascript"></script>
</head>
<body>
<div class="outer">
  Outer...
  <div class="inner">
    Inner...
```

Method	Description
isDefaultPrevented()	Whether or not *preventDefault()* has been called
isImmediatePropagationStopped()	Whether or not *stopImmediatePropagation()* has been called
isPropagationStopped()	Whether or not *stopPropagation()* has been called
preventDefault()	Prevents the default action
stopImmediatePropagation()	Stops any further event handlers on the element from triggering and stops event bubbling
stopPropagation()	Stops event bubbling

Table 7-3 Event Object Methods in jQuery

```
    </div>
    <div class="inner">
      Inner...
    </div>
  </div>
</body>
</html>
```

If you wanted to append some text to each <div> element that is clicked, you might write the following jQuery code (save as *stop-prop.js*):

```
$(document).ready(function() {
  $("div").click(function(event) {
    $(this).append(" You clicked this element!");
  });
});
```

Load the *stop-prop.html* file in your browser and click one of the inner <div> elements. While the intention of the script was probably to simply append the text to any <div> element that was clicked, the event will bubble up to the parent (outer) <div> element as well, which causes both <div> elements to have the text appended, even though you only clicked an inner one. Figure 7-7 shows the initial page, and Figure 7-8 shows the page after the first inner <div> element is clicked.

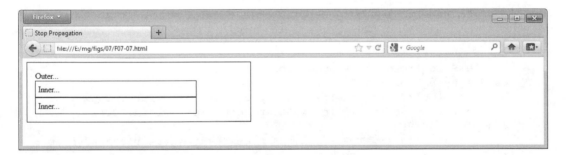

Figure 7-7   The initial page

Figure 7-8   The page after the first inner <div> is clicked.

To fix this to work as intended, you can use the *stopPropagation()* method to prevent the event from bubbling up any further. This will keep the outer <div> element from attempting to handle the event when one of the inner <div> elements is clicked. Edit the *stop-prop.js* file to use the following code and save it:

```
$(document).ready(function() {
  $("div").click(function(event) {
    event.stopPropagation();
    $(this).append(" You clicked this element!");
  });
});
```

The *stopPropagation()* method is used, preventing the event from bubbling up the DOM tree

Reload the *stop-prop.html* file in your browser and click an inner <div>. This time, it won't cause the outer <div> to also have the text appended. The text will now only be appended to the outer <div> if you actually click within the outer <div> outside of any of the inner <div> elements. Figure 7-9 shows the result of clicking an inner <div> element with this in place.

The stopImmediatePropagation() Method

The *stopImmediatePropagation()* method stops the event from bubbling up further and also prevents any further event handlers for that event from running. As an example, you will build on the previous page. Save the following HTML code as *stop-i-prop.html*:

```
<!DOCTYPE html>
<html>
<head>
  <meta charset="utf-8">
  <title>Stop Immediate Propagation</title>
  <style type="text/css">
    .outer { border:solid 1px #000; padding:15px; width:400px; }
    .inner { border:solid 1px #000; padding:5px; width:300px; }
  </style>
  <script src="jquery-1.9.1.min.js" type="text/javascript"></script>
```

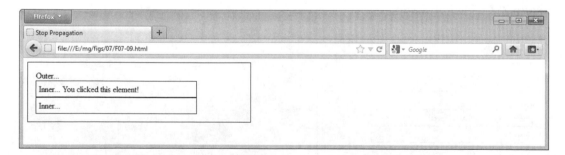

Figure 7-9 The outer <div> no longer gets the text appended when an inner <div> is clicked.

```
    <script src="stop-i-prop.js" type="text/javascript"></script>
</head>
<body>
<div class="outer">
  Outer...
  <div class="inner">
    Inner...
  </div>
  <div class="inner">
    Inner...
  </div>
</div>
</body>
</html>
```

To see the difference between this and *stopPropagation()*, you will first simply add a second *click* event handler for <div> elements, as in the following code (save as *stop-i-pro.js*):

```
$(document).ready(function() {
  $("div").click(function(event) {
    event.stopPropagation();
    $(this).append(" You clicked this element!");
  });
  $("div").click(function(event) {
    $(this).css("background-color", "#FFD");
  });
});
```

This will highlight each <div> when it is clicked by changing the background color. Since *stopPropagation()* is called in the first *click* event handler, this effect won't bubble up and each <div> element is highlighted individually when clicked (additional clicks simply add more text since the element will already be highlighted). Figure 7-10 shows an example of this when the first inner <div> element is clicked.

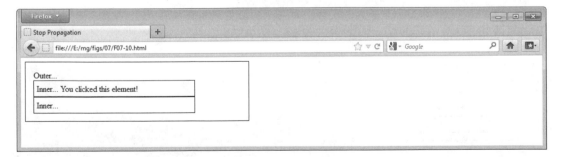

Figure 7-10 The first inner <div> element is highlighted.

Suppose, however, that you do not want the highlight effect and instead just want to run the first event handler, which adds the text. Using *stopImmediatePropagation()* will not only keep the event from bubbling up any further, but it will also stop all additional event handlers for that event from executing. To see this in action, change the *stop-i-prop.js* file to use the following code and save it:

```
$(document).ready(function() {
  $("div").click(function(event) {
    event.stopImmediatePropagation();
    $(this).append(" You clicked this element!");
  });
  $("div").click(function(event) {
    $(this).css("background-color", "#FFD");
  });
});
```

Reload the *stop-i-prop.html* file in your browser and click one of the inner <div> elements. It should now only add the text to the element rather than adding the text and highlighting. Figure 7-11 shows the result after the first inner <div> element is clicked.

The "is" Methods

The *isDefaultPrevented()*, *isPropagationStopped()*, and *isImmediatePropagationStopped()* methods return *true* or *false* depending on whether or not their corresponding methods, *preventDefault()*, *stopPropagation()*, and *stopImmediatePropagation(),* have been called.

For example, *isDefaultPrevented()* can be handy if you need to know whether *preventDefault()* has already been called. In this way, you can call it if needed, as in the following code:

```
$(".special a").click(function(event) {
  if (!event.isDefaultPrevented()) {
    event.preventDefault();
  }
  // Additional code for the click event...
});
```

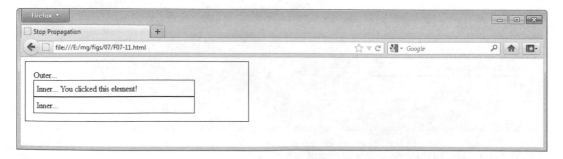

Figure 7-11 The <div> element is no longer highlighted.

The other methods can be used in the same way to test for whether or not *stopPropagation( )* or *stopImmediatePropagation( )* have been called.

Try This 7-2   Practice Stopping Propagation

pr07-02.html
pr07-02.js

This project allows you to practice using the *stopPropagation( )* method of the *Event* object by using it to stop an event from bubbling up to any parent elements.

Step by Step

1. Insert the following HTML code into your editor and save the file as *pr07-02.html*:

```
<!DOCTYPE html>
<html>
<head>
  <meta charset="utf-8">
  <title>Project 7-2</title>
  <style type="text/css">
    .outer { border:solid 1px #000; padding:15px; width:400px; }
    .inner { border:solid 1px #000; padding:5px; width:300px; }
  </style>
  <script src="jquery-1.9.1.min.js" type="text/javascript"></script>
  <script src="pr07-02.js" type="text/javascript"></script>
</head>
<body>
<div class="outer">
  Outer...
  <div class="inner">
    Inner...
  </div>
  <div class="inner">
    Inner...
  </div>
</div>
</body>
</html>
```

2. Create a JavaScript file and save it as *pr07-02*.js. Add jQuery code that will append "
You clicked me!" to any <div> that is clicked. Make sure this will not affect any parent <div> elements.

(continued)

3. When complete, the code should look like this:

```
$(document).ready(function() {
  $("div").click(function(event) {
    event.stopPropagation();
    $(this).append("<br>You clicked me!");
  });
});
```

4. Open the *pr07-02.html* file in your Web browser. Click any <div> element to show the additional text. Clicking it again will repeat the addition of the text.

Try This Summary

In this project, you used your knowledge of *stopPropagation()* to keep an event from bubbling up the DOM tree to be handled by any parent elements. This allowed you to add text to one element at a time.

Chapter 7 Self Test

1. The _____ object contains properties and methods that are helpful when certain events are triggered.

2. The _____ property simply returns the type of event that occurred.

   A. kind

   B. type

   C. category

   D. eventName

3. The *timeStamp* property contains the number of _____ that elapsed from January 1, 1970, to the time the event occurred.

   A. seconds

   B. minutes

   C. milliseconds

   D. hours

4. JavaScript has the _____ method, which allows you to generate a random number.

    A. Number.getRandom()

    B. Math.getRand()

    C. Math.randomNum()

    D. Math.random()

5. The *Math.floor()* method takes off any digits after the decimal point.

    A. True

    B. False

6. The _____ property contains the code of a pressed key or the code for the mouse button that was pressed.

    A. which

    B. code

    C. mouseKeyCode

    D. codeNum

7. When used with mouse events, the *which* property will return *1* if the right mouse button is pressed.

    A. True

    B. False

8. The *which* property allows you to determine what _____ was pressed on the keyboard.

    A. note

    B. type

    C. key

    D. function

9. The *isDefaultPrevented()* method returns true if:

    A. there was no event

    B. the user moved on to another event

    C. the *preventDefault()* method has been called

    D. the *preventDefault()* method has not been called

10. The _____ method returns whether or not the *stopPropagation()* method has been called.

   A. isImmediatePropagationStopped()

   B. isPropagationStopped()

   C. stopPropagation()

   D. isDefaultPrevented()

11. The _____ method stops the event from bubbling up to any further parent elements that could handle the event.

   A. stopPropagation()

   B. preventDefault()

   C. stopBubbling()

   D. stopBubble()

12. To prevent the default action from occurring for an event, you can use the _____ method.

   A. preventUsual()

   B. stopDefault()

   C. preventDefault()

   D. cancelDefault()

13. The *stopPropagation()* method stops the event from bubbling up further and also prevents any further event handlers for that event from running.

   A. True

   B. False

14. jQuery helps make a number of the properties and methods of the *Event* object work consistently cross-browser.

   A. True

   B. False

15. Which of the following properties of the *Event* object does *not* have cross-browser support via jQuery?

   A. pageX

   B. target

   C. which

   D. cancelable

Chapter 8

The DOM and Forms

Key Skills & Concepts

- Form Element Values
- Form Events
- Regular Expressions
- Form Validation

The jQuery library offers a number of helpful tools for dealing with HTML forms. You can use jQuery to get the value of various form element inputs, make use of form events and methods, and put all of these together with techniques such as regular expressions and others that you have learned earlier to validate form input.

Form Element Values

The jQuery library provides a helpful method named *val()*, which allows you to get or set values for matched elements. You can also use various techniques to work with special elements such as check boxes, radio buttons, and select boxes.

The val() Method

The *val()* method allows you to get or set the values of form elements.

Getting Values

The *val()* method can get the value of the first matched element in a set of elements. This can be used with an id as the selector in order to obtain the value of a specific form element. For example, the following code can be used to get the value of an element with an id of *textbox-name*:

```
$("#textbox-name").val();
```

If the selection matches more than one element, then *val()* will only retrieve the value of the first matched element. Consider the following code:

```
$("input[type=text]").val();
```

The selection will be all of the text boxes on the page, but *val()* will only get the value of the first text box.

If instead you want to do something with the value of each of the text boxes, you can iterate over the collection using *each()*, as in the following code:

```
$("input[type=text]").each(function() {
  $("#my-element").append($(this).val() + "<br>");
});
```

This will append each value to *#my-element* to be viewed on the page. You could do several things within the *each()* handling function, from validation to storing the values for later use. You'll look at some of these options later in this chapter.

NOTE
If a text input field is left empty, its value will be an empty string ("") and not "undefined". Otherwise, the value will be the characters that were typed into the field in string format.

To see an example of *val()*, save the following HTML code as *val.html*:

```html
<html>
<head>
  <meta charset="utf-8">
  <title>The val() Method</title>
  <script src="jquery-1.9.1.min.js" type="text/javascript"></script>
  <script src="val.js" type="text/javascript"></script>
</head>
<body>
  <form method="post" action="my-program.php" id="contact-form">
    <label for="name">Name:</label>
      <input type="text" id="name"><br>
    <label for="e-mail">E-mail:</label>
      <input type="text" id="e-mail"><br><br>
    <input type="submit" value="Submit" id="submit">
  </form>
  <div id="show-vals"></div>
</body>
</html>
```

Next, save the following code as *val.js*:

```javascript
$(document).ready(function() {
  $("#contact-form").submit(function(event) {
    $("input[type=text]").each(function() {
      $("#show-vals").append($(this).val() + "<br>");
    });
    event.preventDefault();
  });
});
```

A handler is added for the *submit* event

Each of the text boxes is collected and iterated over using *each()*

The value of each of the text boxes is displayed (followed by a line break) by appending the value to the *#show-vals* element

The default action is prevented (the form is not submitted)

Figure 8-1 shows the initial page, and Figure 8-2 shows how the page would look after entering "John" for the name and "me@scripttheweb.com" for the e-mail address and clicking the Submit button once.

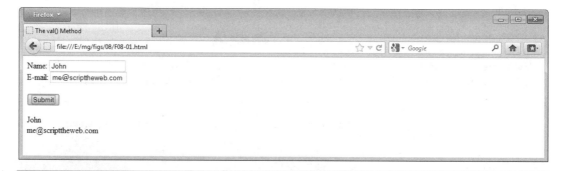

Figure 8-1 The initial page

Figure 8-2 The page after the Submit button is clicked once.

Setting Values

The *val()* method can also be used to set the value for all matched elements. Using the same HTML code (*val.html*), edit the *val.js* file to use the following code and save it:

```
$(document).ready(function() {
    $("input[type=text]").val("Enter Value");
});
```

Notice that this works much like other jQuery methods that set values. This will set the value of all of the text boxes to have an initial value of "Enter Value". Figure 8-3 shows the *val.html* file after being loaded in a browser.

Note that this isn't all that helpful and forces the user to delete the initial text and type the new value. However, setting the value for each field individually could be more useful, especially if you had the user's name and e-mail address stored (such as in a cookie or localStorage) and filled these in for the user so that the information does not need to be typed at all. As with other things, what will be most helpful for you and your visitors will depend on your specific situation.

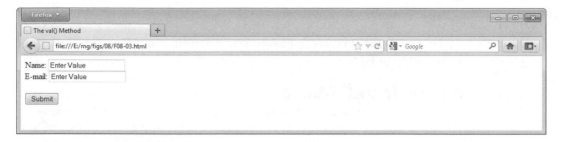

Figure 8-3   Both text boxes have their value set by the script.

Ask the Expert

Q: Does *val()* work with radio buttons and check boxes?

A: Yes! It will return the value of the value attribute for the selected element. However, it will not tell you whether the element was checked or not. For example, suppose you have a radio button as in the following code:

```
<input type="radio" id="food" value="pizza">
```

Using *alert($("#food").val());* will alert "pizza" whether the element was checked or not. You can either select elements that were checked by adding *:checked* to the selector, for example, *$("input[type=radio]:checked")*, or you can used the *checked* property provided in JavaScript to determine whether or not the element is checked.

Q: Well then, does it work with select elements?

A: Yes! For select elements that only allow a single selection, it will return the value of the value attribute for the selected option. If the element allows multiple selections, then *val()* will return a comma-separated list of the value of the value attribute of each selection option.

Q: Can values be obtained via JavaScript instead?

A: Yes, though when selecting more than one element, the jQuery library makes it easier to do so cross-browser so that you do not need to write extra code to account for those differences. If you want to get the value of an element using its id in JavaScript, you can do so like this:

```
var emailValue = document.getElementById("E-mail").value;
```

This would get the value of the "E-mail" field on the page and assign it to the *emailValue* variable.

Form Events

Form elements have a number of events that can be bound to them with their corresponding methods; these are listed in Table 8-1.

The blur() and focus() Methods

The *blur* event occurs when the focus is taken away from an element; for example, clicking outside the element or pressing the TAB key to access another element. This can be used to test input in a field once the user leaves it. As an example, save the following HTML code as *form-events.html*:

```html
<html>
<head>
  <meta charset="utf-8">
  <title>Form Events</title>
  <style type="text/css">
    body { font-family:Verdana, sans-serif; }
    .form-element { margin:0.8em 0; }
    #contact-form label { font-weight:bold; }
    .err-msg { padding-left:12px; color:#900; font-weight:bold; }
  </style>
  <script src="jquery-1.9.1.min.js" type="text/javascript"></script>
  <script src="form-events.js" type="text/javascript"></script>
</head>
<body>
  <h1>Contact Us</h1>
  <form method="post" action="my-program.php" id="contact-form">
    <div class="form-element">
      <label for="name">Name:</label>
        <input type="text" id="name">
        <span class="err-msg" id="err-name"></span>
    </div>
    <div class="form-element">
      <label for="e-mail">E-mail:</label>
```

Some basic CSS is added to provide font styles and spacing; the *.err-msg* class is used in an empty <span> after each element, which will provide messages via jQuery code to the user as needed

Method	Description
blur()	The focus is taken away from an element
change()	The value of the element is changed in some way (typing text, selecting an item, and so on)
focus()	The focus is given to an element
select()	Text is selected within an element (<input type="text"> and <textarea> elements only)
submit()	The form is submitted (<form> elements only)

Table 8-1 Methods That Can Be Bound to Various Elements Within Forms

```
        <input type="text" id="e-mail">
        <span class="err-msg" id="err-e-mail"></span>
    </div>
    <div class="form-element">
      <label for="topic">Topic:</label>
        <select id="topic">
          <option value="Choose..." selected>Choose...</option>
          <option value="Praise">Praise</option>
          <option value="Problems">Problems</option>
        </select>
        <span class="err-msg" id="err-topic"></span>
    </div>
    <div class="form-element">
      <label for="comments">Comments:</label><br>
        <textarea id="comments" cols="25" rows="5"></textarea>
        <span class="err-msg" id="err-comments"></span>
    </div>
    <input type="submit" value="Submit" id="submit">
  </form>
</body>
</html>
```

As you can see, there are two text boxes, a select box, and a text area. Suppose you want to ensure that a name is entered into the *#name* text box once the user removes focus from it. You can do this by using the *blur()* method on the *#name* element.

For example, you could use the following code (save as *form-events.js*):

The selected elements are assigned to variables

```
$(document).ready(function() {
  var $name = $("#name"),
      $errName = $("#err-name");
  $name.blur(function() {
    $errName.empty();
    if ($name.val().length < 1) {
      $errName.empty().append('Name is required!');
    }
  });
});
```

The *blur* event is bound to the *#name* field

Makes sure there is no content in the *#err-name* <span> element before checking it (this ensures it is cleared if there is no error and that the same message doesn't appear more than once if there is an error)

The *val()* method is used to get the current value of the element, and the *length* property is used to determine the number of characters in that value; if less than 1, then the error message is appended to the *#err-name* element

Binding the *blur* event to the *#name* element will cause the handling function to execute when the field loses focus (by clicking another element, tabbing, and so on). When this happens, the *#err-name* <span> element is cleared of any content by using *empty()*. This ensures that the <span> is empty before the message is appended, keeping the message from duplicating if the *blur* event occurs more than once before the error is fixed. The script then checks to see if the length of the element's value is less than 1, which indicates nothing was entered in the field. If that is the case, the empty *#err-name* <span> element has an error message appended to it.

To try this out, load the *form-events.html* page in your browser. Click the "Name:" field, and then anywhere outside the field without entering any information. The error message should display after the field. To remove the error, go back and enter at least one character into the field and then remove the focus from it again. Figure 8-4 shows the initial page, and Figure 8-5 shows the page after the field loses focus without any text being entered.

This is one method that can be used to validate fields as the user moves through the form, but you can also use the *change()* method, which will be discussed in the next section.

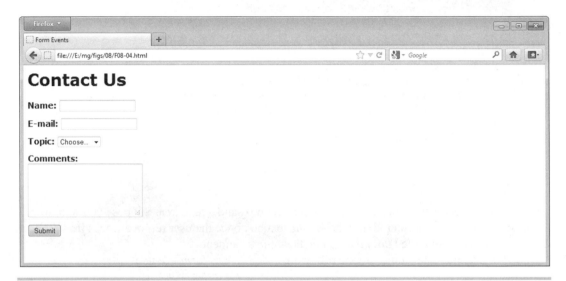

Figure 8-4 The initial page

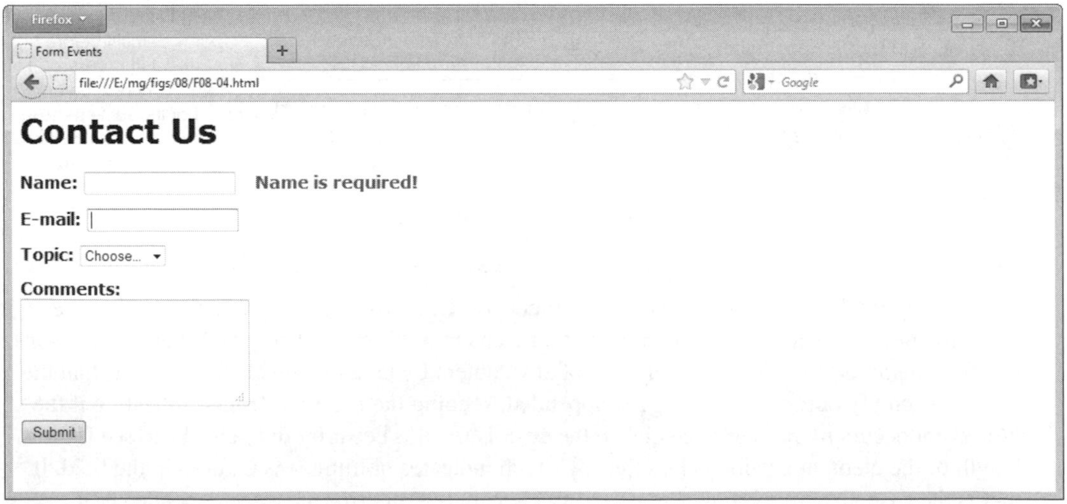

Figure 8-5 The page after the "Name:" field loses focus without any data being entered.

If you want to take the opposite approach—providing a helpful hint for the user when a field receives focus—then the *focus()* method is a good choice. For example, if you wanted to provide users with a message reminding them to include the @ symbol in their e-mail address, you could use the following code:

```
var $eMail = $("#e-mail"),
    $errEMail = $("#err-e-mail");
$eMail.focus(function() {
  $errEMail.append('Remember the @ sign!');
});
```

This is fairly straightforward, appending the message when the user clicks the field. However, it does not remove the message once the user leaves. This can be done by also attaching the *blur()* method, which you can do as part of the chain, as in the following code:

```
var $eMail = $("#e-mail"),
    $errEMail = $("#err-e-mail");
$eMail.focus(function() {
  $errEMail.append('Remember the @ sign!');
}).blur(function() {
  $errEMail.empty();
});
```

When the field loses focus, the message is now removed by using the *empty()* method. You can now update your *form-events.js* file to include this new code. Use the following code:

```
$(document).ready(function() {
  var $name = $("#name"),
      $errName = $("#err-name"),            The variables are
      $eMail = $("#e-mail"),                all placed together
      $errEMail = $("#err-e-mail");
  $name.blur(function() {
    $errName.empty();
    if ($name.val().length < 1) {
      $errName.empty().append('Name is required!');   Code to handle
    }                                                  the #name field
  });
  $eMail.focus(function() {
    $errEMail.append('Remember the @ sign!');
  }).blur(function() {                                 Code to handle the
    $errEMail.empty();                                 #e-mail field
  });
});
```

Save the *form-events.js* file and refresh the *form-events.html* file in your browser. Click the "E-mail" field and the hint will appear after it. Figure 8-6 shows the page once the hint has been displayed.

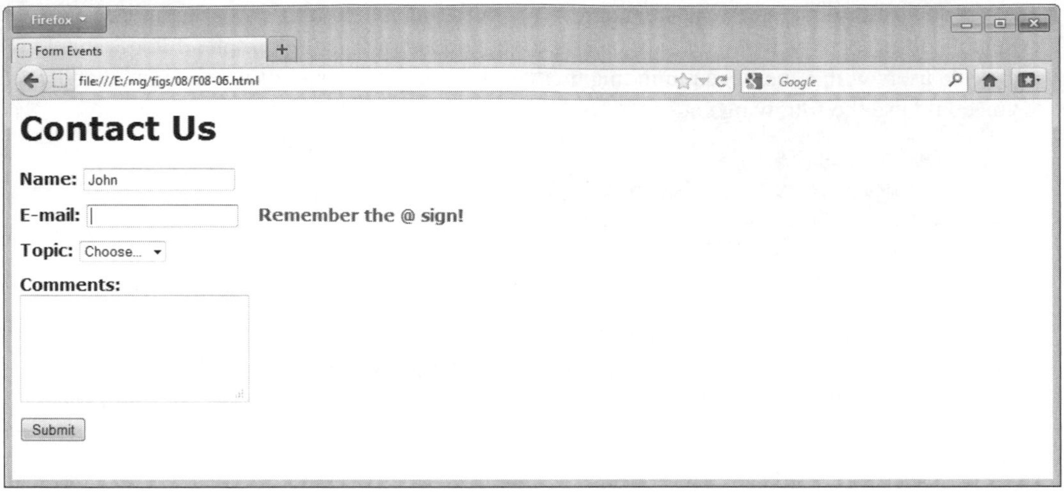

Figure 8-6 The hint is displayed when the "E-mail" field receives focus.

The change() Method

The *change* event occurs when a change is made to an element. For text boxes and text areas, this is when the user enters or deletes characters; for select boxes, when the user makes a different or additional selection; for radio buttons and check boxes, when one is checked or unchecked.

Working with your current *form-events.html* page, you can use the *change()* method for the select box. Suppose you want to provide a different response to each selection the user can make. Since the "Choose…" option is already selected, selecting it will do nothing unless you change it to something else first. The other options will all be available for scripting on the first *change* event.

The following code can be used to make this work:

```
var $topic = $("#topic"),                The elements that will be used
    $errTopic = $("#err-topic");          are assigned to variables
$topic.change(function() {                The change() method is used on the #topic select element
  var choice = $topic.val();              The #err-topic <span> is emptied
  $errTopic.empty();
  switch(choice) {
    case "Praise"   : $errTopic.append("Cool! Thanks!"); break;
    case "Problems" : $errTopic.append("Oh no..."); break;
    default         : $errTopic.append("Please make a selection.");
  }
});
```

A *switch* statement is used to determine which message to append

Here, the same process is followed, but a JavaScript *switch* statement is used to determine which message to append to the <span> element based on the value chosen in the select element.

The switch Statement

The *switch* statement can save you some time when you need to write multiple *if/else* statements based on the same value. In the example, the value selected by the user gets assigned to a variable named *choice*. Since there are multiple values that can be chosen and the list could be expanded in the future, a *switch* statement will help organize the code a bit.

A *switch* statement uses the following basic format:

```
switch(expression) {
  case expression : statements;
  default : statements;
}
```

The expression within the parentheses can be any expression, but is most commonly a variable value, as with the example, which uses the *choice* variable. This is followed by one or more *case* statements, which evaluate whether the value is equal to the *expression*. In the example, you just used the first two possible selections ("Praise" and "Problems"). If the case returns true, then the statements following the colon are executed. If not, then it moves on to the next case, then the next, and so on. If none of the cases returns true, then the *default* case is used. In the example, the "Choose…" option that is a placeholder will go to the *default* case, which asks the user to make a valid selection.

Look at the example code again to see how it works:

```
switch(choice) {
  case "Praise"   : $errTopic.append("Cool! Thanks!"); break;
  case "Problems" : $errTopic.append("Oh no..."); break;
  default         : $errTopic.append("Please make a selection.");
}
```

You will see that if *choice* is equal to "Praise", then the <span> will have the "Cool! Thanks!" message appended to it. This is followed by a *break* statement, which exits the *switch* statement.

The *break* statement is necessary in order to keep the case from "falling through" to the next one and executing those statements as well. For example, forgetting the *break* statement after the "Problems" case will result in both the "Oh no…" and "Please make a selection" messages being appended to the <span> element if "Problems" is selected, because this will cause the default *case* statements to be executed as well.

Adding the New Code to form-events.js

You can now add this to your *form-events.js* file, as shown in the following code:

```
$(document).ready(function() {
  var $name = $("#name"),
      $errName = $("#err-name"),
      $eMail = $("#e-mail"),
```

```
    $errEMail = $("#err-e-mail"),
    $topic = $("#topic"),
    $errTopic = $("#err-topic");
$name.blur(function() {
  $errName.empty();
  if ($name.val().length < 1) {
    $errName.empty().append('Name is required!');
  }
});
$eMail.focus(function() {
  $errEMail.append('Remember the @ sign!');
}).blur(function() {
  $errEMail.empty();
});
$topic.change(function() {
  var choice = $topic.val();
  $errTopic.empty();
  switch(choice) {
    case "Praise"    : $errTopic.append("Cool! Thanks!"); break;
    case "Problems"  : $errTopic.append("Oh no..."); break;
    default          : $errTopic.append("Please make a selection.");
  }
});
});
```

The variables are placed with the others

The remainder of the code is added here

Save the *form-events.js* file and reload the *form-events.html* page in your browser. Try selecting the various options to get the different messages. Figure 8-7 shows the result of selecting the "Problems" option.

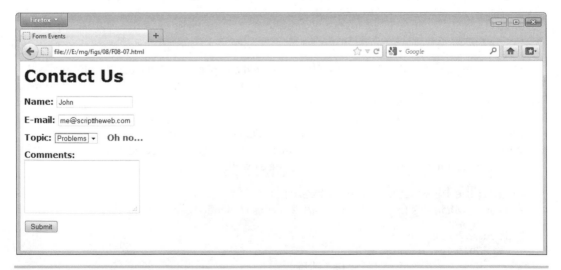

Figure 8-7 The message for selecting the "Problems" option is displayed.

The select() Method

The *select* event occurs when a user selects text within a text box or text area. For example, you could use the following code to offer a tip if the user selects some text:

```
var $comments = $("#comments"),
    $errComments = $("#err-comments");
$comments.select(function() {
  $errComments.empty();
  $errComments.append("If using Windows, Press CTRL+A to select all.");
}).blur(function() {
  $errComments.empty();
});
```

Just as with the other events, the contents of the associated <span> element are first emptied, then the message is appended. The additional *blur()* method is chained on to allow the message to be cleared again once the user leaves the field.

You can now add this to your code. Update the *form-events.js* file to use the following code:

```
$(document).ready(function() {
  var $name = $("#name"),
      $errName = $("#err-name"),
      $eMail = $("#e-mail"),
      $errEMail = $("#err-e-mail"),
      $topic = $("#topic"),
      $errTopic = $("#err-topic"),
      $comments = $("#comments"),
      $errComments = $("#err-comments");          The elements are placed in variables
  $name.blur(function() {
    $errName.empty();
    if ($name.val().length < 1) {
      $errName.empty().append('Name is required!');
    }
  });
  $eMail.focus(function() {
    $errEMail.append('Remember the @ sign!');
  }).blur(function() {
    $errEMail.empty();
  });
  $topic.change(function() {
    var choice = $topic.val();
    $errTopic.empty();
    switch(choice) {
      case "Praise"   : $errTopic.append("Cool! Thanks!"); break;
      case "Problems" : $errTopic.append("Oh no..."); break;
      default         : $errTopic.append("Please make a selection.");
    }
  });
```

```
$comments.select(function() {
    $errComments.empty();
    $errComments.append("If using Windows, Press CTRL+A to select
all.");
}).blur(function() {
    $errComments.empty();
});
});
```

The code to handle the "Comments:" field is added

Save the *form-events.js* file and reload the *form-events.html* file in your browser. Type some text into the "Comments:" field and then make a text selection. The "tip" will appear (which is only helpful to Windows users). Figure 8-8 shows the page after some text is selected.

While this provides an example of the *submit()* method, you can create more useful scripts for text selection by using a jQuery plugin such as jQuery TextRange (http://plugins.jquery .com/textrange/), which will allow you to get, set, and replace selected text. Plugins will be discussed in more detail in Chapter 10.

The submit() Method

The *submit* event occurs when a form is submitted. You have already been using the *submit()* method to handle form submissions and perform various actions. Later in the chapter, you will see how it can be used to provide a final validation on the client side before you submit the form to a server-side program.

Regular Expressions

JavaScript includes regular expressions, which can give you more flexibility when you need to validate form fields for specific character patterns.

Figure 8-8 The "tip" is displayed when text is selected.

For example, you may want to know if a valid phone number or e-mail address was entered. Regular expressions can test the entered data against a pattern you provide to determine whether the data matches the pattern. This gives you the ability to more accurately validate some form fields.

It should be noted that HTML5 provides a means for validating common types of patterns, such as telephone numbers, dates, e-mail addresses, and fields that simply require input. Until this is widely implemented, you may wish to use JavaScript as a fallback for browsers that do not support the new elements and validation routines yet. However, you can also bypass the JavaScript fallback and allow the server-side program to validate the fields in older browsers.

Creating Regular Expressions

You need to create an instance of the JavaScript *RegExp* object or a *RegExp* literal in order to use a regular expression. In this chapter, you will simply use a *RegExp* literal, as it can use the methods needed to test the pattern. To create a *RegExp* literal, you can assign the regular expression to a variable. Instead of using quotation marks to surround the expression, you use forward (/) slashes, as shown here:

```
var varname = /your_pattern/;
```

You replace *your_pattern* with a regular expression pattern.

NOTE

JavaScript uses forward slashes to let the browser know that a regular expression is between them, the same way quote marks are used to set off strings. Thus, if a forward slash is used within the regular expression, it must be escaped with a backslash in order to work properly. For instance, instead of writing /02/03/2009/, you would need to write /02\/03\/2009/.

For example, a simple regular expression pattern, which will match when a specific character sequence occurs anywhere within a string, can be created like this:

```
var myPattern = /our/;
```

The preceding code creates a *RegExp* literal named *myPattern*. If you test the word *our* against the expression, it's a match. If you test *your, sour, pour,* or *pouring* against the pattern, then it also returns a match. If you test *cool, Our, OUR,* or *souR*, then it won't return a match, since none of these strings have "our" in them (capitalization matters unless the *i* flag is used, which is discussed later in this section).

Testing Strings Against Regular Expressions

You can use the *test()* method of the *RegExp* object to test a string against a regular expression. The basic syntax is as follows:

```
regex_pattern.test(string_to_test);
```

For instance, consider the following example:

```
var myPattern = /our/;
var isMatch = myPattern.test("pour");
```

This code will test the "pour" string against the regular expression named "tomatch." The *test()* method returns true if there is a match and *false* if there is not a match. In this case, the value of *isMatch* will be *true*, since the test will return true ("our" is found within "pour").

To create more specific patterns, you'll need to learn additional characters that can be used within regular expressions to create those patterns. These characters are listed in Table 8-2.

As you can see, there is an extensive set of characters that can be used to create patterns. For example, /[a-z]/ would create a range that matches all lowercase letters between a and z. You can build on this by using /^[a-z]{3,5}$/, which would match all lowercase letters from a–z if any of the characters within the range occur in a sequence

Character	Description
^	Matches only from the beginning of a line
$	Matches only at the end of the line
*	Matches the character preceding it if the character occurs zero or more times
+	Matches the character preceding it if it occurs one or more times
?	Matches the character preceding it if it occurs zero or one time
.	Matches any individual character, excluding the newline character
(x)	By replacing x with characters, matches that sequence and keeps it in memory to be used later; used for grouping of expressions
|	Used as a logical OR symbol to allow a match of what is on the left of the symbol OR what is on its right
{x}	Using a number to replace x, matches when there are exactly x occurrences of the character preceding it
{x,}	Using a number to replace x, matches when there are x or more occurrences of the character preceding it
{x,y}	Using numbers to replace x and y, matches when there are at least x occurrences of the character preceding it but no more than y occurrences of it
[]	Matches a character set of your choice; will match when any one of the characters in the brackets (such as [abc]) or any one of a range of characters (such as [a-k]) is present
[^]	Matches when the characters in your character set are *not* present; may be a set (such as [abc]) or a range (such as [a–k])
\	Used to escape special characters or to make a normal character special
[\b]	Matches a BACKSPACE keystroke

Table 8-2 Special Characters in Regular Expressions

Character	Description
\b	Matches when the character before or after it is located at a word boundary, such as before or after a space character
\B	Matches a character that is not located at a word boundary
\cX	Using a letter character to replace X, matches when the user presses the CTRL key followed by typing the letter X
\d	Matches if the character is a single numeric character
\D	Matches a single character if it is *not* a numeric character
\f	Matches if there is a form feed
\n	Matches if there is a new line
\r	Matches if there is a carriage return
\s	Matches a single character if it represents white space (such as a space or a new line)
\S	Matches a single character if it does *not* represent white space
\t	Matches if there is a tab
\v	Matches if there is a vertical tab
\w	Matches any single character that is a letter, number, or underscore
\W	Matches any single character that is *not* a letter, number, or underscore

Table 8-2   Special Characters in Regular Expressions (*continued*)

between three and five times from the start to the end of the string. In other words, strings such as "ace," "cool," and "bikes" would match, while strings such as "as" (valid characters but too short), "234" (invalid characters), "superfluous" (valid characters but too long), and "$me = 2" (invalid characters) would not. This type of pattern can be helpful when validating forms, since you can determine the type and number of characters a field will accept.

Using Flags

In addition to all of the characters, you can use flags after the ending forward slash (/) to further refine a regular expression pattern, as listed in Table 8-3.

For example, if you want to make a pattern case insensitive, you can easily do so by adding *i* to the end of the regular expression, as in the following code:

```
var myPattern = /[a-z]/i;
```

This pattern now accepts all lowercase and all uppercase letters.

Flag(s)	Purpose
i	Makes the match case insensitive
g	Makes the match global
m	Makes the match work in multiline mode

Table 8-3 Flags That Can Be Added at the End of Regular Expressions

If you are interested in delving further into regular expressions, a more in-depth study of regular expressions can be found at www.regular-expressions.info/tutorial.html. For the purposes of this beginner's book on jQuery, you will use some fairly straightforward patterns to assist in form validation, but you can learn much more on regular expressions if desired by visiting the referenced site.

Try This 8-1   Practice Using Regular Expressions

```
pr08-01.html
pr08-01.js
```

This project allows you to practice using regular expressions by applying one to a form input and validating that the data entered matches the regular expression pattern.

Step by Step

1. Place the following HTML code into your editor and save the file as *pr08-01.html*:

```
<!DOCTYPE html>
<html>
<head>
  <meta charset="utf-8">
  <title>Project 8-1</title>
  <script src="jquery-1.9.1.min.js" type="text/javascript"></script>
  <script src="pr08-01.js" type="text/javascript"></script>
</head>
<body>
<form method="post" action="my-program.php" id="contact-form">
<label for="name">Name:</label>
 <input type="text" id="name">
 <span class="err-msg" id="err-name"></span>
 <br><br>
<input type="submit" id="submit" value="Submit">
</form>
</body>
</html>
```

2. In the *pr08-01.js* file, add jQuery/JavaScript code that will check the value of the *#name* element when it loses focus to ensure that it matches the following regular expression:

```
/^[a-z ]+$/i
```

   If it does not match, display an error message that states "Only letters and spaces are allowed." If it does match, the message should not display.

3. Save the file. When complete, the code should look like this:

```
$(document).ready(function() {
  var $name = $("#name"),
      $errName = $("#err-name");
  $name.blur(function() {
      var myPattern = /^[a-z ]+$/i;
      $errName.empty();
      if (!myPattern.test($name.val())) {
         $errName.append("Only letters and spaces are allowed");
      }
  });
});
```

4. Open the *pr08-01.html* file in your Web browser. Try entering different types of data into the field. If the field contains anything other than letters and spaces, you should receive the error message when you leave the field.

Try This Summary

In this project, you used your knowledge of regular expressions and form events to validate a field once the user leaves it. This allowed you to ensure that the field contained only your predefined set of characters.

Form Validation

Form validation can be quite a task to undertake, since there are a number of tasks that must be accomplished to not only validate the form, but also to make the form as user-friendly as possible to assist those who are filling in the information.

The following is a list of some of the things you will need to consider while you are developing a form for users:

- What can be done to help the user in the HTML code? (Accessibility, helpful input types or attributes, and so on.)

- What can be done to help the user via client-side scripting? (Helpful hints or other indications.)

● What validation can be performed on the client side prior to the submission of the form to a server-side program? (Validate character patterns, whether required information is filled in, and so on.)

● Everything *must* be validated on the server side to prevent security issues and allow as little bad data as possible to be entered.

Since you are learning a client-side technology, you won't need to deal with the final point at this time (though it is still very important). The remainder of the tasks can be taken care of on the "front end" (the server-side programming would be the "back end").

To deal with the first three points, you will look at each in sequence while building a short contact form. First, you will look at what can be done with the HTML code, briefly covering accessibility and helpful HTML5 elements and attributes. Next, you will look at one method of adding helpful hints for the users as they move through the form. After that, you will perform a final client-side validation routine when the user clicks the "Submit" button.

Helpful HTML for Forms

With forms, there are helpful things you can do to make them accessible, as well as helpful new HTML5 input types and attributes that can enhance the experience for those who have the latest browsers. First, take a look at form accessibility.

Form Accessibility

The first thing you will want to do with a form is to make sure it is accessible to everyone who needs to be able to use it. If customers are filling out your form to purchase items, you certainly don't want to lose any of them simply because they do not have the latest browser, don't have JavaScript enabled, or use assistive technology to navigate your Web site.

While this book cannot go into great detail, there are a few basic things you can do to help ensure that your forms are usable for as many people as possible:

● Using proper element and label order

● Using <label> elements

● Using <fieldset> elements

● Marking required fields

● Not assuming client-side scripting is available

Element and Label Order   The order of form input elements and their label text can make a difference. In most cases (text boxes, text areas, select boxes, and so on), it is preferable to have the label text directly before the input field, as in the following code:

```
Name: <input type="text" id="name">
```

Most assistive technology can pick up that the label text is intended for the field directly following it, even if the <label> element is missing for some reason.

For radio buttons and check boxes, it is preferable to have the label text directly *after* the field, as in the following code:

```
<input type="checkbox" id="Pizza" value="Pizza"> Pizza
```

Again, this helps assistive technologies to more easily determine which label text goes with which element, though the <label> element may be missing.

Using <label> Elements   You can use the <label> element to specify what field the enclosed label text is intended to describe. This strengthens the tie between the two when they are already ordered as described previously, but can also help when the label text and input field are separated for some reason, such as being in different table cells or in an unexpected order.

To use the <label> element, you simply wrap the label text within it, and use the for attribute to point to the id of the form field it should describe, as in the following code:

```
<label for="name">Name:</label> <input type="text" id="name">
```

As you can see, the value of the for attribute matches the value of the id attribute of the field it is describing.

Using <fieldset> Elements   The <fieldset> element can be used to group elements together in a logical way. While it can be used with any group of elements that are tied together by a common theme, <fieldset> is particularly helpful with radio buttons and check boxes, where the label text refers to each individual choice, rather than the overall request. For example, consider the following code:

```
What is your favorite food?
<input type="radio" name="food" id="food-Pizza" value="Pizza">
  <label for="food-Pizza">Pizza</label>
<input type="radio" name="food" id="food-Burgers" value="Burgers">
  <label for="food-Burgers">Burgers</label>
<input type="radio" name="food" id="food-Chocolate" value="Chocolate">
  <label for="food-Chocolate">Chocolate</label>
```

Each label is tied to its individual radio button, which leaves the overall question on its own. To tie these together, you can wrap everything inside a <fieldset> element and the question within a <legend> element, as in the following code:

```
<fieldset>
  <legend>What is your favorite food?</legend>
  <input type="radio" name="food" id="food-Pizza" value="Pizza">
    <label for="food-Pizza">Pizza</label>
  <input type="radio" name="food" id="food-Burgers" value="Burgers">
    <label for="food-Burgers">Burgers</label>
  <input type="radio" name="food" id="food-Chocolate"
value="Chocolate">
```

```
    <label for="food-Chocolate">Chocolate</label>
</fieldset>
```

This helps to tie everything together for the user and assistive technology.

Most browsers implement some default styling for <fieldset> elements (many use a border), so you may need to adjust the styling in your CSS code to fit the needs of your form.

Marking Required Fields

When a field is required, it is helpful for users to know this in advance so that they can be sure to fill in any necessary information. While marking a field in a different color, such as red, can be helpful, color should not be used as the only way of conveying essential information. Instead, marking required fields is often done either using an asterisk or by adding text to state the requirement.

For example, one way to add an asterisk is shown in the following code:

```
<label for="name">Name <span title="Required">*</span></label>
  <input type="text" id="name">
```

The asterisk is additionally wrapped in an element with a title attribute that states it is required.

Alternatively, you can explicitly state the requirement, as in the following code:

```
<label for="name">Name (required):</label>
  <input type="text" id="name">
```

Either method can help the user determine what fields must contain information to proceed.

Not Assuming Client-Side Scripting

In order to ensure that the form will be usable for all of your visitors, you will need to make sure that any actions the users need to take can be performed without client-side scripting like jQuery/JavaScript.

One example of this is when scripting is used in such a way that the user cannot submit the form without scripting enabled. Consider the following code:

```
<form method="post" action="my-program.php" id="contact-form">
<!-- form elements -->
<a href="javascript:submitForm();">Submit</a>   ← This won't work without
</form>                                             JavaScript enabled!
```

Notice that a link is used rather than a standard submit button and that the destination of the link is to run some JavaScript code, which would then submit the form via the script. Unfortunately for users without JavaScript enabled, the form can be completely filled out, but the link will not do anything at all!

This can be avoided by using a standard submit button and performing any scripting via the *submit* event for the form. The following code changes the link to a submit button to fix this:

```
<form method="post" action="my-program.php" id="contact-form">
<!-- form elements -->
<input type="submit" id="submit" value="Submit">
</form>
```

From here, you can perform any scripting you need to do, such as validation, by including a separate .js file and using the *submit* event to perform any scripting for those that have JavaScript enabled. Those that do not will still be able to submit the form to the server-side program for validation and completion.

Helping the User

With all of the previous information in mind, you can now do some additional things that can be helpful to the user and assist you in the validation process. First, you will take a look at some new HTML5 input types and attributes. You will then use your knowledge of form events to provide some messages to users as they move through your form to assist them in entering the information in the format you need.

New Input Types and Attributes in HTML5

HTML5 provides a number of new input types and attributes that can assist you and your users. The input types are new values that can be used for the type attribute of the <input> element. These new types offer more flexible input options for the user and can help you validate the information more easily. Table 8-4 shows the new input types available in HTML5.

Each of the new input types can be helpful in browsers that support them. For example, the *email* type will validate that the entered e-mail address uses valid characters and contains the @ symbol. An example of using this is shown in the following code:

```
<label for="e-mail">E-mail:</label> <input type="email" id="e-mail">
```

Type	Description
color	Provides a tool to choose a color
date	Provides a tool to choose a date
datetime	Provides a tool to choose a date and time (UTC time)
datetime-local	Provides a tool to choose a date and time (not UTC)
email	Designed for e-mail address entry
month	Provides a tool to enter a year value and a month value
number	Designed to accept only numerical input
range	Provides a tool to choose a range
search	Designed for entering a value to be placed in a search
tel	Designed for entering a telephone number
time	Designed for a time value to be entered with hours, minutes, seconds, and fractional seconds
url	Designed for entering a URL
week	Designed for entering a week

Table 8-4   New HTML5 Input Types

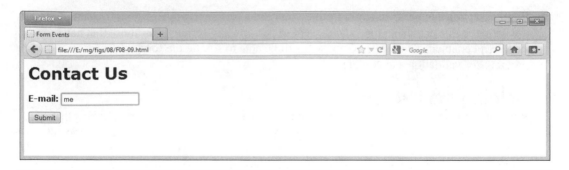

Figure 8-9 An invalid e-mail address is highlighted by the browser.

Figure 8-9 shows what happens in Firefox when an invalid e-mail address is entered into an email field.

In addition to the new input types, there are a number of new attributes that can be used with forms and/or form elements. These are listed in Table 8-5.

For the purposes of this chapter, you will look at the required and pattern attributes. Further information on the remaining HTML5 form elements and attributes can be found at www .adobe.com/devnet/dreamweaver/articles/html5-forms-pt1.html in a helpful series from Adobe.

Attribute	Description
autocomplete	Determines whether or not autocomplete will be available for form fields
autofocus	An element with this attribute will have the focus placed on it when the page loads
dirname	Indicates the direction of the input
form	Specifies the form with which the element is associated
formaction	For <submit> elements—overrides the value of the <form> element's action attribute
formenctype	For <submit> elements—overrides the value of the <form> element's enctype attribute
formmethod	For <submit> elements—overrides the value of the <form> element's method attribute
formnovalidate	For <submit> elements—overrides the value of the <form> element's novalidate attribute
formtarget	For <submit> elements—overrides the value of the <form> element's target attribute
pattern	Validates the contents of a field against a regular expression
placeholder	Specifies text that will be used as a placeholder in a form field
novalidate	Disables the validation performed on form elements by the browser
required	Specifies that the field is required

Table 8-5 New Attributes for Forms/Form Elements

The required Attribute   The required attribute tells the browser that the field must be completed to submit the form. If it is left blank, the browser will bring attention to the error. An example of this is shown here:

```
<label for="e-mail">E-mail:</label>
  <input type="email" id="e-mail" required>
```

In supported browsers, leaving the field blank will cause an error that may be indicated once you leave the field, on a submission attempt, or both. This is a handy way to ensure that a necessary field does not get left blank in modern browsers.

The pattern Attribute   The pattern attribute allows you to provide a regular expression that must be matched by the entered data in order to be valid for submission. An example of this is shown in the following code:

```
<label for="first-name">First Name:</label>
  <input type="text" id="first-name" pattern="[A-Za-z]">
```

By default, the field will be optional (so a blank field will pass), but when pattern is used in tandem with the required attribute, the field will both be required and the data will have to match your specified pattern. The following code gives the field a pattern and also makes it required:

```
<label for="first-name">First Name:</label>
  <input type="text" id="first-name" pattern="[A-Za-z]" required>
```

Thus, you can choose whether the pattern must be matched always, or whether the field is optional and only needs to match the pattern when filled in.

The regular expression used as the pattern does have some differences from the way you used them with JavaScript previously:

- The ^ and $ (to match the string from beginning to end) are automatically used, so the pattern must be fully matched to pass validation.

- The forward slashes (//) are not used to enclose the pattern; only the regular expression characters are used.

- Flags (such as *i* and *g*) cannot be used.

The first two differences are fairly straightforward. If you use *pattern*, you will need to make sure your regular expression accounts for any additional allowed characters, since it will have to be a complete match rather than a partial match. Leaving off the slashes is not a problem, since they are just delimiters.

Being unable to use flags means that if you want the pattern to be case insensitive, you will have to specify that within the regular expression rather than placing an *i* afterward. So, rather than using /[a-z]/i as the regular expression, you would specify the additional character range of A–Z to allow for both lowercase and uppercase letters, as in the following code:

```
<input type="text" id="first-name" pattern="[A-Za-z]">
```

Both the required and pattern attributes are quite helpful in browsers that support them. In those that don't, you can provide fallback validation using JavaScript/jQuery (as you will do later in this chapter) or simply send the data to the server-side program for validation.

Providing Inline Hints

With what you have learned so far, you are ready to create the example page that will be used throughout the remainder of the chapter. This will be similar to the form you created earlier, but will use some HTML5 code to provide initial validation in supported browsers.

Save the following HTML code as *validation.html*:

```html
<html>
<head>
  <meta charset="utf-8">
  <title>Form Events</title>
  <style type="text/css">
    body { font-family:Verdana, sans-serif; }
    .form-element { margin:0.8em 0; }
    #contact-form label { font-weight:bold; }
    .err-msg { padding-left:12px; color:#900; font-weight:bold; }
  </style>
  <script src="jquery-1.9.1.min.js" type="text/javascript"></script>
  <script src="validation.js" type="text/javascript"></script>
</head>
<body>
<body>
  <h1>Contact Us</h1>
  <form action="my-program.php" id="contact-form">
    <div class="form-element">
      <label for="e-mail">E-mail (required):</label>
        <input type="email" id="e-mail" class="fields" required>
        <span class="err-msg" id="err-e-mail"></span>
    </div>
    <div class="form-element">
      <label for="name">Name (optional):</label>
        <input type="text" id="name" class="fields" maxlength="20"
          pattern="[A-Za-z ]{2,20}">
        <span class="err-msg" id="err-name"></span>
    </div>
    <div class="form-element">
      <label for="comments">Comments (required):</label><br>
        <textarea id="comments" class="fields" cols="25" rows="5"
          maxlength="100" required></textarea>
        <span class="err-msg" id="err-comments"></span>
    </div>
    <input type="submit" name="submit" id="submit">
  </form>
</body>
</html>
```

The special *email* input type is used, as well as the required attribute

The text box is optional, but is validated against a pattern if filled in

The text area is required, and also must have a maximum length of 100 characters

At this point, the only new thing to point out is the fact that HTML5 allows the maxlength attribute to be set on <textarea> elements as well as text boxes. This allows you to have the browser stop any further data from being entered in the field once the maximum length is reached, and is used for the "Comments" field in this form.

You also already know how to use the *focus()* and *blur()* methods to display and remove messages next to each form field. You will use this to provide users with helpful hints about what is expected in each field as they enter the field. Save the following code as *validation.js*:

```
$(document).ready(function() {
  var $eMail = $("#e-mail"),
      $msgEMail = $("#err-e-mail"),
      $name = $("#name"),
      $msgName = $("#err-name");
      $comments = $("#comments"),
      $msgComments = $("#err-comments"),
      $cForm = $("#contact-form");
  $eMail.focus(function() {
      $msgEMail.empty().append("Example: john@doe.com");
  }).blur(function() {
      $msgEMail.empty();
  });
  $name.focus(function() {
      $msgName.empty().append("Letters and spaces only");
  }).blur(function() {
      $msgName.empty();
  });
  $comments.focus(function() {
      $msgComments.empty().append("Enter up to 100 characters");
  }).blur(function() {
      $msgComments.empty();
  });
});
```

This will add helpful hints each time the user focuses on a field, and remove each one when the focus is removed. In addition to providing helpful information, this can assist the user in knowing which form field is currently in focus to be filled in. The last variable declaration (*$cForm*) assigns the <form> element to *$cForm* to be used later for the *submit* event.

The calls to *empty()* prior to appending the message will help when you add the error messages later, since you will want to clear (empty) those and show the hint again when the user returns to the field.

Open the *validate.html* file in your browser and move into the various fields. Each one should provide a helpful message to indicate what type of data should be entered. If you are using a supported browser, it will also indicate when entered data is not valid. Figure 8-10 shows how the page looks when the "Name" field is given focus.

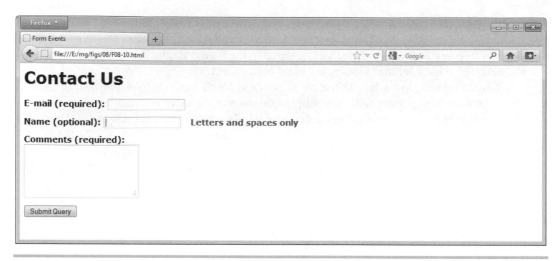

Figure 8-10 The hint for the "Name" field displays.

Validating the Form

Now that you have your hints and HTML5 initial validation in place, you can perform a final client-side validation of the data in the form before sending it to the server-side program. Basically, you will perform the same checks as the HTML5 validation, which will work as both a fallback and a way to provide any additional validation you may require before allowing the submission to proceed.

First, you have the "E-mail" field, which is required. Validation of an e-mail address can be done using a regular expression. Since the field is required, you can simply test the content of the field for a match, as in the following code:

```
$cForm.submit(function(event) {
  var emailPattern = /^[A-Z0-9._%+-]+@[A-Z0-9.-]+\.[A-Z]{2,4}$/i;
      namePattern = /^[A-Za-z ]{2,20}$/,
  if (!emailPattern.test($eMail.val())) {
    // Show error message, etc.
  }
});
```

The regular expression pattern here is more in-depth than the validation used by the browser, so it may catch some additional errors the browser did not. More information on this regular expression and what it does can be found at www.regular-expressions.info/email.html.

When an error occurs on the submission, this script is going to do several things:

- Keep a count of errors and place a message at the top of the form if there is at least one error

- Clear any current "hint" messages next to the fields

● Change the background color of any fields that have errors

● Write a message next to the fields that have errors

To do this, you first need to add a variable to count the number of errors, which will be increased by one each time an error is found. You will also add two variables to hold the default field color and the color of fields when they contain errors. The *submit()* handler will now look like this:

```
$cForm.submit(function(event) {
  var emailPattern = /^[A-Z0-9._%+-]+@[A-Z0-9.-]+\.[A-Z]{2,4}$/I,
      namePattern = /^[A-Za-z ]{2,20}$/,
      errors = 0,
      fieldColor = "#FFF",
      errColor = "#FDD";
  if (!emailPattern.test($eMail.val())) {
    // Show error message, etc.
  }
});
```

This variable will keep track of the number of errors and is set to zero when the form is submitted

These variables set the default field background color (#FFF) and the error background color (#FDD)

Notice that *errors* is initialized to 0. This will happen each time the form is submitted. The count will only go up if an error is found. You now need to make sure that both the default background color is reset each time and that any current messages are cleared from the *.err-msg* <span> elements. This can be done by adding two lines of code, as follows:

```
$cForm.submit(function(event) {
  var emailPattern = /^[A-Z0-9._%+-]+@[A-Z0-9.-]+\.[A-Z]{2,4}$/I,
      namePattern = /^[A-Za-z ]{2,20}$/,
      errors = 0,
      fieldColor = "#FFF",
      errColor = "#FDD";
  $(".fields").css("background-color", fieldColor);
  $(".err-msg").empty();
  if (!emailPattern.test($eMail.val())) {
    // Show error message, etc.
  }
});
```

Sets the background color of all the form fields to the default color (#FFF)

Empties all of the .err-msg <span> elements

With this in place, you can now work on the e-mail validation. Since you have the test in place, you simply need to add the functionality. Here, if an error is found, you will change the background color of the field to the error color, append an error message to its corresponding <span> element, and add 1 to the *errors* variable. This is done with the following code:

```
if (!emailPattern.test($eMail.val())) {
  $eMail.css("background-color", errColor);
  $msgEMail.append("Required: Must be a valid e-mail address");
  errors += 1;
}
```

As you can see, if the validation is not passed, then the necessary elements are selected, changes are made, and the *errors* variable is increased. Since you want nothing to happen if the validation does pass, no else statement is used.

Finally, before the form is sent on to the server-side program, you want to check to make sure no errors were encountered. If so, you want to write a message at the beginning of the form and prevent the default action. This is done by adding the following code:

```
if (errors > 0) {
  $cForm.prepend('<div class="err-msg">Please edit the marked fields ' +
                 'below to fix errors.</div>');
  event.preventDefault();
}
```

This places a message at the top of the form alerting the user to the fact that there are errors and to update the marked fields. The submission to the server-side script is cancelled by using *event.preventDefault()*.

When the *submit* handler code is all put together, it should look like the following:

```
                                                 Sets up the necessary variables
$cForm.submit(function(event) {
  var emailPattern = /^[A-Z0-9._%+-]+@[A-Z0-9.-]+\.[A-Z]{2,4}$/i,
      namePattern = /^[A-Za-z ]{2,20}$/,
      errors = 0,
      fieldColor = "#FFF",
      errColor = "#FDD";
  $(".fields").css("background-color", fieldColor);          Resets field background
  $(".err-msg").empty();                                     colors, clears messages
  if (!emailPattern.test($eMail.val())) {
    $eMail.css("background-color", errColor);
    $msgEMail.append("Required: Must be a valid e-mail address");
    errors += 1;
  }                                           If the validation is not passed, then an
  if (errors > 0) {                           error is created and indicated to the user
    $cForm.prepend('<div class-"err-msg">Please edit the marked fields ' +
                   'below to fix errors.</div>');
    event.preventDefault();
  }
});
                          If there is at least one error, then a message is added to
                          the top of the form and the default action is prevented
```

With this done, there are two fields left to validate. The code shown for these fields will be added immediately prior to the final *if* statement: *if (errors > 0)*.

The *name* field used a pattern for HTML5 validation, so that pattern will be used again (this is already placed in the *namePattern* variable in your code). Since it is an optional field, you will only check the pattern if the length of the data in the field is at least one character.

If there is an error, you will perform the same tasks as you did with the "E-mail" field. The
following code will be used for the name validation:

This keeps the field optional by only performing the
validation if there is at least one character in the field

```
if ($name.val().length > 0) {
  if (!namePattern.test($name.val())) {
    $name.css("background-color", errColor);
    $msgName.append("Must contain only letters and spaces - between " +
                    "2 and 20 characters");
    errors += 1;
  }
}
```

Tests the name against the regular
expression pattern

If the input does not pass validation, the background color of the field is
changed, a message is appended, and the *errors* variable is increased

This is very much like the E-mail field, except that the validation is wrapped within another *if*
statement, which ensures that it is OK if the field is left blank, making the field optional.

Next, you want to validate the "Comments" text area. This is required, but cannot be more
than 100 characters. Thus, you need only check the length of the input, as in the following
code:

```
if (($comments.val().length < 1) || ($comments.val().length > 100)) {
  $comments.css("background-color", errColor);
  $msgComments.append("Requried: Maximum 100 characters");
  errors += 1;
}
```

This ensures that the field has between 1 and 100 characters. If not, then the same procedure is
performed.

Finally, you can put all of the code together to finish up the JavaScript file. The final code
for the *validate.js* file should look like this:

```
$(document).ready(function() {
  var $eMail = $("#e-mail"),
      $msgEMail = $("#err-e-mail"),
      $name = $("#name"),
      $msgName = $("#err-name");
      $comments = $("#comments"),
      $msgComments = $("#err-comments");
      $cForm = $("#contact-form");
  $eMail.focus(function() {
      $msgEMail.empty().append("Example: john@doe.com");
  }).blur(function() {
      $msgEMail.empty();
  });
  $name.focus(function() {
      $msgName.empty().append("Letters and spaces only");
  }).blur(function() {
```

```
        $msgName.empty();
    });
    $comments.focus(function() {
        $msgComments.empty().append("Enter up to 100 characters");
    }).blur(function() {
        $msgComments.empty();
    });
    $cForm.submit(function(event) {
        var emailPattern = /^[A-Z0-9._%+-]+@[A-Z0-9.-]+\.[A-Z]{2,4}$/i,
            namePattern = /^[A-Za-z ]{2,20}$/,
            errors = 0,
            fieldColor = "#FFF",
            errColor = "#FDD";
        $(".fields").css("background-color", fieldColor);
        $(".err-msg").empty();
        if (!emailPattern.test($eMail.val())) {
          $eMail.css("background-color", errColor);
          $msgEMail.append("Required: Must be a valid e-mail address");
          errors += 1;
        }
        if ($name.val().length > 0) {
          if (!namePattern.test($name.val())) {
            $name.css("background-color", errColor);
            $msgName.append("Must contain only letters and spaces - between " +
                            "2 and 20 characters");
            errors += 1;
          }
        }
        if (($comments.val().length < 1) || ($comments.val().length > 100)) {
          $comments.css("background-color", errColor);
          $msgComments.append("Requried: Maximum 100 characters");
          errors += 1;
        }
        if (errors > 0) {
          $cForm.prepend('<div class="err-msg">Please edit the marked
fields ' +
                         'below to fix errors.</div>');
          event.preventDefault();
        }
    });
});
```

Save the file and open *validate.js* in your browser. You should now have the form and validation fully functioning, aside from an actual server-side program. Try out some different types of input or different browsers to see how the validation is handled (whether it is done in the browser via HTML5, done with jQuery, or sent to the server side with JavaScript off).

Try This 8-2 Practice Validation

pr08-02.html
pr08-02.js

This project allows you to practice using the validation techniques learned in this chapter. You will validate a form similar to the one you created (*validate.js*), except that it will use a different HTML5 input type (*number*) and won't have a "Comments" field.

Step by Step

1. Insert the following HTML code into your editor and save the file as *pr08-02.html*:

```
<!DOCTYPE html>
<html>
<head>
  <meta charset="utf-8">
  <title>Project 8-2</title>
   <style type="text/css">
    body { font-family:Verdana, sans-serif; }
    .form-element { margin:0.8em 0; }
    #contact-form label { font-weight:bold; }
    .err-msg { padding-left:12px; color:#900; font-weight:bold; }
  </style>
  <script src="jquery-1.9.1.min.js" type="text/javascript"></script>
  <script src="pr08-02.js" type="text/javascript"></script>
</head>
<body>
  <h1>Send a Number</h1>
  <form action="my-program.php" id="contact-form">
    <div class="form-element">
      <label for="name">Name (optional):</label>
        <input type="text" id="name" class="fields" maxlength="20"
          pattern="[A-Za-z ]{2,20}">
        <span class="err-msg" id="err-name"></span>
    </div>
    <div class="form-element">
      <label for="num">Enter a Number (required):</label>
        <input type="number" id="num" class="fields" required>
        <span class="err-msg" id="err-num"></span>
    </div>
    <input type="submit" name="submit" id="submit">
  </form>
</body>
</html>
```

2. Create a JavaScript file and save it as *pr08-02.js*. Add code that will add "hints" for each field. For the "Name" field, the hint should say "Letters and spaces only." For the "Enter a Number" field, the hint should say "Digits 0-9 only."

(continued)

3. Add code to work as a fallback for the HTML5 methods already used to validate the input. If there are errors, place a message at the top of the form to alert the user. For each field, add an error message beside it and change the background color of the field if there is an error. For the "Name" field, the message should say "Must contain only letters and spaces—between 2 and 20 characters." For the "Enter a Number" field, the message should say "Required: Must contain only digits—between 0 and 9."

4. When complete, the code should look like this:

```
$(document).ready(function() {
  var $name = $("#name"),
        $msgName = $("#err-name");
        $num = $("#num"),
        $msgNum = $("#err-num");
        $cForm = $("#contact-form");
  $name.focus(function() {
        $msgName.empty().append("Letters and spaces only");
  }).blur(function() {
        $msgName.empty();
  });
  $num.focus(function() {
        $msgNum.empty().append("Digits 0-9 only");
  }).blur(function() {
        $msgNum.empty();
  });
  $cForm.submit(function(event) {
    var namePattern = /^[A-Za-z ]{2,20}$/,
          numPattern = /^\d+$/,
          errors = 0,
          fieldColor = "#FFF",
          errColor = "#FDD";
    $(".fields").css("background-color", fieldColor);
    $(".err-msg").empty();
    if ($name.val().length > 0) {
      if (!namePattern.test($name.val())) {
        $name.css("background-color", errColor);
        $msgName.append("Must contain only letters and spaces - between" +
                      "2 and 20 characters");
        errors += 1;
      }
    }
    if (!numPattern.test($num.val())) {
      $num.css("background-color", errColor);
      $msgNum.append("Required: Must contain only digits - between 0 and 9");
      errors += 1;
    }
```

```
      if (errors > 0) {
        $cForm.prepend('<div class="err-msg">Please edit the marked fields' +
                       'below to fix errors.</div>');
        event.preventDefault();
      }
    });
  });
```

5. Open the *pr08-02.html* file in your Web browser. Try filling in the form elements and testing different scenarios to see how the form validation is handled.

Try This Summary
In this project, you used your knowledge of HTML5, jQuery, and JavaScript to create a form that assists the user in filling in the necessary information. This form validated a number using both the HTML5 *number* input type and using jQuery/JavaScript code as a fallback.

Chapter 8 Self Test

1. The _____ method allows you to get or set values for matched elements.

2. Which of the following would get the value of a text box element with an id of *#yourname*?

    A. $("#name").val();

    B. $("#yourname").val();

    C. $("element").val("#yourname");

    D. $("#yourname").value();

3. Which of the following could be used to set the same value of "Enter Value" for all of the plain text boxes on a page (<input type="text"> elements)?

    A. $("input[type=email]").val("Enter Value");

    B. $("input[type=text]").value("Enter Value");

    C. $("input").val("Enter Value");

    D. $("input[type=text]").val("Enter Value");

4. The _____ event occurs when focus is taken away from an element.

    A. blur

    B. focus

    C. select

    D. submit

5. The *change* event occurs when the user selects text within an input box.

    A. True

    B. False

6. The _____ method can be used to perform actions when focus is given to an element.

    A. change()

    B. blur()

    C. focus()

    D. select()

7. The *break* statement should be used at the end of each *case* within a *switch* statement to keep the case from "falling through" to the next *case* and executing those statements as well.

    A. True

    B. False

8. The _____ event occurs when a user selects text within a text box or text area.

    A. change

    B. textSelect

    C. text

    D. select

9. Given the regular expression pattern of /^[a-z]$/, which of the following strings would return a match?

    A. "Very Cool"

    B. "cool"

    C. "2 cool"

    D. "cool!"

10. You can use the _____ method of the *RegExp* object to test a string against a regular expression.

   A. test()

   B. regExTest()

   C. preg_match()

   D. eregi()

11. The _____ flag can be added to a regular expression to make it case insensitive.

   A. m

   B. g

   C. i

   D. c

12. In most cases (text boxes, text areas, select boxes, and so on), it is preferable to have the label text directly _____ the input field.

   A. after

   B. before

   C. within

   D. below

13. You can use the <label> element to specify what field the enclosed label text is intended to describe.

   A. True

   B. False

14. In order to ensure that the form will be usable for all of your visitors, you will need to make sure that any actions the users need to take can only be performed with client-side scripting, like jQuery/JavaScript, enabled.

   A. True

   B. False

15. The _____ attribute in HTML5 tells the browser that the field must be completed to submit the form.

   A. necessary

   B. obligatory

   C. required

   D. mandatory

Chapter 9

Working with AJAX

Key Skills & Concepts

- Introduction to AJAX

- Creating AJAX Requests

- Two-Way AJAX Requests

- Security Issues and Further Information

The jQuery library offers numerous helpful methods for working with AJAX requests. This makes it easy to send information to the server or retrieve information from the server and do so in a way that works across modern browsers.

Introduction to AJAX

The acronym AJAX stands for Asynchronous JavaScript and XML. The term was used by Jesse James Garrett in 2005 in his article "Ajax: A New Approach to Web Applications" (www.adaptivepath.com/ideas/ajax-new-approach-web-applications). While the term originally dealt with XML as the means of transferring data, it can now mean transferring data in any form between the client and the server.

In modern JavaScript applications, you can request data from the server using the *XMLHttpRequest* object. This allows you to send to or receive information from the server without reloading the current page (*asynchronously*). Before this was possible, you had to send the request to the server *synchronously*, wait for the response from the server, and load the new information, requiring a page reload or a redirect to another page. When making calls to the server asynchronously, you can do this behind the scenes without the need to reload the whole page in the browser window. Instead, you can simply load the retrieved information into a specified location on the current page when it arrives.

This chapter will discuss basic AJAX requests, two-way AJAX requests, and offer some resources to further your study of AJAX security and server-side programming if you don't already have this knowledge.

Creating AJAX Requests

There are several methods available in jQuery for requesting information from the server. Technically, you can request just about any type of text file: *txt*, *html*, *xml*, *json*, *js*, and numerous other file types are possible. In this section, you will look at the most commonly used file types (*html*, *xml*, and *json*) and how you can use different jQuery methods to obtain the needed data.

First, you will need a document that needs some data from the server to get you started. This HTML document will be used for the examples in this chapter. Save the following code as *ajax.html*:

```
<!DOCTYPE html>
<html>
<head>
  <meta charset="utf-8">
  <title>AJAX</title>
  <style type="text/css">
    body { font-family:Verdana, sans-serif; }
    #our-products { margin:0 30% 0 0; }
    .product { margin:1.2em 0em; }
    .product-title { font-weight:bold; }
  </style>
  <script src="jquery-1.9.1.min.js" type="text/javascript"></script>
  <script src="ajax.js" type="text/javascript"></script>
</head>
<body>
<h1>Our Special Products</h1>
<a id="view-products" href="view-products.html">View Products</a>
<div id="our-products"></div>
</body>
</html>
```

This document has some very basic styles applied to it, and contains an empty *#our-products* <div> element.

You will also need a *.js* file, so save the following code as *ajax.js*:

```
$(document).ready(function() {
  $("#view-products").click(function(event) {
  });
});
```

At this point, this just has an empty function to handle a *click* event on the "View Products" link. The HTML and jQuery/JavaScript code will be adjusted as you move through the upcoming sections of the chapter.

Retrieving HTML

The easiest type of AJAX request to perform is one that loads an HTML file from the server. The jQuery library provides the *load()* method for loading HTML content into a document. To use it, you select an element in the current document where the retrieved content will be loaded and provide the URL of the document containing the additional content to the *load()* method.

For example, to load the contents of *my-file.html* into an element with an id of *#my-element*, you could use the following code:

```
$("#my-element").load("my-file.html");
```

This would load any HTML within *my-file.html* into *#my-element* in the current document.

NOTE

This *load()* method has the same name as the *load()* event-handling method. To keep this from being problematic, jQuery determines which of the methods is being called based on the arguments that are sent to it.

To make use of this with your current example document (*ajax.html*), you will need to create an additional HTML document that has the content that will be added to *ajax.html*. So, save the following code as *more-content.html*:

```
<div class="product">
  <div class="product-title">Super Programmer Robot 3000</div>
  <div class="product-price">Price: $1,635,343.99</div>
  <div class="product-desc">
    Need code written in a hurry? No time to hire a human programmer?
    This is the product for you! Fluent in over 30 programming
    languages: C#, C, Java, PHP, Ruby, Python, JavaScript, Perl,
    Basic, COBOL, FORTRAN, ADA, PASCAL, and many more. Just explain
    to the robot what you need and it automatically converts your
    request into a perfectly coded, bug-free application!
  </div>
  <div class="product-more"><a href="product-01.html">More...</a></div>
</div>
<div class="product">
  <div class="product-title">Web Programmer Robot 2000</div>
  <div class="product-price">Price: $675,287.99</div>
  <div class="product-desc">
  Need a quick Web application? While not fluent in as many
  programming languages as the Super Programmer Robot 3000, this robot
  can code Web applications like no other! Why? Because in addition
  to knowing Web programming languages like PHP, Python, and Ruby,
  this robot knows HTML and CSS as well! A great buy at this price!
  </div>
  <div class="product-more"><a href="product-02.html">More...</a></div>
</div>
<div class="product">
  <div class="product-title">The Dougnick Res, I.G.</div>
  <div class="product-price">Price: $1,002,875.99</div>
  <div class="product-desc">
  The Dougnick Res, Internet Guru is a specialized JavaScript
  programming robot. It can literally make anything in JavaScript! We
  currently have a limited supply so act today!
  </div>
  <div class="product-more"><a href="product-03.html">More...</a></div>
</div>
```

Figure 9-1 The initial page

One thing you will notice here: This is not a complete HTML file with the doctype, head section, and so on included. Instead, you have a snippet of HTML code specifically for the purpose of providing content to the *#our-products* element in the main HTML document (you will see how to access content within complete HTML documents later in this section).

With this HTML snippet file available, you can simply plug it into the *load()* method to add its content to the *ajax.html* document. Make the following changes to your *ajax.js* file and save it:

```
$(document).ready(function() {
  $("#view-products").click(function(event) {
    event.preventDefault();
    $("#our-products").load("more-content.html");
  });
});
```

Prevents the link from performing its default action

Loads the content from *more-content.html* into the *#our-products* element in the *ajax.html* document

Load the *ajax.html* file in your browser and click the "View Products" link. The content will be loaded into the page once you click the button! Figure 9-1 shows the initial page, and Figure 9-2 shows the page once the "View Products" link is clicked.

Loading a Portion of a Complete HTML Document

Sometimes the HTML you will need won't be in a handy snippet file. You may need to get content from a complete HTML document. This means that the other document will have its own doctype, head section, body tags, and possibly other elements that are not needed in the document where you will use the content.

Fortunately, jQuery makes it possible to select a portion of the document using its selector syntax as part of the argument to the *load()* method. As an example, suppose the *more-content .html* file contained the following code rather than an HTML snippet:

```
<!DOCTYPE html>
<html>
<head>
```

Lines of code that aren't needed in the other document!

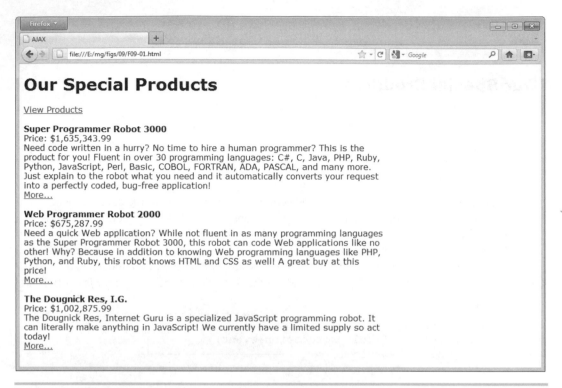

Figure 9-2 The page after the link is clicked

Lines of code that aren't needed in the other document!

```
    <meta charset="utf-8">
    <title>AJAX</title>
    <link rel="stylesheet" type="text/css" href="styles.css">
</head>
<body>
<h1>Special Products</h1>
<p>We have numerous experimental products that you may want to test.
   Keep checking back as we add to this list!</p>
<div id="product-list">
 <div class="product">
   <div class="product-title">Super Programmer Robot 3000</div>
   <div class="product-price">Price: $1,635,343.99</div>
   <div class="product-desc">
     Need code written in a hurry? No time to hire a human programmer?
     This is the product for you! Fluent in over 30 programming
     languages: C#, C, Java, PHP, Ruby, Python, JavaScript, Perl,
     Basic, COBOL, FORTRAN, ADA, PASCAL, and many more. Just explain
     to the robot what you need and it automatically converts your
     request into a perfectly coded, bug-free application!
```

```
    </div>
    <div class="product-more"><a href="product-01.html">More...</a></div>
  </div>
  <div class="product">
    <div class="product-title">Web Programmer Robot 2000</div>
    <div class="product-price">Price: $675,287.99</div>
    <div class="product-desc">
    Need a quick Web application? While not fluent in as many
    programming languages as the Super Programmer Robot 3000, this robot
    can code Web applications like no other! Why? Because in addition
    to knowing Web programming languages like PHP, Python, and Ruby,
    this robot knows HTML and CSS as well! A great buy at this price!
    </div>
    <div class="product-more"><a href="product-02.html">More...</a></div>
  </div>
  <div class="product">
    <div class="product-title">The Dougnick Res, I.G.</div>
    <div class="product-price">Price: $1,002,875.99</div>
    <div class="product-desc">
    The Dougnick Res, Internet Guru is a specialized JavaScript
    programming robot. It can literally make anything in JavaScript! We
    currently have a limited supply so act today!
    </div>
    <div class="product-more"><a href="product-03.html">More...</a></div>
  </div>
</div>
</body>
</html>
```

— Lines of code that aren't needed in the other document!

While the needed code is here, there is also a bit of extra content that you don't need: the <doctype>, <html>, and <head> elements; the opening and closing <body> tags; and the additional <h1> and <p> elements. Instead, you just want all of the *product* elements to be loaded.

You can do this by placing a space after the URL of the document you are retrieving, followed by a jQuery selector. For example, the following code would get all of the *product* elements from *more-content.html*:

```
$("#our-products").load("more-content.html .product");
```

With this, you can now update *ajax.js* to use the following code and save it:

```
$(document).ready(function() {
  $("#view-products").click(function(event) {
    event.preventDefault();
    $("#our-products").empty().load("more-content.html .product");
  });
});
```

Note that the *empty()* method is now added to prevent the loaded document from displaying more than once if the link is clicked more than once. Open *ajax.html* in your browser and click the "View Products" link. You should get the same result as before, with the product content being displayed once the link is clicked.

Using Animation and the Callback Function

When loading the content, you may wish to use one of the animation effects, such as *slideDown()*. At first, this would seem fairly easy to do by simply adding it to the chain, as in the following code:

```
$("#our-products").empty().load("more-content.html .product")
.slideDown(2000);
```

Replacing the *load()* call in *ajax.js* with this line will not appear to make any difference! The content will simply appear once it loads, with no sliding. So why doesn't this work?

The first issue is that the content being loaded is already visible, so *slideDown()* won't reshow it. This is easy enough to fix by adding *hide()* to the chain before calling *load()* so that the content that is loaded within *#our-products* will be hidden before loading, then displayed afterward by using *slideDown()*. Thus, the following code could be used instead:

```
$("#our-products").empty().hide()
    .load("more-content.html .product").slideDown(2000);
```

Trying this out, unfortunately, doesn't change things much, except to potentially add an extra delay before the content is displayed. Why is this?

AJAX methods load content *asynchronously*. This means that the typical order of execution for your statements may be altered. Most jQuery/JavaScript code runs *synchronously*. In other words, each task is run only after the previous task has completed. There is a strict order that is maintained so that no unexpected tasks are completed before their turn in the order.

With an *asynchronous* request, the asynchronous task is started, but the script immediately returns to the next task at hand rather than waiting for the asynchronous task to be completed. The asynchronous task will at some later time receive a response from the server and be executed.

What this means for the last code listing is that the *hide()* method will execute, and the *load()* method will begin execution (but may be waiting for a response). While the *load()* method waits for a response, the script execution is immediately handed back to the next task, which is to execute the *slideDown()* method. Thus, even though you might not have the content loaded yet, *slideDown()* is executed right away. Since this particular call uses a duration of two seconds, nothing else can be done until that time elapses. Once it is complete, the asynchronous task can then be completed if it has received a response and can load the data.

Given that you are working locally at this time, you will likely have the data load immediately after the two-second delay. If there were any additional lag time, the request might not complete until a longer wait (or until even more synchronous tasks are completed). To keep this from happening, you can use a callback function to be executed once the asynchronous *load()* method has completed its task. This is done by adding the callback function as an argument to the *load()* method, as in the following code (save these changes to your *ajax.js* file):

```
$(document).ready(function() {
  $("#view-products").click(function(event) {
    event.preventDefault();
    $("#our-products").empty().hide()
      .load("more-content.html .product", function() {  ◄── The second argument
      $(this).slideDown(2000);  ◄──┐                         is a callback function
    });
  });                          This executes only after the load()
});                            method has completed its task
```

Reload the *ajax.html* file in your browser and click the "View Products" link. This time, the new content should slide down as expected once it is loaded. Figure 9-3 shows the slide-down in progress after the link is clicked.

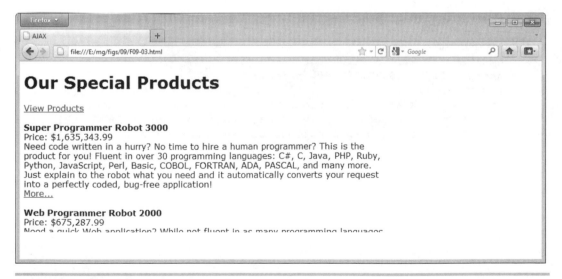

Figure 9-3   The slide-down now works as expected.

Retrieving XML

Another type of document you can retrieve is one in XML format. To retrieve the data, you can use the *$.get()* method, which sends back the text of the document in most cases. However, if a response is received from the server that the document's MIME type is XML, its callback function will receive the XML DOM tree.

Using an XML Document

To work with this method, you will first need an XML document. The following code shows how the same data you were retrieving via an HTML document could be represented in an XML document (save this file as *more-content.xml*):

```xml
<?xml version="1.0" encoding="utf-8"?>
<products>
  <product>
    <title>Super Programmer Robot 3000</title>
    <price>Price: $1,635,343.99</price>
    <description>
    Need code written in a hurry? No time to hire a human programmer?
    This is the product for you! Fluent in over 30 programming
    languages: C#, C, Java, PHP, Ruby, Python, JavaScript, Perl,
    Basic, COBOL, FORTRAN, ADA, PASCAL, and many more. Just explain
    to the robot what you need and it automatically converts your
    request into a perfectly coded, bug-free application!
    </description>
    <url>product-01.html</url>
  </product>
  <product>
    <title>Web Programmer Robot 2000</title>
    <price>Price: $675,287.99</price>
    <description>
    Need a quick Web application? While not fluent in as many
    programming languages as the Super Programmer Robot 3000, this
    robot can code Web applications like no other! Why? Because in
    addition to knowing Web programming languages like PHP, Python,
    and Ruby, this robot knows HTML and CSS as well! A great buy at
    this price!
    </description>
    <url>product-02.html</url>
  </product>
  <product>
    <title>The Dougnick Res, I.G.</title>
    <price>Price: $1,002,875.99</price>
    <description>
    The Dougnick Res, Internet Guru is a specialized JavaScript
    programming robot. It can literally make anything in JavaScript!
```

```
    We currently have a limited supply so act today!
    </description>
    <url>product-03.html</url>
  </product>
</products>
```

As you can see, the XML document simply describes the content, rather than providing HTML code. With an XML file, you will need to retrieve the document structure and build the HTML code from the structure and data contained in the XML file.

The *$.get()* method is a global jQuery method—it is not tied to a jQuery object (such as a selection of elements) like most methods you have used. Instead, you simply call the method to get the information, then use it in the document where needed (using *append()*, *prepend()*, and so on). First, you will need to get the data, so you will need to call the method. Since this document is XML, you will use the callback function to obtain the DOM structure of the document, which you can then easily traverse using jQuery, as in the following code:

```
$(document).ready(function() {
  $("#view-products").click(function(event) {
    event.preventDefault();
    $.get("more-content.xml", function(dom) {
      var phtml = '';
      // Traverse XML DOM and build HTML code...
    });
  });
});
```

The first argument specifies the URL of the file to retrieve. The second argument is the callback function, which executes when the response has been received and the DOM information has been loaded. This information is stored in the argument used in the callback function, which can use any name you wish (*dom* is used in this case). The *phtml* variable will be used to build and store the HTML that will be used to fill in the product information.

You now need a way to traverse the XML DOM structure and build your HTML code from it. For this purpose, the jQuery *find()* method will be most helpful.

The find() Method

The jQuery *find()* method allows you to search all descendant elements of the specified element and select any needed elements using a second selector as the argument. For example, to find all of the <product> elements in the XML document, you can use the *dom* object obtained from the XML file and select any <product> elements within it using the following code:

```
$(dom).find('product')
```

You can now use the jQuery methods you already know to work with those elements. In this case, the selection includes all of the <product> elements in the XML document, so you can use *each()* to cycle through each of the <product> elements and build your HTML from their content, as in the following code (update your *ajax.js* file to use this code and save it):

```
$(document).ready(function() {
  $("#view-products").click(function(event) {
    event.preventDefault();
    $.get("more-content.xml", function(dom) {
      var phtml = '';
      $(dom).find('product').each(function() {
        var $prod = $(this);
        phtml += '<div class="product">';
        phtml += '<div class="product-title">';
        phtml += $prod.find('title').text() + '</div>';
        phtml += '<div class="product-price">';
        phtml += $prod.find('price').text() + '</div>';
        phtml += '<div class="product-desc">';
        phtml += $prod.find('description').text() + '</div>';
        phtml += '<div class="product-more">';
        phtml += '<a href="' + $prod.find('url').text() + '">More
        </a></div>';
        phtml += '</div>';
      });
      $("#our-products").empty().hide().append(phtml).
      slideDown(2000);
    });
  });
});
```

The XML document is retrieved and the callback function is used to obtain the DOM structure

A variable is defined to hold the HTML content that will be built

$(this), which is the current <product> element, is assigned to a variable, *$prod*, for reuse

The final HTML code (after all of the *each()* iterations are executed) is appended to the *#our-products* element and is shown using *slideDown()*

The product <div> is closed

The URL is used to build a link to more information on the product

The same process is used to fill in the price and description content

The text of the <title> element from the XML DOM is used as the content of the <div> element; the <div> element is closed

The <div> element is created to hold the product title

Since you have the <product> element selected, create the corresponding <div> element HTML

The <product> elements are selected and *each()* is used to run code for each of the <product> elements

Notice how *find()* is used throughout the code to select the necessary elements and how their content can be retrieved using *text()*. The DOM structure and content within the XML document is used to build the corresponding HTML that will be inserted into the *ajax.html* document.

After the last iteration of *each()*, the content is appended and shown using *slideDown()*. Notice that simply adding *slideDown()* to the chain works here, since you are already within the callback function of the asynchronous request from *$.get()*.

Reload the *ajax.html* file in your browser and click the "View Products" link. This should work exactly as it did before, but now is using an XML document to obtain its necessary data.

Retrieving JSON

Another popular file from which you can obtain data is a *json* file. JSON (JavaScript Object Notation) was developed by Douglas Crockford as a means to transport data easily among the different applications that may need it. JSON formats data in such a way that everything is described as an object (map) or array. A map can have properties (which can be values or further maps/arrays), and arrays can contain items (which can also be values or further maps/arrays). This formatting allows JSON data to be used easily by numerous applications. In fact, most languages have some type of JSON parser available so that JSON data can be either retrieved or sent out as needed.

An example of JSON-formatted data is shown here:

```
{
  "name": "John",
  "schedule": { "M-F": "Work", "Weekend": "Sleep" },
  "foods": ["pizza", "burger", "salad"]
}
```

As you can see, there is a root object (you could also use an array here), which contains three name/value pairs. Each value can, in turn, be another object or array if needed, as "schedule" and "foods" demonstrate here. One more thing that you should notice: When creating JSON data, the names of any object properties must be within quote marks, where in JavaScript, this is optional for simple names.

To load JSON data, jQuery has another global method named *$.getJSON()*, where you can pass the file to load and the callback function as arguments. For example, the following code could be used to get the data from a file named *more-content.json*:

```
$.getJSON("more-content.json", function(data) {
  // Statements...
});
```

The *data* argument will contain the JSON data to be parsed, which can be done using the global version of *each*, which is *$.each()*. Instead of working on a selection, *$.each()* can be passed an object or an array as the first argument and a callback function as the second argument. This callback function can use two arguments: current iteration index (0, 1, 2, and so on) and the current item or property from the array or map. For your example, you can use the current item/property to easily obtain its value.

First, you will need your data in JSON format. The following code shows how the same data you have been using could be represented in JSON (save the file as *more-content.json*):

```
[
  {
    "title": "Super Programmer Robot 3000",
    "price": "Price: $1,635,343.99",
    "desc": "Need code written in a hurry? No time to hire a human
programmer? This is the product for you! Fluent in over 30 programming
languages: C#, C, Java, PHP, Ruby, Python, JavaScript, Perl, Basic,
COBOL, FORTRAN, ADA, PASCAL, and many more. Just explain to the robot
what you need and it automatically converts your request into a
perfectly coded, bug-free application!",
    "url": "product-01.html"
  },
  {
    "title": "Web Programmer Robot 2000",
    "price": "Price: $675,287.99",
    "desc": "Need a quick Web application? While not fluent in as many
programming  languages as the Super Programmer Robot 3000, this robot
can code Web applications like no other! Why? Because in addition to
knowing Web programming languages like PHP, Python, and Ruby, this
robot knows HTML and CSS as well! A great buy at this price!",
    "url": "product-02.html"
  },
  {
    "title": "The Dougnick Res, I.G.",
    "price": "Price: $1,002,875.99",
    "desc": "The Dougnick Res, Internet Guru is a specialized
JavaScript programming robot. It can literally make anything in
JavaScript! We currently have a limited supply so act today!",
    "url": "product-03.html"
  }
]
```

In this case, the root is an array, and each of the three maps within it can easily be iterated over using *$.each()*.

CAUTION
Each of the descriptions runs over multiple lines in the code listing, but should not do so in your actual source code in order to avoid errors. Also, your Web server needs to have .json (application.json) configured in the server MIME types in order for JSON files to be properly parsed.

With the JSON file in place, you can now update your *ajax.js* file to make use of it. Update your *ajax.js* code to the following and save the file:

The *$.getJSON()* method is called to read the JSON file and execute the callback function

```
$(document).ready(function() {
  $("#view-products").click(function(event) {
    event.preventDefault();
    $.getJSON("more-content.json", function(data) {
      var phtml = '';                                    ← Variable to store and build the HTML code
        $.each(data, function(index, prod) {
          phtml += '<div class="product">';
          phtml += '<div class="product-title">' + prod.title +
          '</div>';
          phtml += '<div class="product-price">' + prod.price +
          '</div>';
          phtml += '<div class="product-desc">' + prod.desc +
          '</div>';
          phtml += '<div class="product-more">';
          phtml += '<a href="' + prod.url + '">More</a></div>';
          phtml += '</div>';
        });
        $("#our-products").empty().hide().append(phtml)
        .slideDown(2000);
    });
  });
});
```

The finished HTML is appended to the *#our-products* element as you have been doing previously

Each time through *$.each()*, *prod* contains the current object from the JSON file; you can then grab the values using the properties of the object

The *$.each()* method iterates over the array, with each object being sent as the *prod* argument

Notice how *$.each()* works well with the JSON data. The JSON file contains an array of objects, each of which contains property/value pairs. The *prod* argument contains the object/array of the current iteration. In this case, you are iterating over an array of objects, so the *prod* argument will represent each object in the array. You can then use each object's property names to access the corresponding values, just as you would with a typical JavaScript object (refer back to Chapter 5 if needed). In the end, the same effect is achieved, with the content being loaded and displayed with a slide-down effect after the link is clicked.

Try This 9-1   Practice Basic AJAX

```
pr09-01.html
pr09-01-jp.html
pr09-01-kd.html
pr09-01.js
```

This project allows you to practice a simple AJAX request by using the *load()* method to load some HTML code from another page. You will need to be sure to request only the code you need from the other HTML page.

Step by Step

1. Place the following HTML code into your editor and save the file as *pr09-01.html*:

```
<!DOCTYPE html>
<html>
<head>
  <meta charset="utf-8">
  <title>Site Authors</title>
  <style type="text/css">
    body { font-family:Verdana, sans-serif; width:50%; }
  </style>
  <script src="jquery-1.9.1.min.js" type="text/javascript"></script>
  <script src="pr09-01.js" type="text/javascript"></script>
</head>
<body>
<h1>Authors</h1>
<h2>John Pollock</h2>
<a id="author-jp" href="bio-jp.html">View Details</a>
<div id="details-jp"></div>
<h2>Kool Dude</h2>
<a id="author-kd" href="bio-kd.html">View Details</a>
<div id="details-kd"></div>
</body>
</html>
```

2. Place the following HTML code into your editor and save the file as *pr09-01-jp.html*:

```
<!DOCTYPE html>
<html>
<head>
  <meta charset="utf-8">
  <title>Bio - John Pollock</title>
</head>
<body>
<h1>John Pollock</h1>
<div id="bio">
<p>
```

```
John Pollock has written a book on JavaScript and one
 on jQuery. He also runs a Web site where he writes
 articles on Web development. He is also an odd
 character, so we let him write some stuff here, too.
</p>
<p>
You can contact him on his site (which I can't find
 in a search right now) or on Twitter (he says he has
 one but he must not have any followers because I can't
 find it). Just keep searching until you find him.
</p>
</div>
</body>
</html>
```

3. Place the following HTML code into your editor and save the file as *pr09-01-kd.html*:

```
<!DOCTYPE html>
<html>
<head>
  <meta charset="utf-8">
  <title>Bio - Kool Dude</title>
</head>
<body>
<h1>Kool Dude</h1>
<div id="bio">
<p>
Kool Dude is one enigmatic character. I don't know if
 he actually exists or is someone's alter ego on this
 Web development forum I visit. Something tells me he
 is actually just a real person like you and me, though.
</p>
<p>
I can't find any real contact information for him. The
 site he lists in his forum profile doesn't work and
 his e-mail address bounces. He could be on a social
 network but I just can't find his profile...
</p>
</div>
</body>
</html>
```

4. Notice how both "bio" pages have a <div> element with an id of *bio*. In the *pr09-01.js* file, add jQuery/JavaScript code that will load the appropriate bio information from the corresponding HTML file when the "View Details" link is clicked for that person.

(continued)

5. Save the file as *pr09-01.js*. When complete, the code should look like this:

```
$(document).ready(function() {
  var $dJP = $("#details-jp"),
      $dKD = $("#details-kd");
  $("#author-jp").click(function(event) {
    event.preventDefault();
    $dJP.empty().hide().load("pr09-01-jp.html #bio", function(data) {
      $dJP.slideDown(1000);
    });
  });
  $("#author-kd").click(function(event) {
  event.preventDefault();
   $dKD.empty().hide().load("pr09-01-kd.html #bio", function(data) {
    $dKD.slideDown(1000);
    });
  });
});
```

6. Open the *pr09-01.html* file in your Web browser. Click each link to view the details about the chosen author, which will be loaded from a separate HTML file.

Try This Summary

In this project, you used your knowledge of the AJAX *load()* method to load information from outside HTML files. Depending on the link that was clicked, a different HTML file was used to obtain the necessary data to display on the page.

Two-Way AJAX Requests

In addition to simply loading data from a file, jQuery provides AJAX methods that allow you to also send data to be processed by an application on the server. In this way, you can provide an even more interactive experience that gathers information based on user decisions or user input.

Using Get and Post Requests

The jQuery library provides the global *$.get* and *$.post* methods. These can be used to pass information to an application on the server, which can then return data to your application on the client side.

For these examples, you will be adding a PHP file to the project you have been working on in this chapter. This file will take data from your AJAX request and send data back to you based on the data you sent. While this book will use a simple PHP script, the same tasks can be performed by any server-side language (Ruby, Python, ASP.NET, Java, and so on). Since this book is about using jQuery on the client side, the PHP script will be discussed according to concepts more than the specifics of the code. Resources for learning server-side programming languages will be provided at the end of the chapter.

Using Get

The *$.get()* method can be used to send and receive data. The general format is shown in the following code:

```
$.get(url, map, function(data, status, jqXHR) {
  //function code...
}, type);
```

Up to four arguments can be used as needed. These include (as seen in the previous code):

- **url**   The URL of the file to get

- **map**   An object of property/value pairs that can be sent to the server/application

- **function(data, status, jqXHR)**   The callback function that executes on success

  - **data**   The data returned from the server/application

  - **status**   The text of the status response

  - **jqXHR**   The jQuery XHR object

- **type**   The type of data expected from the server

The *url* argument is required, where the others are optional. If nothing is used for *type*, jQuery will try to determine the data type of the requested file.

An example of *$.get()* is shown in the following code:

```
$.get('app.php', { num: 1 }, function(data) {
  // Function code
});
```

This will get the url *app.php* and will send it an object map that includes the property *num* with a value of *1*. When the request has been completed successfully, the callback function is executed and can make use of any data that has been returned using the *data* variable.

As a more complete example, you will update the *ajax.html* file you have been using. This update will move the CSS code to an external style sheet so that it can be used for multiple files. This is shown in the following code (save as *ajax.html*):

```
<!DOCTYPE html>
<html>
<head>
  <meta charset="utf-8">
  <title>AJAX</title>
  <link href="ajax.css" rel="stylesheet" type="text/css">
  <script src="jquery-1.9.1.min.js" type="text/javascript"></script>
  <script src="ajax.js" type="text/javascript"></script>
```

The CSS code is moved to an external style sheet named *ajax.css*

```
</head>
<body>
<h1>Our Special Products</h1>
<a id="view-products" href="view-products.php">View Products</a>
<div id="our-products"></div>
</body>
</html>
```

The link is altered so that it calls a PHP script rather than a static HTML file when JavaScript is unavailable

You will now create the external CSS file. Place the following code into a new file and save it as *ajax.css*:

```
body { font-family:Verdana, sans-serif; }
#our-products { margin:0 30% 0 0; }
.product { margin:1.2em 0em; }
.product-title { font-weight:bold; }
```

This is the same code used within the <style></style> tags previously.

The idea behind the example script will be to load the title of each product (Super Programmer Robot 3000, Web Programmer Robot 2000, and so on) when the "View Products" link is clicked and make each title a link that will display the details about the product when clicked.

This will use two different AJAX requests, both of which will request return data from a PHP script. Depending on the data sent to the PHP script from the *$.get()* method, the PHP script will return either a list of linked product titles or the product details for a single product.

To ensure the user can obtain the data once the "View Products" link is clicked, the PHP script will also check to see whether the request was made as an AJAX request or not. If not, then the product titles and data will simply be displayed as you have done previously.

The PHP file will simply be a concept file. You'll see notes pointing to different parts of the PHP code to describe what is being done. You will then see how this affects the jQuery code you need to write to make the necessary requests and work with the returned data.

NOTE

To run the code as it is, you will need a server with PHP and MySQL installed (the product data also needs to be entered into a MySQL database named "products" within a table named "special"). If you have another configuration (a different programming language or database type), you can code the same concept file in the alternate language and/or adjust the database portions of the code to suit your setup.

The code for the PHP file you will use is shown here (save as *view-products.php*):

```php
<?php
require_once("config.php"); // defines $dbhost, $dbuser, $dbpass
$dbname='products';
$conn = new mysqli($dbhost, $dbuser, $dbpass, $dbname) or
            die ('Error connecting to mysql');
if (mysqli_connect_error()) {
    die('Connect Error (' . mysqli_connect_errno() . ') '
                            . mysqli_connect_error());
}
$sql = "SELECT * FROM special;";
$data = mysqli_query($conn, $sql);
$ajaxRequest = isset($_SERVER['HTTP_X_REQUESTED_WITH']) &&
            $_SERVER['HTTP_X_REQUESTED_WITH'] == 'XMLHttpRequest';
if (!$ajaxRequest):
?>
<!DOCTYPE html>
<html>
<head>
  <meta charset="utf-8">
  <title>Product Details</title>
  <link href="ajax.css" rel="stylesheet" type="text/css">
</head>
<body>
<h1>Our Special Products - Details</h1>
<p><a href="ajax.html">Back</a></p>
<div id="our-products">
<?php
while ($row = mysqli_fetch_array($data, MYSQLI_ASSOC)) {
  echo '<div class="product">';
```

If it is not an AJAX request, the program simply displays a page with all of the data that is retrieved from the earlier query results *($data)*

Defines a variable named *$ajaxRequest*, which will be *true* if the request is made as an AJAX request and *false* if not

Defines a general database query to get all of the items in the *special* table of the *products* database and then assigns the result to *$data*

Connects to the database using the host, user, password, and name information; exits the program if a connection is not made

Defines the database host, user, password, and name (the first three are defined in a separate file named *config.php*, which is then required by the script)

If it is not an AJAX request, the program simply displays a page with
all of the data that is retrieved from the earlier query results *($data)*

```php
echo '<div class="product-title">' . $row['title'] . '</div>';
echo '<div class="product-price">Price: $' . $row['price'] . '</div>';
echo '<div class="product-desc">' . $row['description'] . '</div>';
echo '<div class="product-more">';
echo '<a href="' . $row['url'] . '">More...</a></div>';
echo '</div>';
}
?>
</div>
</body>
</html>
<?php endif; ?>
<?php
function getData($conn, $data) {
  $html = '';
  if ((isset($_GET['page'])) && (!isset($_GET['prod']))) {
    while ($row = mysqli_fetch_array($data, MYSQLI_ASSOC)) {
        $html .= '<div class="product">';
        $html .= '<div class="product-title">';
        $html .= '<a href="product-0' . $row['item'] . '.html">';
        $html .= $row['title'] . '</a></div>';
        $html .= '<div class="product-details"></div>';
        $html .= '</div>';
    }
  }
  elseif ((isset($_GET['prod'])) && (!isset($_GET['page']))) {
    $prod = mysqli_real_escape_string($conn, trim($_GET['prod']));
    $psql = "SELECT * FROM special WHERE title='" . $prod . "' LIMIT
    1;";
    $pdata = mysqli_query($conn, $psql);
    $row = mysqli_fetch_array($pdata, MYSQLI_ASSOC);
```

Checks to see if the request contains a *page* property
and does not contain a *prod* property either in the
query string (for example, *view-products.php?page=1*)
or in the data sent by the jQuery *$.get()* method

Begins a function that will be executed
if the request is an AJAX request

Creates an empty *$html* variable that will
have HTML code added to it as needed

A new query is run on the database to limit the result
set to a single product, based on the product title sent
via the *prod* property and stored in *$prod*

Checks to see if there is a *prod* property
and not a *page* property in the request

Since the value of the *prod* property *could* be input by the user in the query
string, this helps ensure that it does not contain any characters that will alter the
MySQL database; the value of the *$prod* variable is the result of this action

If there is a *page* property, then the results of the query stored in *$data* are used to
retrieve the product item number and title of each item from the database, ultimately
creating the three *.product* <div> elements with the product titles as clickable links

Builds the HTML code with the product
details obtained from the database

```php
$html .= '<div class="product-price">Price: $' . $row['price'] .
'</div>';
$html .= '<div class="product-desc">' . $row['description'] .
'</div>';
$html .= '<div class="product-more">';
$html .= '<a href="' . $row['url'] . '">More...</a></div>';
}
else {
    $html = '';
}
return $html;
}
if ($ajaxRequest) {
  echo getData($conn, $data);
}
mysqli_close($conn);
?>
```

If neither properties exist (or both do), then
the value of *$html* is set to an empty string
(will display nothing)

The value of *$html* is returned, which will be sent to
an echo command that calls the *getData()* function

If the request is an AJAX request, the
getData() function is executed and the
results are sent back via the *echo* statement

Closes the connection to the database

This PHP program is what reacts to a click on the "View Products" link. In summary, it performs one of four general actions, based on the type of request and the information sent to it:

- Simply display a page with all of the data if the request is not an AJAX request (for example, if the user has JavaScript disabled)

- Return a list of products in HTML format (where each title can be clicked to display further details)

- Return the details of a single product in HTML format

- Return nothing for the HTML if the request is made improperly (does not contain either the *page* or *prod* properties, and only one of those properties at a time)

The PHP program does the major work here: It makes the application accessible for those without JavaScript and returns the relevant data to allow you to enhance the application via jQuery/JavaScript for those that have it enabled. Since the data has been placed into a database for this application, the PHP program also does the work of connecting to and retrieving information from the database.

NOTE

This PHP program is used here to present the concept, but should only be used in a test environment. It should not be used in a production environment where you will need to double-check application and data security, among other needs.

The task now is to use jQuery and its *$.get()* method to put this PHP program to use and create an application that responds to the various elements that can be clicked by the user to request further information.

First, you need to determine how a click on the "View Products" link will be handled. In this case, you want to retrieve the list of clickable links. Since the PHP script checks for the existence of the *page* to return the links, you can use the *$.get()* method to send the program what it needs. Consider the following code (save this as the new code for your *ajax.js* file):

The *click()* method is used on the "View Products" link

```
$(document).ready(function() {
  $("#view-products").click(function(event) {
    event.preventDefault();
    $.get('view-products.php', { page: 1 }, function(products) {
      $("#our-products").empty().hide().append(products).
      slideDown('slow');
    });
  });
});
```

Since the returned data stored in *products* is HTML code, this simply appends it to the *#our-products* element as you have done with HTML code previously

The *$.get()* method is used—the *view-products.php* file is executed, the *page* property with a value of *1* is sent to the server-side application, and any data returned from the PHP application is sent to the callback function using a variable named *products*

The default action of the link is prevented

This handles the first click to view the product list. It sends the PHP program the *page* property as part of the get request, which you will recall is used by the PHP program to determine that the list of product links should be returned (rather than the details of a single product, which happens when you send it the *prod* property). Figure 9-4 shows how the *ajax.html* page looks after the "View Products" link is clicked.

The next task is to react any time one of the product links is clicked. The details of the product need to be loaded and shown to the user. The first issue is that you will need to access elements that were not a part of the DOM when the page loaded. You will recall from Chapter 3 that the *on()* method allows you to use event delegation, allowing you to attach an event handler to a parent element, which can then target the specific child element later.

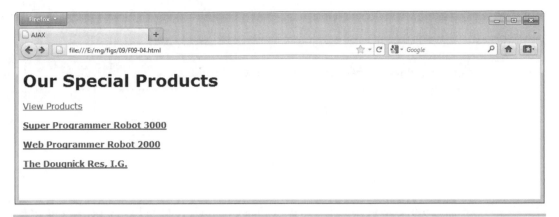

Figure 9-4 The products are displayed as a list of clickable links.

In this case, the *#our-products* element was already in place when the document loaded, and the <div> elements with the *.product-title* class were loaded after the "View Products" link was clicked. Thus, we can use *on()* to delegate the event and allow clicks on any <div> elements with the *.product-title* class to work once they are a part of the DOM, as in the following code:

```
$("#our-products").on("click", "div.product-title", function(event) {
    // Function code...
});
```

With this in place, you now need to see whether the container element (*.product-details*) for all of the elements containing details exists. This will accomplish a particular goal here: to determine whether the data is already in the DOM and can simply be shown/hidden, or whether the data needs to be loaded into the DOM via an AJAX request.

To accomplish this, you will need to search for a <div> element with the *.product-details* class within the current *.product* <div> element. This can be done using the *find()* method. The following code illustrates what you will be doing:

A variable is created for the current *.product* <div>; *$(this)* points to *.product-title*, so you can use its parent element to execute the *find()* method

```
$("#our-products").on("click", "div.product-title", function(event) {
    var $prodDiv = $(this).parent(),
        $prodDetails = $prodDiv.find(".product-details")
    event.preventDefault();    The default action (following the link) is prevented
```

The *.product-details* <div> is assigned to *$prodDetails* if it exists; otherwise, an empty object will be assigned to it

```
if($prodDetails.text().length > 0) {
    // Show or hide the element since it has already been loaded
}
else {
    // Get the data, load it into the DOM, and show it
}
});
```

If the element is not found, *$prodDetails* will have a length
of zero (empty object), so you will need to load the data

If the *.prod-details* element is found, the length property
of *$prodDetails* will be greater than zero, so you can
simply show/hide the element

As you can see, with jQuery's selectors and the *find()* method, you can locate the *.prod-details* element if it exists. Assigning the result of the selection to a variable (*$prodDetails*) gives you a way to determine if the element is there: If so, the object will have a length of 1 or more; otherwise, the length will be 0.

With this information, you can handle the click in a different way when the *.prod-details* <div> is present. If it exists, you will simply show or hide the data that has been loaded. If it does not exist, then you need to obtain the data with *$.get()* and load it into the DOM.

So, if you want to use a slide animation, you can use *slideToggle()* when the element is present. If not, you can load the data and then use *slideDown()*, as in the following code:

With the data already loaded, you can simply
toggle between sliding down and sliding up

```
$("#our-products").on("click", "div.product-title", function(event) {
  var $prodDiv = $(this).parent(),
      $prodDetails = $prodDiv.find(".product-details")
  event.preventDefault();
  if($prodDetails.text().length > 0) {
    $prodDetails.slideToggle('slow');
  }
  else {
    $.get('view-products.php', { prod: $(this).text() }, function(p) {
      $prodDetails.hide().append(p).slideDown('slow');
    });
  }
});
```

Once the data is retrieved, it can be
appended and shown via *slideDown()*

The request sends the *prod* property with the value of the text
in the *.prod-title* <div>; this prompts the PHP script to locate the
corresponding product in the database, obtain its details, and
send them back with HTML markup

As you can see, *slideToggle()* is used when the element is present, while *$get()* is used to obtain the information and add it to the document if not. Notice that the PHP program is sent the property *prod* with a value of *$(this).text()* from *$.get()*. *$(this).text* refers to the text within the element *.prod-title* element, which means that the product title is sent. This allows the PHP program to check the database for the product title and return the product details for that title.

With that taken care of, you can now complete the *ajax.js* file. Use the following code for *ajax.js* and save the file:

```
$(document).ready(function() {
  $("#view-products").click(function(event) {
    event.preventDefault();
    $.get('view-products.php', { page: 1 }, function(products) {
      $("#our-products").empty().hide().append(products).
      slideDown('slow');
    });
  });
  $("#our-products").on("click", "div.product-title", function(event) {
    var $prodDiv = $(this).parent(),
        $prodDetails = $prodDiv.find(".product-details")
    event.preventDefault();
    if($prodDetails.text().length > 0) {
      $prodDetails.slideToggle('slow');
    }
    else {
      $.get('view-products.php', { prod: $(this).text() },
      function(p) {
      $prodDetails.hide().append(p).slideDown('slow');
    });
    }
  });
});
```

If you are able to use this example in a test server environment, you can load the *ajax.html* page and go through the process. Click the "View Products" link to get the list of products, then click a product title to view/hide its details. Figure 9-5 shows the result of clicking the "Web Programmer Robot 2000" link.

Using Post

The *$.post()* method works the same way as get, but sends the data via a post request rather than get. The biggest difference here is that a post request can transport more data than a get request.

For example, to call the first request from the previous example using *$.post()* rather than *$.get()*, you would simply swap out the method name, as in the following code:

```
$.post('view-products.php', { page: 1 }, function(products) {
  $("#our-products").empty().hide().append(products).
```

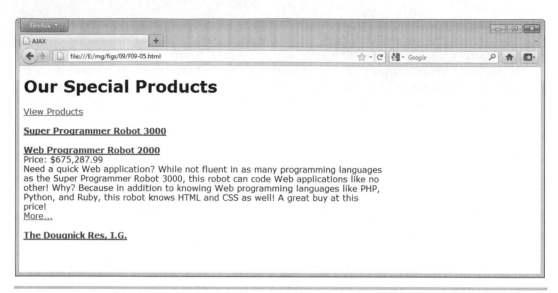

Figure 9-5 The details are displayed when the link is clicked.

```
    slideDown('slow');
});
```

The PHP program would then need to be updated accordingly to look for $_POST information rather than $_GET. If your application is transmitting large amounts of data, *$.post()* may be a better option for you.

Handling Errors

Sometimes when gathering information from the server, things do not go as planned. Perhaps the file you are trying to access doesn't get loaded due to a network error or a slow connection. In such cases, it is good to be able to handle the error in some way so that the user knows that something went wrong.

For any AJAX function other than *load()*, you can chain the *error()* function to it in order to handle errors with an AJAX request. For example, consider the following code:

```
$.get('my-script.php', function(products) {
  // Show loaded information
}).error(function() {
  $("#my-element").empty().append("Load Error!");
});
```

Here, the *error()* method is chained to the *$.get()* method. In this way, a function can be executed to alert the user to the error.

In your *ajax.js* file, you can now use this to provide a quick error message to users if an AJAX request fails for some reason. This example will simply display some text, but you could do any number of things (provide a "try again" link or other helpful information, for instance). Save the new code, shown here, in your *ajax.js* file:

An error message for
the product list request

```
$(document).ready(function() {
  $("#view-products").click(function(event) {
    event.preventDefault();
    $.get('view-products.php', { page: 1 }, function(products) {
      $("#our-products").empty().hide().append(products).
      slideDown('slow');
    }).error(function() {
      $("#our-products").empty().append("Load Error!");
    });
  });
  $("#our-products").on("click", "div.product-title", function(event) {
    var $prodDiv = $(this).parent(),
        $prodDetails = $prodDiv.find(".product-details")
    event.preventDefault();
    if($prodDetails.text().length > 0) {
    $prodDetails.slideToggle('slow');
    }
    else {
      $.get('view-products.php', { prod: $(this).text() }, function(p) {
        $prodDetails.hide().append(p).slideDown('slow');
      }).error(function() {
        $prodDiv.after("Load Error!");
      });
    }
  });
});
```

An error message for the
product details request

To see the error work, you may need to manually create one by altering the name of the requested file in the code to one that doesn't exist (creates a 404 error). So, instead of "view-products.php," you might use "not-here.php" or anything else so that an error will occur. Figure 9-6 shows the page when there is an error after clicking the "View Products" link.

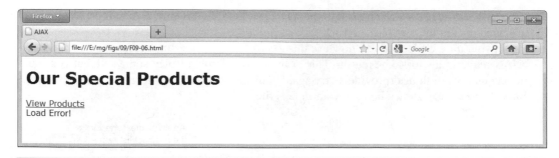

Figure 9-6 Oops! The content was not loaded!

Form Input Serialization

The jQuery library offers a helpful method named *serialize()* for sending form input data to the server, which allows you to submit the form behind the scenes, avoiding the typical page reload or redirect for the user once a form is submitted.

You can serialize individual input fields, but most likely you will want to send all the form input to the server. By selecting the form and using *serialize()*, this can be done easily using jQuery.

As an example, suppose you have a contact form that allows users to send you a message. Rather than redirecting the users back to the same page or a new one for confirmation, you would like to simply display a message on the page once the submission is complete. Using *serialize()*, you can submit the form data and then use *$.get()* or *$.post()* to send the serialized data to an application. In the callback function that executes on the completion of the request, you can insert a message letting the user know the message was sent successfully.

First, you will need a page with an HTML form. Save the following code as *form-ajax.html*:

```
<!DOCTYPE html>
<html>
<head>
  <meta charset="utf-8">
  <title>Form AJAX</title>
  <script src="jquery-1.9.1.min.js" type="text/javascript"></script>
  <script src="form-ajax.js" type="text/javascript"></script>
</head>
<body>
  <h1>Contact Us</h1>
  <form method="post" id="contact-form" action="form-sub.php">
    <label for="name">Name:</label>
     <input type="text" name="name" id="name"><br>
    <label for="email">E-mail:</label>
```

```
      <input type="text" name="email" id="email"><br>
      <label for="msg">Message:</label><br>
      <textarea name="msg" id="msg"></textarea>
      <br><br>
      <input type="submit" value="Submit">
    </form>
    <p id="sub-msg"></p>
  </body>
</html>
```

This sets up a simple form with three input fields. The name attribute is used with all of the fields. This is because *serialize()* will only include input fields that have the name attribute (used by server-side scripts to collect form data). Also, only fields that contain input are sent as part of the serialized string to the server. Thus, empty text boxes, unchecked radio buttons, and so on will not be included. You can use form validation (refer back to Chapter 8) to ensure that the fields you require data from have been completed.

To avoid another long PHP code example, assume that the server-side PHP program that handles the form (*form-sub.php*) can perform the following tasks:

● Redirect the user to a completion/error message if it is not an AJAX request/JavaScript is disabled

● Return a "success" message if the information was successfully submitted

The details on how to accomplish these tasks are handled by the server-side program, so you need only work on the client-side task of making sure the information is sent to it.

Using *serialize()* and *$.post()*, the following code submits the form data behind the scenes with an AJAX request and simply appends a message to the page when complete (save the file as *form-ajax.js*):

```
$(document).ready(function() {
  $("#contact-form").submit(function(event) {
    var formInput = $(this).serialize();  ◄─────── The form data is serialized
    event.preventDefault();
    $.post("form-sub.php", formInput, function(data) { ◄
      $("#sub-msg").empty().append("Message sent successfully."); ◄─┐
    }).error(function() {
      $("#sub-msg").empty().append("Load Error!");
    });
  });                              Once the request is complete, the message
});                               is displayed on the page by appending it

          The serialized data is sent to the server for processing
```

As you can see, the form is selected and *submit()* is used to handle the form when it is submitted. By using the form itself as the selection for *serialize()*, each form input field that is filled in will be sent as part of a formatted string to the server. For example, entering "blah" in all three fields will send the following string to the server:

```
name=blah&email=blah&msg=blah
```

This works the same way as if it had been submitted via a regular get or post request to the server, and the server-side program can handle the data in its usual syntax.

Since the data returned is not being used, all that displays upon completion is the message, "Message sent successfully." You could also choose to return a message, the input data, or other items from the server-side program, depending on your needs. Figure 9-7 shows the initial page, and Figure 9-8 shows how the page would look with a server-side program returning a completed request, which displays the success message.

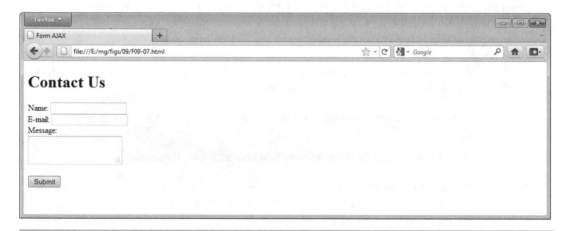

Figure 9-7 The initial page

Figure 9-8 The page after successful submission

Try This 9-2 Practice Serialization

pr09-02.html
pr09-02.js
pr09-02.php

This project allows you to practice using the *serialize()* method to serialize form input. You will create a form that submits without reloading the page, like the example in this chapter. Upon completion, a success message will be displayed.

Step by Step

1. Insert the following HTML code into your editor and save the file as *pr09-02.html*:

```
<!DOCTYPE html>
<html>
<head>
  <meta charset="utf-8">
  <title>Project 9-2</title>
  <script src="jquery-1.9.1.min.js" type="text/javascript"></script>
  <script src="pr09-02.js" type="text/javascript"></script>
</head>
<body>
 <h1>Contact Us</h1>
   <form method="post" id="contact-form" action="pr09-02.php">
     <label for="name">Name:</label>
      <input type="text" name="name" id="name"><br>
     <label for="email">E-mail:</label>
      <input type="text" name="email" id="email"><br>
     <label for="msg">Message:</label><br>
      <textarea name="msg" id="msg"></textarea>
     <br><br>
      <input type="submit" value="Submit">
   </form>
   <p id="sub-msg"></p>
</body>
</html>
```

2. Next, you will create an empty PHP file. This will allow the script to succeed if you are not able to work with a server (if you are able to use a server, you can adjust the program and/ or language and write some code to return information if desired). Insert the following PHP code in your editor and save the file as *pr09-02.php*:

```
<?php ?>
```

3. Create a JavaScript file and save it as *pr09-02.js*. Add jQuery/JavaScript code so that the form input is serialized and used as part of a post request using the *$.post()* method. If the

(continued)

request is successful, send a success message with the text "Message sent successfully." If there is an error, send the message "Load Error!"

4. When complete, the code should look like this:

```
$(document).ready(function() {
  $("#contact-form").submit(function(event) {
    var formInput = $(this).serialize();
    event.preventDefault();
    $.post("pr09-02.php", formInput, function(data) {
      $("#sub-msg").empty().append("Message sent successfully.");
    }).error(function() {
      $("#sub-msg").empty().append("Load Error!");
    });;
  });
});
```

5. Open the *pr09-02.html* file in your Web browser. Fill in some form fields and submit the form to see the success message.

Try This Summary

In this project, you used your knowledge of the *$.post()* method and the *serialize()* method in order to serialize and submit form information behind the scenes without reloading the page. Once this process was complete, a success message was displayed for the user.

Security Issues and Further Information

Due to the risk of cross-site scripting and other potential attacks, AJAX requests must request files on the same server. This helps to prevent malicious code from running, or from another site changing the code from something helpful to something malicious.

If you do have a trusted source, however, there are some methods being drafted for allowing requests from another server, such as Cross-Origin Resource Sharing (CORS). You can read more about this at www.w3.org/TR/cors/.

When dealing with data sent to and from the server, it is often possible for users to input information of their own in some way. Form elements provide an easy way for users to input information, but get and post requests can also be sent information (the user simply needs to know the name of the file you are requesting, for example, *view-products.php*). Rather than running the program from your intended action, users could, for instance, type their own URLs for get requests to see if malicious code could be run.

It is best to always test user input before running a database query or displaying it on a Web page. Some resources for this, as well as for learning some common server-side languages, are provided next.

Further Information

Further information on AJAX and server-side programming is provided here so that you can further explore the topics.

AJAX Security

- **AJAX Security Basics**   www.symantec.com/connect/articles/ajax-security-basics

- **OWASP AJAX Security Guidelines**   https://www.owasp.org/index.php/OWASP_AJAX_Security_Guidelines

- **Common Ajax Security Vulnerabilities and How to Resolve Them**   www.securitygeeks .net/2013/06/common-ajax-security-vulnerabilities.html

Server-Side Programming Resources

- **PHP**   http://php.net

- **ASP.NET**   www.asp.net/get-started

- **Ruby**   www.ruby-lang.org

- **Python**   www.python.org

- **Java**   www.java.com/en/download/faq/develop.xml

- **Perl**   www.pcrl.org/lcarn.html

Ask the Expert

Q: Are there other methods for creating AJAX requests?

A: Yes, jQuery offers the *$.ajax()* method, which allows you to create a customized AJAX request if you need to do so. It offers you the ability to supply a multitude of arguments that alter how the request operates. To find out more about the *$.ajax()* method, visit the jQuery site at http://api.jquery.com/jQuery.ajax/.

Q: So the data sent or received doesn't need to be in XML format?

A: No, the data can be in any text format you need to use. You can send a string of text, text in JSON format, XML, HTML, or in various other formats.

Q: Can AJAX be done via JavaScript instead?

A: Yes, using the *XMLHttpRequest* object, you can create AJAX requests in JavaScript. For more information on using native JavaScript, see www.webmonkey.com/2010/02/ajax_for_beginners/.

Chapter 9 Self Test

1. The acronym AJAX stands for _____.

   A. Asynchronous JavaScript and HTML

   B. Alternative JQuery and XML

   C. Asynchronous JavaScript and XML

   D. Absolute JavaScript aside XML

2. While the term AJAX originally dealt with XML as the means of transferring data, it can now mean transferring data in any form between the client and the _____.

   A. server

   B. modem

   C. phone

   D. browser

3. In modern JavaScript applications, you can request data from the server using the _____ object.

   A. XMLHttpRequest

   B. AJAX

   C. RequestAJAX

   D. ServerRequest

4. The jQuery library provides the _____ method for loading HTML content into a document.

   A. getHTML()

   B. load()

   C. loadHTML()

   D. HTML()

5. The jQuery library makes it possible to select a portion of the document using its selector syntax as part of the argument to the *load()* method.

   A. True

   B. False

6. AJAX methods load content _____.

    A. synchronously

    B. immediately

    C. constantly

    D. asynchronously

7. When using *$.get( )*, if a response is received from the server that the document's MIME type is XML, its callback function will receive the XML DOM tree.

    A. True

    B. False

8. The jQuery _____ method allows you to search all descendant elements of the specified element and select any needed elements using a second selector as the argument.

    A. search()

    B. locate()

    C. find()

    D. select()

9. JSON stands for _____.

    A. JQuery Standard Object Nodes

    B. JavaScript Object Notation

    C. Java Server Over Network

    D. JSON: Standard Object Notation

10. To load JSON data, jQuery has a global method named _____.

    A. $.getJSON()

    B. $.JSON()

    C. $.retrieveJSON()

    D. $.JSONget()

11. The jQuery library provides the global _____ and _____ methods.

    A. $.get(), $.getMore()

    B. $.grab(), $.post()

    C. $.get(), $.post()

    D. $.getAJAX(), $postAJAX()

12. The *$.get()* and *$.post()* methods provide a _____ function that is executed if the request is successful.

    A. return

    B. callback

    C. sendback

    D. finished

13. You can use only PHP programming on the server side when performing AJAX requests.

    A. True

    B. False

14. In order to ensure that the user is aware of any errors loading data from an AJAX request, the *error()* method can be added to the chain after any AJAX method other than the *load()* method, which will execute any code within it if there is a load error.

    A. True

    B. False

15. The _____ method allows you to format form input data to be sent as a server-side request behind the scenes without reloading the page.

    A. serious()

    B. cerealize()

    C. surmise()

    D. serialize()

Chapter 10

Using Plugins

Key Skills & Concepts

- Introduction to jQuery Plugins
- Using a Plugin
- Helpful Plugins

The jQuery library supports the addition of plugins, which can further extend the capabilities of the scripts you write. In this chapter, you will learn what jQuery plugins are, how to make use of them, and get a quick overview of some plugins that you may find useful in developing your scripts and applications.

Introduction to jQuery Plugins

Up to this point, you have been using the core components of the jQuery library, which have allowed you to perform numerous tasks with ease and cross-browser compatibility. While the jQuery library by itself is very helpful, you may find occasions where you need additional functionality or features that are not part of the core library.

To assist with this, jQuery allows developers to create methods that can extend the jQuery library to provide additional features, which are called plugins. By simply adding another JavaScript file and calling a new method, you can use a plugin to harness the extra features it brings to the table.

The jQuery site houses numerous plugins at http://plugins.jquery.com/. The site displays helpful information for each plugin, such as the version number, the home page for the plugin, bug reports, and more. Some information, such as the number of "watchers," can be helpful to see if the plugin is a popular one.

You can also search for plugins on the Web via Google, Bing, DuckDuckGo, or other search engines. Needless to say, there are numerous plugins available all over the Web. This means that you will need to be mindful when choosing a plugin for use to ensure that it does what you need it to do and is still supported and/or bug-free. Many have documentation on the author's Web site or on GitHub, a popular code repository (http://github.com). If you are in doubt, you can always visit the jQuery forums to ask other users and developers for help or recommendations. The forum is at http://forum.jquery.com (shows all categories). Plugin-specific questions can be posted in the "Using jQuery Plugins" category at http://forum.jquery .com/using-jquery-plugins/.

Using a Plugin

Using a plugin is typically an easy process of including the new files and calling a new method within your script. Some plugins require just an extra JavaScript file, while others will also

Ask the Expert

Q: Will using plugins slow down my site?

A: Many plugins are optimized as much as possible in order to keep the additional code and overhead to a minimum. Depending on the plugin you choose, you could potentially add a large codebase to what you are already using, thus creating longer download times. When choosing plugins, you will want to be sure that each one does what you need without containing too many additional features that you don't plan to use.

Q: So does this mean I shouldn't use plugins?

A: Not at all. Many plugins provide very helpful features with a minimum of additional overhead. You may also need a lot of features, in which case a larger plugin may be what you need. What you do will largely depend on your needs and the needs of your users.

Q: What if I can't find what I need? Can I create my own plugins?

A: Yes! Chapter 11 will introduce plugin development and provide additional resources for you if you wish to pursue this. There are certainly cases where a custom plugin can be helpful. For example, you may have a need that is not currently addressed, or you may need a single feature but can only find plugins that include that feature with numerous others you do not need. In such cases, you may wish to develop a custom plugin to meet your needs or to ensure that only the features you need are added.

need you to include CSS files, images, or other media. In addition, most plugins can be used by simply calling a method, but many allow you to set options by adding arguments to the method call in your script.

Downloading and Installing a Plugin

First, you will need to download a plugin. For an example, you will download a plugin named Chosen, which takes plain select elements and transforms them into a more user-friendly selection tool (which is especially helpful for select elements with a lengthy number of options).

You can download the files you will need by going to http://plugins.jquery.com/chosen/ and clicking "Download Now." This will take you to the developer's GitHub site where you can download the zip file. You will need to extract the zip file into the same folder where you have jQuery installed (you can, of course, choose a different folder as long as you remember to alter the <script> element's src attribute appropriately).

Once you have the files in place, take note of what is included. In some cases, you may wish to delete files you don't intend to use. This plugin contains developer and production versions of the plugin JavaScript file and the CSS file. Also, it includes some example pages and a version of the plugin for the *Prototype* library. If you decide to delete some of these to save space, you will need to be sure to keep at least the following files:

```
chosen.jquery.min.js
chosen.min.css
chosen-sprite@2x.png
chosen-sprite.png
```

The next step is to include the necessary CSS and JavaScript files in your HTML document. For this example, you will use a simple contact form, which includes both a single and a multiple select box so that you can see what the plugin does. Save the following HTML code as *selects.html*:

```
<!DOCTYPE html>
<html>
<head>
  <meta charset="utf-8">
  <title>Select Boxes</title>
  <link rel="stylesheet" type="text/css" href="chosen.min.css">
  <script src="jquery-1.9.1.min.js" type="text/javascript"></script>
  <script src="chosen.jquery.min.js" type="text/javascript"></script>
  <script src="selects.js" type="text/javascript"></script>
</head>
<body>
<h1>Contact Us</h1>
<form method="post" action="contact.php">
  <label for="name">Name:</label>
    <input type="text" id="name">
    <br><br>
  <label for="ref">Referred By:</label>
    <select id="ref" class="use-chosen">
      <option value="Search">Search</option>
      <option value="Site">Another Site</option>
      <option value="Word">Word of Mouth</option>
      <option value="Social">Social Media</option>
    </select>
    <br><br>
    <label for="foods">Foods You Like:</label>
    <select id="foods" class="use-chosen" multiple>
      <option value="Pizza">Pizza</option>
      <option value="Burgers">Burgers</option>
      <option value="Salads">Salads</option>
      <option value="Fried Asparagus">Fried Asparagus</option>
      <option value="Steamed Asparagus">Steamed Asparagus</option>
      <option value="Chocolate">CHOCOLATE!</option>
    </select>
    <br><br>
    <label for="comments">Comments:</label><br>
    <textarea id="comments"></textarea><br><br>
```

The Chosen plugin is included —
The jQuery library is included —
The accompanying CSS file is included —

Your own JavaScript file is included ┘

```
        <input type="submit" value="Submit">
</form>
</body>
</html>
```

You will notice that the companion CSS file is included, as well as the additional JavaScript file. The order in which the JavaScript files are included is important: You must include jQuery first, any plugins after that, and your own JavaScript file last. This ensures that the plugins can use jQuery, and that your script can use both jQuery and the included plugins! Once this is in place, the plugin is installed and ready to use.

Calling the Method

Your next task will be to invoke the plugin by calling the method that it uses. In most cases, you do this as you would most other jQuery methods, by chaining it to a jQuery object (a collection of one or more elements). You will need to refer to the documentation for each plugin you use to determine what the name of the method will be.

In this case, you have two select elements: a single select and a multiple select. Both of these have the class *use-chosen*, so you can use this to make the Chosen plugin work for both select elements by calling the *chosen()* method, as in the following code (save as *selects.js*):

```
$(document).ready(function() {
  $(".use-chosen").chosen();
});
```

That's it! The plugin will now transform both select boxes to be more user-friendly. Open the *selects.html* file in your browser and try making selections. You'll notice some changes, such as a "search" box being available for the single select box and that selecting items in the multiple select box pops each selected item into a list at the top of the box rather than allowing each of them to potentially be hidden from view by a long list of options (this makes it easy to see what you have selected).

There are also some visual changes and other things you may notice. As you can see, simply using the plugin with the default options already helps to make the select boxes easier to use. Figure 10-1 shows the page before the plugin is used (plain select boxes), and Figure 10-2 shows the page after the plugin is used and some items have been selected (this is what you have saved).

Setting Plugin Options

As with many other plugins, Chosen allows you to set numerous options. Most often, options are set by including one or more arguments to the method that you call. Often, you are able to send a single argument: a map of property names and values, as in the following example code:

```
$("#my-element").methodName({ name: value, name: value });
```

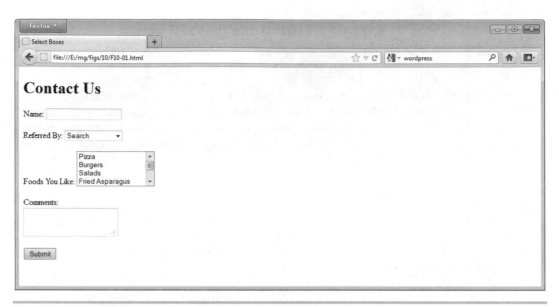

Figure 10-1 How the page would look without the plugin installed

Figure 10-2 The plugin adds some new features to the select boxes.

You have used this pattern many times throughout this book, so you are already familiar with the syntax you will need to use.

In the case of the Chosen plugin, you can tell it not to display the search box for the single select lists if there are fewer than a certain number of options in the list. You can also tell it what text to use as the default (when no options are selected) for select boxes with the multiple attribute. These are set using the *disable_search_threshold* and *placeholder_text_multiple* properties. Update your *selects.js* file to use the following code and save it:

```
$(document).ready(function() {
  $(".use-chosen").chosen({
    disable_search_threshold: 5,
    placeholder_text_multiple: "Choose Options..."
  });
});
```

Reload the *selects.html* page in your browser. Since the single select is now set to not display the search box when there are fewer than five options, you will now get no search box when you activate the select box, since there are only four options. The multiple select box will now display the default text "Choose Options..." until you make a selection. Figure 10-3 shows the single select box when it is activated after the options have been set.

Of course, this plugin has numerous other options that you can set by adding them to the map you pass to the *chosen()* method. Also, Chosen allows the use of attributes and classes as additional means of setting particular options. You can view the full list by going to the Chosen options page at http://harvesthq.github.io/chosen/options.html.

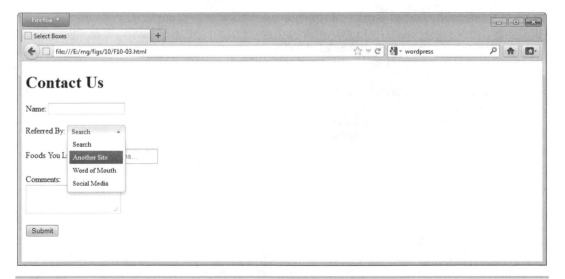

Figure 10-3　The select box no longer has the search box since there aren't many options.

Practice Using a Plugin

pr10-01.html
pr10-01.js

This project allows you to practice using a plugin. You will again use the Chosen plugin, but this time you will have a particularly long list of options to choose from in a select box (the fifty U.S. states plus the District of Columbia). To make it easier, you will apply the Chosen plugin, which will allow you to search the options list more easily.

Step by Step

1. Place the following HTML code into your editor and save the file as *pr10-01.html*:

```
<!DOCTYPE html>
<html>
<head>
  <meta charset="utf-8">
  <title>Project 10-1</title>
  <link rel="stylesheet" type="text/css" href="../figs/10/chosen.
  min.css">
  <script src="jquery-1.9.1.min.js" type="text/javascript"></script>
  <script src="chosen.jquery.min.js" type="text/javascript"></
  script>
  <script src="pr10-01.js" type="text/javascript"></script>
</head>
<body>
<h1>Contact Us</h1>
<form method="post" action="contact.php">
  <label for="name">Name:</label>
    <input type="text" id="name">
    <br><br>
  <label for="state">State:</label>
    <select name="state" id="state" class="use-chosen">
      <option value="AL">Alabama (AL)</option>
      <option value="AK">Alaska (AK)</option>
      <option value="AZ">Arizona (AZ)</option>
      <option value="AR">Arkansas (AR)</option>
      <option value="CA">California (CA)</option>
      <option value="CO">Colorado (CO)</option>
      <option value="CT">Connecticut (CT)</option>
      <option value="DC">District of Columbia (DC)</option>
      <option value="DE">Delaware (DE)</option>
      <option value="FL">Florida (FL)</option>
      <option value="GA">Georgia (GA)</option>
      <option value="HI">Hawaii (HI)</option>
      <option value="ID">Idaho (ID)</option>
```

```
            <option value="IL">Illinois (IL)</option>
            <option value="IN">Indiana (IN)</option>
            <option value="IA">Iowa (IA)</option>
            <option value="KS">Kansas (KS)</option>
            <option value="KY">Kentucky (KY)</option>
            <option value="LA">Louisiana (LA)</option>
            <option value="ME">Maine (ME)</option>
            <option value="MD">Maryland (MD)</option>
            <option value="MA">Massachusetts (MA)</option>
            <option value="MI">Michigan (MI)</option>
            <option value="MN">Minnesota (MN)</option>
            <option value="MS">Mississippi (MS)</option>
            <option value="MO">Missouri (MO)</option>
            <option value="MT">Montana (MT)</option>
            <option value="NE">Nebraska (NE)</option>
            <option value="NV">Nevada (NV)</option>
            <option value="NH">New Hampshire (NH)</option>
            <option value="NJ">New Jersey (NJ)</option>
            <option value="NM">New Mexico (NM)</option>
            <option value="NY">New York (NY)</option>
            <option value="NC">North Carolina (NC)</option>
            <option value="ND">North Dakota (ND)</option>
            <option value="OH">Ohio (OH)</option>
            <option value="OK">Oklahoma (OK)</option>
            <option value="OR">Oregon (OR)</option>
            <option value="PA">Pennsylvania (PA)</option>
            <option value="RI">Rhode Island (RI)</option>
            <option value="SC">South Carolina (SC)</option>
            <option value="SD">South Dakota (SD)</option>
            <option value="TN">Tennessee (TN)</option>
            <option value="TX">Texas (TX)</option>
            <option value="UT">Utah (UT)</option>
            <option value="VT">Vermont (VT)</option>
            <option value="VA">Virginia (VA)</option>
            <option value="WA">Washington (WA)</option>
            <option value="WV">West Virginia (WV)</option>
            <option value="WI">Wisconsin (WI)</option>
            <option value="WY">Wyoming (WY)</option>
        </select>
        <br><br>
        <label for="comments">Comments:</label><br>
        <textarea id="comments"></textarea><br><br>
        <input type="submit" value="Submit">
    </form>
</body>
</html>
```

(continued)

2. In the *pr10-01.js* file, add jQuery code that will implement the Chosen plugin. Also, set an option when implementing—set the *no_results_text* property to the value "No state found for."

3. Save the file. When complete, the code should look like this:

```
$(document).ready(function() {
    $(".use-chosen").chosen({
      no_results_text: "No state found for"
    });
  });
```

4. Open the *pr10-01.html* file in your Web browser. Activate the select box and perform some searches. If a state cannot be found for a search, then the string "No state found for" will be displayed followed by the text you entered.

Try This Summary

In this project, you used your knowledge of implementing plugins in order to enhance a select box for users with the Chosen plugin. This allowed you to take a select element with 51 options and make it easier for users to select one by providing a search function for them.

Helpful Plugins

There are numerous plugins available for the jQuery library, so you can almost always find something that will suit your needs. In this section, some popular and/or helpful plugins will be highlighted so that you can see what type of features can be achieved with them.

jQuery UI

The jQuery UI plugin is a library of related plugins that are designed to help Web applications feel more like desktop applications. It adds the ability to drag and drop items, resize items, sort items, and more. In addition, there are a number of widgets included that can do anything from adding a progress bar to adding a date picker.

The first thing to do is go to the jQuery UI site at http://jqueryui.com/ and download the package. You can download everything or customize it to include only what you need. If you are customizing, you may wish to read further into the documentation to see what features you are adding or removing from the plugin.

Once you have the plugin library downloaded and unpacked, you can make use of it by including the necessary files in your HTML code. At minimum, you will need the *jquery-ui .min.css* and *jquery-ui.min.js* files included in the page. Some features or widgets may require additional file inclusions.

As an example, you will add these two files to an HTML document. Since the package is large, it will be stored in a subfolder for access. For offline use, you can simply insert the files from their default locations within the package, as shown in the following HTML code (the package has been stored in a subfolder named *jqui*):

```
<!DOCTYPE html>
<html>
<head>
  <meta charset="utf-8">
  <title>jQuery UI</title>
  <style type="text/css">
    .cool { width:300px; height:50px; border:1px solid #000; }
    .cooler { background-color:#CCC; border:5px solid #444;
            width:500px; height:200px; }
  </style>
  <link rel="stylesheet" type="text/css"
        href="jqui/themes/base/minified/jquery-ui.min.css">
  <script src="jquery-1.9.1.min.js" type="text/javascript"></script>
  <script src="jqui/ui/minified/jquery-ui.min.js" type="text/
javascript"></script>
  <script src="jqueryUIdemo.js" type="text/javascript"></script>
</head>
<body>
<h1>My Page</h1>
<div class="cool">
  This div could be a lot cooler.
  <form>
    <input type="submit" action="cooler.html" id="sub" value="Make
Cooler!">
  </form>
</div>
</body>
</html>
```

Save the file as *jqueryUIdemo.html*. As you can see, the files are included as with other plugins. This page creates a <div> with a button that claims it will make the <div> "cooler." This will be done using classes, which you can see within the <style></style> tags. With this installed, you can now use some of the core components of the library.

Additional Animation Options

One helpful feature is the addition of extra animation options. You will recall that the core jQuery library had the *addClass()*, *removeClass()*, and *toggleClass()* methods. These allowed you to simply add or remove classes, but they provided no animation on their own (you would need to use *animate()* or one of the included animation methods such as *slideDown()* along with them).

The jQuery UI plugin allows you to add arguments to these method calls (and others such as the *show()* and *hide()* methods) that will animate the changes to the element. For example, by providing a *speed* and *easing* argument to *toggleClass()*, you can animate each of the changes to the element that are made by adding or removing the specified classes. Using your *jqueryUIdemo.html* page, you can take the <div> with the class "cool" and add the class "cooler" when the button is clicked. The "cooler" class has a larger width, height, and border, and also has different colors for the background and border. Using the following code will animate the addition or removal of the "cooler" class (save as *jqueryUIdemo.js*):

```
$(document).ready(function() {
  $("#sub").click(function(event) {
      event.preventDefault();
      if ($(this).val() === "Make Cooler!") {
        $(this).val("Make Less Cool.");
      }
      else {
        $(this).val("Make Cooler!");
      }
      $(".cool").toggleClass("cooler", 1000, "easeInOutCubic");
  });
});
```

Code to change the button text based on the toggle state

Notice the additional arguments that are added: a speed and an easing function

Open the *jqueryUIdemo.html* page in your browser and click the "Make Cooler!" button. The <div> will expand and change color. You can return it to its original state by clicking the button again. Figure 10-4 shows the initial page, and Figure 10-5 shows the page after the button is clicked.

You will notice that the *easing* function is not one you have been able to use before with the jQuery library alone, which only included *linear* and *swing*. The jQuery UI plugin adds a number of additional *easing* options that you can use. A complete listing can be found on the jQuery UI site at http://api.jqueryui.com/easings/.

Example Widget

The jQuery UI plugin includes numerous widgets to enhance the user experience, which simply require you to call a method to make use of them. One of these is the date picker, which can turn a plain text input element into an element that allows the user to choose a date from a calendar that displays when the field is clicked.

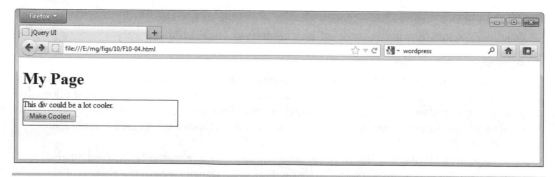

Figure 10-4 The initial page

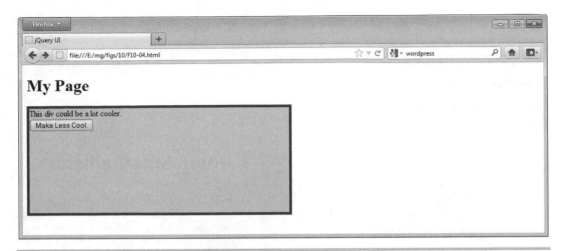

Figure 10-5 The page after the button is clicked

To see this in action, you will add a form with a simple text field to your *jqueryUIdemo* *.html* page. Add the following code just prior to the closing </body> tag and save the file:

```
<br><br>
<div>
<form method="post" action="contact.php">
  <label for="date">Date:</label>
    <input type="text" id="date">
    <br><br>
    <input type="submit" id="submit" value="Submit">
</form>
</div>
```

This adds a form with a simple text field with an id of *date*.

Next, you simply need to apply the *datepicker()* method from the jQuery UI plugin to the *date* text field. You can do this by adding a line of code to your *jqueryUIdemo.js* file. Update the file to use the following code and save it:

```
$(document).ready(function() {
  $("#date").datepicker();        ◄——————— The datepicker() method is used on the date element
  $("#sub").click(function(event) {
      event.preventDefault();
      if ($(this).val() === "Make Cooler!") {
        $(this).val("Make Less Cool.");
      }
      else {
        $(this).val("Make Cooler!");
      }
    $(".cool").toggleClass("cooler", 1000, "easeInOutCubic");
  });
});
```

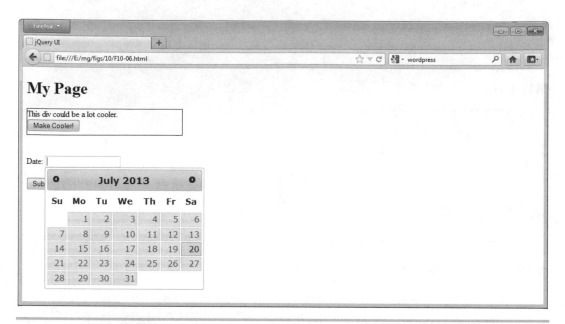

Figure 10-6 The date picker calendar is displayed.

Reload the *jqueryUIdemo.html* page in your browser and click the text field. A calendar will appear that allows you to choose a date to be entered into the field. Figure 10-6 shows the date picker displayed once the field is clicked.

Further Information

The jQuery UI plugin is very extensive, so it cannot be covered in full detail here. However, you can find additional information and help on using the plugin, the API, and more on the jQuery UI plugin site at http://jqueryui.com/. Helpful links within the site include

- **jQuery UI API**   http://api.jqueryui.com/
- **jQuery UI Demos**   http://jqueryui.com/demos/
- **jQuery UI Support**   http://jqueryui.com/support/

Parsley.js

The Parsley.js plugin is designed to perform client-side validation of forms. It allows you to set particular HTML attributes and values in order to have it validate a simple form without the need to write additional jQuery/JavaScript code. If needed, however, you can write some jQuery/JavaScript code to handle a more complex form.

More information on Parsley.js can be found at http://parsleyjs.org/.

ParamQuery Grid

The ParamQuery Grid plugin helps you add functionality to data tables, especially when dealing with AJAX applications. This includes the ability to perform many tasks with table cells, columns, or rows, such as sort, page, select, show, hide, resize, group, and more.

More information on ParamQuery Grid can be found at http://paramquery.com/.

jKit

The jKit plugin is a UI plugin that uses the data-jkit attribute within an element to add functionality. This keeps you from even needing to write any additional jQuery/JavaScript code if you choose not to do so. The plugin can display elements randomly, and can create light boxes, slide shows, tabs, photo galleries, and more.

More information on jKit can be found at http://jquery-jkit.com/.

jCanvas

The jCanvas plugin is designed to make working with the HTML <canvas> element and its JavaScript API easier, as well as allow a canvas to work on both desktop and mobile devices.

More information on jCanvas can be found at http://calebevans.me/projects/jcanvas/.

Try This 10-2   Practice with jQuery UI

```
pr10-02.html
jquery-ui.min.css
pr10-02.js
jquery-ui.min.js
```

This project allows you to practice using two effects that are a part of the jQuery UI plugin: *shake* and *bounce*. Both of these effects can be used by calling the *effect()* method that is part of the jQuery UI plugin.

Step by Step

1. Insert the following HTML code into your editor and save the file as *pr10-02.html*:

```
<!DOCTYPE html>
<html>
<head>
  <meta charset="utf-8">
  <title>jQuery UI</title>
  <style type="text/css">
    .question { width:40%; height:auto; border:1px solid #000;
    padding:7px; }
    .question label { font-weight:bold; }
    .right { background-color:#99FFCC; }
    .wrong { background-color:#FCC; }
```

(continued)

```
    </style>
    <link rel="stylesheet" type="text/css"
        href="jqui/themes/base/minified/jquery-ui.min.css">
    <script src="jquery-1.9.1.min.js" type="text/javascript"></script>
    <script src="jqui/ui/minified/jquery-ui.min.js" type="text/
javascript"></script>
    <script src="pr10-02.js" type="text/javascript"></script>
</head>
<body>
<h1>My Page</h1>
<div class="question">
    <form id="qform">
        <label for="ans">Where are you?</label><br>
            <input type="text" id="ans" size="3"><br><br>
        <input type="submit" action="answer.html" id="sub" value="Check
        Answer">
    </form>
</div>
</body>
</html>
```

This page asks the user for the answer to a question. You want to add the *right* class to the input field if the submitted answer is right and the *wrong* class if the answer is wrong. In addition, you will want to "bounce" the input field if the answer is right and "shake" the field if the answer is wrong. The *effect()* method can be used in the following general format to create the effects:

```
$("#my-element").effect(effectName, duration);
```

2. Create a JavaScript file and save it as *pr10-02*.js. Add jQuery/JavaScript code so that if the answer is not "here," the input field will "shake" and have the *wrong* class added to it. If the answer is "here," then the input field should "bounce" and have the *right* class added to it. Remember to prevent the default action and to remove all classes from the field once the submit button is clicked but before performing the test. Also, assign the *#ans* element to a variable so that it can easily be reused.

3. When complete, the code should look like this:

```
$(document).ready(function() {
  $("#qform").submit(function(event) {
    var $ans = $("#ans");
    event.preventDefault();
    $ans.removeClass("right wrong");
      if ($ans.val() !== "here") {
        $ans.addClass("wrong").effect("shake", 800);
      }
      else {
        $ans.addClass("right").effect("bounce", 800);
```

```
        }
    });
});
```

4. Open the *pr10-02.html* file in your Web browser. Answer the question wrong and click the Submit button. The field should shake and turn light red. Answer correctly and submit again. This time, the field should bounce and turn light green.

Try This Summary

In this project, you used your knowledge of the jQuery UI plugin and learned the new *bounce* and *shake* effects that are available using the *effect()* method. You used all of this to create a simple question and to alter the input field in different ways based on whether or not the answer was correct.

Chapter 10 Self Test

1. jQuery allows developers to create methods that can extend the jQuery library to provide additional features, which are called _____.

    A. add-ons

    B. plugins

    C. additions

    D. themes

2. Some plugins require just an extra _____ file, while others will also need you to include CSS files, images, or other media.

    A. JavaScript

    B. HTML

    C. PHP

    D. Python

3. Most plugins can be used by simply calling a method, but many allow you to set options by adding _____ to the method call in your script.

    A. a callback function

    B. methods

    C. arguments

    D. AJAX requests

4. The order in which the JavaScript files are included is important: You must include jQuery _____.

   A. last

   B. after your own script file

   C. after the plugin script file

   D. first

5. The JavaScript file for a plugin should be included in your HTML code before your own JavaScript file.

   A. True

   B. False

6. Often when calling a method for a jQuery plugin, you are able to send a single argument: a map of property _____ and _____.

   A. names, codes

   B. names, values

   C. codes, values

   D. types, codes

7. Plugins always require that additional options be set when calling a method.

   A. True

   B. False

8. Which of the following correctly calls a method named *start( )* on *#my-element* with a map where *time* is set to *1000* and *repeat* is set to "none"?

   A. $("#my-element").startUp({ time: 1000, repeat: "none" });

   B. $("#my-element").start({ timer: 1000, repeat: "none" });

   C. $("#my-element").start({ time: 1000, repeat: "none" });

   D. $("#my-element").start({ time: 1000, repeat: 1 });

9. The jQuery UI plugin is a library of related plugins that are designed to help Web applications feel more as if they are _____ applications.

   A. desktop

   B. mobile

   C. enterprise

   D. console

10. When using the jQuery UI plugin, you will need to include at least the _____ and _____ files.

 A. jquery.css, jquery-ui-first.js

 B. jquery-ui.min.css, jquery-ui.min.js

 C. ui.css, ui.min.js

 D. jqui.max.css, jquery-ui.max.js

11. The jQuery UI plugin allows you to add arguments to certain method calls (such as *show()*, *hide()*, *addClass()*, and so on) that will _____ the changes to the element.

 A. stop

 B. inhibit

 C. animate

 D. post

12. The jQuery UI plugin includes numerous _____ to enhance the user experience, which simply require you to call a method to make use of them.

 A. functions

 B. widgets

 C. numbers

 D. statistics

13. The jQuery UI plugin allows you to add a date picker to a text field by simply applying the *datepicker()* method to the element.

 A. True

 B. False

14. The Parsley.js plugin allows you to set particular HTML attributes and values in order to have it validate a simple form without the need to write additional jQuery/JavaScript code.

 A. True

 B. False

15. The _____ plugin is designed to make working with the HTML <canvas> element and its JavaScript API easier, as well as allow a canvas to work on both desktop and mobile devices.

 A. canvasUI

 B. canvasEase

 C. simpleCanvas

 D. jCanvas

Chapter 11

Creating Plugins

Key Skills & Concepts

- Global Methods and the $ Alias
- Creating jQuery Object Methods
- Adding a Callback Function

While you can find numerous jQuery plugins on the Web that provide all sorts of features, you may come to a point where you need to have a custom plugin to fit your needs. For instance, you may need to add something that no plugin addresses yet, or you may want only a specific set of features but find that the plugins available with those features also have many more that you do not need.

In either case, jQuery allows you to create custom plugins to extend the jQuery library as needed. You can either write plugins specifically for you or your organization, or you can create plugins that are meant to be shared with others and add them to the jQuery plugin repository. In this chapter, you will learn how to create a basic plugin. You will see how to use global methods, how to use jQuery object methods (most common), and also how to add a callback function to your plugin methods.

Global Methods and the $ Alias

While not as common, there are times when a plugin does not act on a jQuery object, and thus may be a candidate for a global method. When creating a plugin such as this, you will need to consider the availability of the $ alias and how to minimize the chances of having naming conflicts with other jQuery methods and plugins.

Ensuring $ Is Available

There are times where jQuery may be available but the $ alias may not, such as when the *.noConflict()* method is used. To ensure that your plugin works whether $ is available or not, you can prefix jQuery methods with the full *jQuery.methodName()* syntax, or you can enclose your plugin code within an immediately invoked function that defines the $ alias for your plugin internally.

To make use of $ internally, you can use what is called an *immediately invoked function expression*, which encloses a function call within parentheses. This syntax ensures that the function is executed immediately rather than waiting for another statement to call it. The following code shows an example of this and how it can be used to define the jQuery $ alias internally:

```
(function($) {
  // Plugin code...
})(jQuery);
```

The outer parentheses provide a wrapper, which sends the global *jQuery* object as the argument to the function contained within it. The function then assigns the *jQuery* object to $ when it runs, making $ available within the function and allowing your plugin code to use it as you normally would.

Creating Methods and Minimizing Naming Conflicts

To create your global method plugin, you can simply add a named function within the immediately invoked function, as in the following code:

```
(function($) {
  $.chooseRandom = function() {
    // Plugin code...
  };
})(jQuery);
```

Here, the global method is named *$.chooseRandom()*. Since this plugin will use only this single method, you simply need a method name that is unique (doesn't conflict with other jQuery global methods or other plugin global methods).

NOTE
Avoiding conflicts with names in other plugins is more difficult, since it is harder to discover all other possible plugins that could be using the name. However, choosing a meaningful and descriptive name will help to keep the chance of a conflict to a minimum.

Using a Single Method

With the method function set up, you simply need to fill in some code so that it will perform a task. Suppose you want this function to choose a random number between zero and another number, which will be defined by the user. The following code can be used (save as *choose-random.js*):

```
(function($) {
  $.chooseRandom = function(items) {
    return (Math.floor(Math.random() * items));
  };
})(jQuery);
```

This code uses the *Math.floor()* and *Math.random()* methods in JavaScript to generate a random number. This syntax produced a number between zero and one less than the value of *items* (sent as an argument). For example, if the value of *items* is 5, then this will return a random inclusive number between zero and four (the number could be 0, 1, 2, 3, or 4).

This type of selection is great if you are planning to use the chosen number to select an item in an array. However, you may prefer the result to be a number between one and *items* (one-based) rather than zero-based. For example, you may want the user to guess a number between 1 and 10 and generate a random number within this range as the correct answer.

You can add a second argument to allow the user to determine whether the random number returned will be zero-based or one-based, as in the following code (update your *choose-random.js* file and save):

```
(function($) {
  $.chooseRandom = function(items, start) {
    if (!parseInt(items) || !parseInt(start)) {
      return ("Error: Arguments must be integers.");
    }
    if (items < 1) {
      return ("Error: First argument must be 1 or greater");
    }
    return (Math.floor(Math.random() * items)) + start;
  };
})(jQuery);
```

The method now accepts two arguments: the number of possible random numbers and the starting number

If an integer cannot be derived from either of the arguments, an error message is returned

The random number is generated and returned; notice that the value of *start* is added to the generated number (zero-based) so that the number will be *start*-based

If the first argument (*items*) is not at least 1, then an error message is returned

Notice that in addition to adding the extra option, this updated method adds a safeguard to ensure that only integers are sent to it as arguments. If not, an error will be returned. Also, if the value of *items* is less than one, then an error is generated, since the assumption is that at least one possible number should be available to return.

The final *return* statement generates a random number between zero and one less than the value of *items*, and then adds the value of *start* to it. This allows the default to be zero-based (adding zero will not affect it) and also allows the start of the range to be defined by the user. For example, if the value of *1* is sent as the second argument, then *1* will be added to the zero-based result (0 becomes 1, 1 becomes 2, and so on). Some further examples are shown here:

```
var randNum = $.chooseRandom(5); // Error
var randNum = $.chooseRandom(5, 2); // randNum is between 2 and 6
var randNum = $.chooseRandom(10, 1); // randNum is between 1 and 10
var randNum = $.chooseRandom(-5); // Error
var randNum = $.chooseRandom(5, -5); // randNum is between -5 and -1
```

As you can see, this offers the user a variety of options in the type of random number that is returned, while checking for errors with the arguments that are sent.

To make use of your new plugin (*choose-random.js*), you will need to create an HTML page, attach jQuery and your plugin to it, and then attach your own JavaScript file (which will use your new plugin). First, save the following HTML code as *random-page.html*:

```
<!DOCTYPE html>
<html>
<head>
  <meta charset="utf-8">
```

```
      <title>How Random!</title>
      <style type="text/css">
        body { font-family:Verdana, sans-serif; }
      </style>
      <script src="jquery-1.9.1.min.js" type="text/javascript"></script>
      <script src="choose-random.js" type="text/javascript"></script>
      <script src="random-page.js" type="text/javascript"></script>
  </head>
  <body>
      <h1>How Random!</h1>
  <p>
  This page has some very random stuff on it!
  </p>
  <div id="rand-num"></div>
  </body>
  </html>
```

This simply creates a basic page that inserts all the necessary script files and creates an empty *rand-num* element where you will place your random number once you retrieve it.

Next, save the following file as *choose-random.js* (this is where you will write the code that uses jQuery and your plugin):

```
$(document).ready(function() {
    var randNum = $.chooseRandom(10, 1); ◄
    $("#rand-num").html('<h2>Random Number</h2>' + randNum); ◄
});
```

The *randNum* variable is created to hold the result if calling the plugin method

The chosen random number is displayed on the page

Here, the *$.chooseRandom()* method is called, which is the method used for the plugin. Calling it with the arguments 10 and 1 will return a random number from 1 to 10. The result is then displayed in the *#rand-num* element.

Open the *random-page.html* file in your browser. A random number will display. You can refresh the page to get different random numbers. Figure 11-1 shows an example of the page with one of the random numbers loaded.

Using Multiple Methods

If your plugin will require multiple methods, then making each method global increases the risk that one or more of them will conflict with another method name within the global scope. For example, if you want to have a plugin that uses one method to return a random number and a second method to return a random quote from a specified set of elements, you could place both methods in the global scope, as in the following code:

```
(function($) {
  $.randomNum = function(items, start) {
    // method code...
  };
```

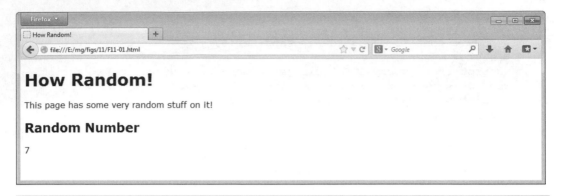

Figure 11-1 A random number is displayed by the plugin.

```
$.randomQuote = function($elements) {
  // method code...
};
})(jQuery);
```

A second global method is added!

In this code, you have both a *$.randomNum()* and a *$.randomQuote()* method in the jQuery global scope. With each additional method, you increase the chances that one of the method names will conflict with another global name or plugin that will be used on the page.

To help prevent this, it is a good idea to place all the methods your plugin will use within an object that contains as unique a name as possible. This allows you to use as many methods as needed with less possibility for conflicts. For example, the following code goes back to your original name (*$.chooseRandom*), but allows for methods within it to be called by using *$.chooseRandom.methodName*. This means that *$.chooseRandom* will be in the global scope, but its methods can only be called by first accessing the *$.chooseRandom* object, thus removing its methods from the global scope.

An example of this technique is shown next:

```
(function($) {
  $.chooseRandom = {
    num: function(items, start) {
      // method code...
    },
    quote: function($quoteDivs) {
      // method code...
    }
  }
})(jQuery);
```

Notice how *$.chooseRandom* is a map (object) with properties and values. Since the value of each property (*num* and *quote*) is a method, the names become method names. This allows you to choose a random number by calling *$.chooseRandom.num()* and to choose a random quote by calling *$.chooseRandom.quote()*.

To finish this example, you can fill in the code for each method. Update your *choose-random.js* plugin file to use the following code and save it:

The random number method that was used previously will choose a random number

```
(function($) {
  $.chooseRandom = {
    num: function(items, start) {
      var startNum = start || 0;
      if (!parseInt(items) || !parseInt(startNum)) {
        return ("Error: Arguments must be numeric.");
      }
      if (items < 1) {
        return ("Error: First argument must be 1 or greater");
      }
      return (Math.floor(Math.random() * items)) + startNum;
    },
    quote: function($quoteDivs) {
      var items = $quoteDivs.length;
      return $quoteDivs.eq(Math.floor(Math.random() * items)).text();
    }
  }
}) (jQuery);
```

The *quote()* method takes in a collection of elements, gets the number of elements in the collection, and returns a random quote from the text of one of the elements

Notice how the *quote()* method works: It takes in a collection of elements (which contain quotes for their text), then determines how many elements are in the collection. This is used to then determine the index of a quote within the collection that matches a random number chosen from zero (since element collections are zero-based) up to one less than the number of elements. The text of the random element that is chosen is then returned, giving the user a random quote.

To see this in action, you will also need to update your HTML and JavaScript files to make use of the updated plugin. First, update your *random-page.html* file to use the following code and save it:

```
<!DOCTYPE html>
<html>
<head>
  <meta charset="utf-8">
  <title>How Random!</title>
  <style type="text/css">
    body { font-family:Verdana, sans-serif; }
  </style>
  <script src="jquery-1.9.1.min.js" type="text/javascript"></script>
```

```
  <script src="choose-random.js" type="text/javascript"></script>
  <script src="random-page.js" type="text/javascript"></script>
</head>
<body>
<h1>How Random!</h1>
<p>
This page has some very random stuff on it!
</p>
<div id="rand-num"></div>
<div id="rand-quote">
  <h2>Random Quotes</h2>
  <div class="quote">Well, this is really random!</div>
  <div class="quote">I have been randomly selected!</div>
  <div class="quote">That's the amulet!</div>
  <div class="quote">Did you randomly arrive here?</div>
  <div class="quote">Serendipity is a happy happenstance.</div>
</div>
</body>
</html>
```

This adds a *#rand-quote* element that contains a number of odd quotes. Each quote is contained within a <div> element with a class of *quote*. By sending this collection to the *.chooseRandom.quote()* method, you can retrieve one of them to display instead of seeing the entire set at once (displaying it this way initially allows those without JavaScript enabled to still view the quotes).

Next, update your *random-page.js* file to use the following code and save it:

```
$(document).ready(function() {          Executes code to use the $.chooseRandom.num() method
  var randNum = $.chooseRandom.num(5, 1);
  $("#rand-num").html('<h2>Random Number</h2>' + randNum);
    var $qWrapper = $("#rand-quote"),
        $qDivs = $("#rand-quote div.quote"),
        randQuote = $.chooseRandom.quote($qDivs);
  $qWrapper.html('<h2>Random Quote</h2>');
  $qWrapper.append('<div class="quote">' + randQuote + '</div>');
});
```

Replaces the content of the *#rand-quote* element with the new heading and the returned random quote

Retrieves the text of a random <div> element within the collection and returns the random quote text

Assigns the collection of <div> elements within the *#rand-quote* element to a variable, *$qDivs*, for later use

Assigns the *#rand-quote* <div> element to a variable, *$qWrapper*, for later use

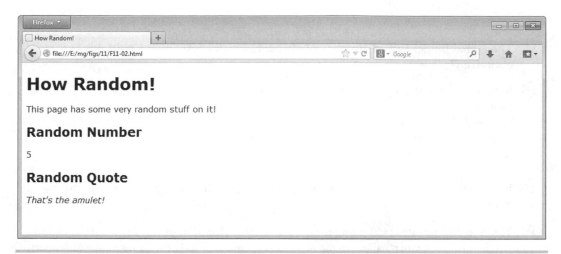

Figure 11-2 A possible result of using your $.chooseRandom plugin

Here, the *#rand-quote* element is assigned to *$qWrapper* and the collection of <div> elements within it that have the *quote* class is assigned to *$qDivs*. The result of running *$.chooseRandom.quote()* on this collection is then assigned to *randQuote*, which will now contain the text of one of those <div> elements chosen at random. Finally, the result is displayed on the page, overwriting the original content of the *#rand-quote* <div> by using the *html()* method (the *append()* that follows is for readability here; you can simply continue to concatenate within the *html()* method if desired).

Reload the *random-page.html* file in your browser. You'll see a random number and a random quote displayed. You can reload the page to see different results. Figure 11-2 shows one of the possible results of this script.

Ask the Expert

Q: Should I create a plugin that uses a global method? I'm not sure that is the best way to do what I need to do.

A: A global method is not typically what you would create, as you will see in the next section. Most plugins are designed to work on a jQuery object (a collection of elements), which is more commonly what a user would need. A global method would be better suited for something that works outside of the document structure (for example, the jQuery global methods *$.get* and *$.post* retrieve information from another document, so calling these methods on an element within the current document wouldn't necessarily be helpful).

(continued)

Q: The global plugin sure required a lot of coding for the developer. Could this be optimized?

A: In the examples, the *$.chooseRandom.num()* method required less of the developer (call the method with arguments, use the result). The *$.chooseRandom.quote()* required more, since you needed to determine the wrapper element and which elements to select to obtain the random quote. This method would definitely be better suited as a jQuery object method, which you will learn about in the next section.

Q: I would like to have the plugin work without sending it any arguments. Can this be done?

A: Yes! You will just need to be sure to set default values for each of the arguments so that the plugin will work when called. In the next section, you will see how using a map of property names and values can ease this process for both you and the user.

Creating jQuery Object Methods

While a plugin using a global method can be useful for some tasks, it is often preferable to create a plugin that acts on one or more elements in a collection. This allows the plugin to use syntax that is more familiar to users, since it will be much like calling any other jQuery method, such as *show()* or *append()*.

When creating object methods, there are several things you will need to consider: extending the jQuery object using *$.fn*, ensuring that implicit iteration will work with the plugin, and allowing the user to send a map of customized options to the plugin if desired.

Extending the jQuery Object

To create a new jQuery object method, you will need to extend the jQuery object using *jQuery .fn*, which can be shortened to *$.fn* when you assign the $ shortcut to your plugin code. This will look quite similar to creating a global method, aside from using *$.fn*. The following code shows an example of this:

```
(function($) {
  $.fn.chooseRandom = function() {
    // plugin code...
  };
})(jQuery);
```

With this syntax in place, the plugin can be used just like any other jQuery method on an element or collection of elements, as in the following code:

```
$(".my-elements").chooseRandom();
```

As you can see, this allows you to call your method directly on one or more elements within the DOM.

Within your plugin method, the bare keyword *this* will refer to the current jQuery object, which is the collection of elements that was used to call it. For the code example you just used, *this* would refer to the *$(".my-elements")* collection. You can refer to *this* within your plugin method at any time to refer to the collection and use any necessary jQuery methods on it, for example, *find()* or *each()*.

To begin, you will update your *random-page.html* file to use the following code and save it:

```
<!DOCTYPE html>
<html>
<head>
  <meta charset="utf-8">
  <title>How Random!</title>
  <style type="text/css">
    body { font-family:Verdana, sans-serif; }
  </style>
  <script src="jquery-1.9.1.min.js" type="text/javascript"></script>
  <script src="choose-random.js" type="text/javascript"></script>
  <script src="random-page.js" type="text/javascript"></script>
</head>
<body>
<h1>How Random!</h1>
<p>
This page has some very random stuff on it!
</p>
<div class="rand-quote">
  <h2>Random Quotes</h2>
  <div>Well, this is really random!</div>
  <div>I have been randomly selected!</div>
  <div>That's the amulet!</div>
  <div>Did you randomly arrive here?</div>
  <div>Serendipity is a happy happenstance.</div>
</div>
<div class="rand-quote">
  <h2>Random Quotes</h2>
  <div>Another set of random quotes? Really?</div>
  <div>I can't believe there could be more random quotes!</div>
  <div>Why?</div>
  <div>John put you up to this, didn't he?</div>
  <div>Please let this be the last random quote!</div>
</div>
</body>
</html>
```

Here, the random number piece is removed and the *#rand-quote* element has been replaced by two *.rand-quote* elements so that you can see your new plugin work on multiple elements. The class="quote" attribute was also removed from the inner <div> elements. You'll access these in a different way for the plugin (which will save the user from supplying that class on each of those elements).

Next, you will need to create your plugin by extending the jQuery object using *$.fn*. This plugin will need to be called on any element with a class of *.rand-quote*. It will then need to determine how many child <div> elements are within each of the *.rand-quote* elements and display the random result for each of the elements. Update your *choose-random.js* file to use the following code and save it:

```
(function($) {  ◄─────────────   The jQuery object is extended with the new
  $.fn.chooseRandom = function() {   chooseRandom() method
    var $coll = this.children("div");
    items = $coll.length,
    rQuote = $coll.eq(Math.floor(Math.random() * items)).text();
    this.html('<h2>Random Quote</h2><div>' + rQuote + '</div>');
  };
})(jQuery);
```

The current element's HTML is updated to include a heading and the selected random quote

A variable named *rQuote* will hold the result of selecting a random element's text from the *$coll* collection

A variable named *items* will hold the number of matching elements

A variable named *$coll* will be assigned the collection of <div> elements within the current element *(this)*

This appears to be a straightforward process. The jQuery object is extended, and the <div> elements within the selected element are collected and placed in *$coll*. The number of items in *$coll* is assigned to *items*, *eq()* is used along with *Math.random()* and *text()* to get the text of the element at a randomly selected index within *$coll*, and the result replaces the content of the currently selected element.

With this in place, you can update your *random-page.js* file to use the following code and save it:

```
$(document).ready(function() {
  $(".rand-quote").chooseRandom();
});
```

That's it! You now have a plugin that you can use without a lot of code needing to be inserted by the user. Your plugin method can simply be called once your plugin code is inserted in the page.

Reload the *random-page.html* file in your browser. You will see two "Random Quote" sections; however, there appears to be a problem! Figure 11-3 shows an example of the page when it is loaded in a browser.

Figure 11-3 What happened to the first set of quotes?

The plugin worked, but it is overwriting both elements that use the *.rand-quote* class with the chosen quote from the last element that has the class. That certainly was not the plan! It appears as though jQuery is using implicit iteration to update all of the elements that use the *.rand-quote* class each time your plugin is run, which means that only the last change will be displayed in the final result. To fix this, your plugin will need to enable implicit iteration internally so that each element is treated according to its own content within your plugin.

Using Implicit Iteration and Returning a jQuery Object

To fix the issue and use implicit iteration within your plugin, you can make use of the jQuery *each()* method, which can be used to iterate over each element within the collection on which your method was called (stored in *this*).

By using *each()* and making some adjustments to the code, you can get the plugin working as expected for each of the elements that has the *.rand-quote* class. Update your *choose-random.js* file to use the following code and save it:

```
(function($) {
  $.fn.chooseRandom = function() {
    this.each(function() {
      $elmt = $(this),
      $coll = $elmt.children("div"),
      items = $coll.length,
      rQuote = $coll.eq(Math.floor(Math.random() * items)).text();
      $elmt.html('<h2>Random Quote</h2><div>' + rQuote + '</div>');
    });
  }
})(jQuery);
```

The *each()* method is used on this, which will cycle through each of the elements within the selection; in this case, these will be the two elements that have the *.rand-quote* class

Another update to use *$elmt* rather than *this*

This line is updated to use *$elmt* rather than the bare *this* keyword

$(this), which is the current element when within the *each()* method, gets assigned to *$elmt*

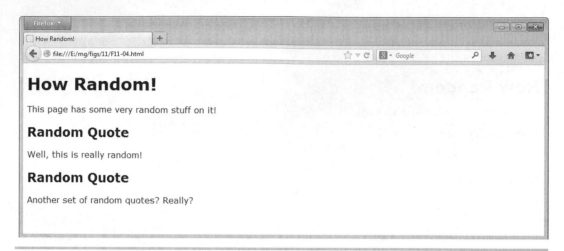

Figure 11-4 The two random quote sections now display a quote from within their own content.

This time, *each()* is called to iterate over each of the elements within *this* internally. Within the *each()* method, the current element is referred to by *$(this)*, so this value is assigned to *$elmt* to make things more clear. The *$elmt* variable is then used to get the child <div> elements of the current element and place them into *$coll*. The length and random quote are obtained as before, then the result is displayed using *$elmt.html()* to place the new content into the proper element.

Reload the *random-page.html* file in your browser and view the results. You should now have a random quote from each set of quotes, rather than one overwriting the other. Figure 11-4 shows one of the possible results.

This now works as expected, but there is one more thing you will want to do. Since the plugin does not return a jQuery object, it cannot be chained along with other jQuery methods, so calling *$(".rand-quote").hide().chooseRandom().slideDown(1000)* would not work. It would instead return undefined for one of the methods and cause the plugin to fail.

To fix this, you simply return the jQuery object on which your method was called by adding *return* before your *this.each()* iteration. Update your *choose-random.js* file to use the following code and save it:

```
(function($) {
  $.fn.chooseRandom = function() {
    return this.each(function() {
      $elmt = $(this),
      $coll = $elmt.children("div"),
      items = $coll.length,
      rQuote = $coll.eq(Math.floor(Math.random() * items)).text();
      $elmt.html('<h2>Random Quote</h2><div>' + rQuote + '</div>');
```

The *return* keyword is added so that the method will return the jQuery object on which the method was called

```
    });
  }
})(jQuery);
```

By adding the *return* keyword, the jQuery collection is returned and allows the method to be used as part of a method chain. You can now focus on providing users of your plugin with additional options by allowing them to use an options map as an argument to your plugin method.

User Customization with an Options Map

To allow users to set options using a map, you will need to have your plugin obtain the values from the map and use them as needed. The first change is straightforward: You will need to update your method so that it takes an argument (which will be the map submitted by the user), as in the following code:

```
(function($) {
  $.fn.chooseRandom = function(custom) {  ⟵——  The custom argument is added to
    return this.each(function() {               receive the user map, if supplied
      // plugin code...
    });
  }
})(jQuery);
```

To use values included in the map, you can simply use the property names that are available. For example, suppose the user called your plugin as shown in this code:

```
$(".rand-quote").chooseRandom({ weight: "bold", style: "italic" });
```

In your method, these values can be accessed through the argument name (*custom*), which acts as an object since it is sent a map. In this way, you can get the value of the properties by using *custom.weight* and *custom.style*, as in the following code:

```
(function($) {
  $.fn.chooseRandom = function(custom) {
    return this.each(function() {
      var fontWeight = custom.weight,
          fontStyle = custom.style;
      // continue plugin code...
    });
  }
})(jQuery);
```

While this works if the user sends both properties in the map, it could cause the remainder of your plugin to fail if it is depending on these values. To ensure that everything will work, you need a stable method of providing default values that are only overwritten if the user supplies new values.

The jQuery library gives you a helpful method named *$.extend()*, which takes in two arguments: a map of default values and a map that will overwrite any default values with the new ones supplied while leaving any unchanged values alone. This offers an excellent way to allow the user to set as many or as few options as desired, or even to call your plugin method with no arguments and simply use your default values.

The following code illustrates the use of *$.extend()* applied within your plugin method:

```
(function($) {
  $.fn.chooseRandom = function(custom) {
    return this.each(function() {
      var defs = {
                weight: "normal",
                style: "normal"
                },
          custOps = $.extend(defs, custom),
      // continue plugin code...
    });
  }
})(jQuery);
```

A map of default values is defined

The *$.extend()* method is used to update the property values in *defs* with the values of any properties in *custom* by the same name; other values are left alone

As you can see, a default map named *defs* is defined and provides default values for *weight* and *height*. Next, *$.extend()* is used to overwrite the property values in *defs* with the values of any properties in *custom* (sent by the user) that have the same property name, while leaving any remaining values unchanged (thus using the default value). The result of this is a new map, which will look like one of the following: all default values (if no values were changed by the user), some default values and some custom values from the user, and all new values (every default value was changed by the user). This new map is assigned to *custOps*, which can then be used to access the needed values.

With this in place, you can update your plugin method to set the font weight and font style for the <div> element that is output around the chosen random quote. Update your *choose-random.js* file to use the following code and save it:

```
(function($) {
  $.fn.chooseRandom = function(custom) {
    return this.each(function() {
      var defs = {
                weight: "normal",
                style: "normal"
                },
          custOps = $.extend(defs, custom),
          $elmt = $(this),
          $coll = $elmt.children("div"),
          items = $coll.length,
```

```
        rQuote = $coll.eq(Math.floor(Math.random() * items)).text();
    $elmt.html('<h2>Random Quote</h2><div style="font-weight:' +
    custOps.weight +'; font-style:' + custOps.style + ';">' + rQuote
    + '</div>');
    });
  }
})(jQuery);
```

The values of the custom/default options are applied to update the style settings of the <div> element; note that these three lines should be on a single line in your editor to avoid errors!

As you can see, this updates the <div> element that displays the quote by altering its style attribute and using the values of the *weight* and *style* properties in *custOps* (*custOps.weight* and *custOps.style*).

Your plugin will now use "normal" for either or both of the values if not customized by the user within an options map. In this way, the user can call your plugin with no arguments, or can send an options map that customized one or more of the properties to specific values.

Update your *random-page.js* file to use the following code and save it:

```
$(document).ready(function() {
  $(".rand-quote").chooseRandom({ weight: "bold", style: "italic" });
});
```

Reload the *random-page.html* file in your browser and view the results. You will see that the quote has been made bold and italic by sending your customized options map. Figure 11-5 shows one possible result when viewed in a browser.

You can further test this by setting just one of the options or setting none. As you will see, this gives you a lot of flexibility that you can provide to the users of your plugin!

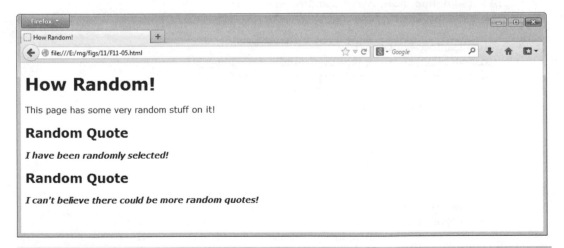

Figure 11-5 A random quote is displayed, bold and italic.

Try This 11-1 Practice Plugin Options

```
pr11-01.html
pr11-01.js
choose-random.js
```

This project allows you to practice working with plugin options maps by having you add more options to your chooseRandom plugin. These new options will allow the user to specify the level of the heading displayed with the random quote and the text that will display within the heading.

Step by Step

1. Place the following HTML code into your editor and save the file as *pr11-01.html:*

```html
<!DOCTYPE html>
<html>
<head>
  <meta charset="utf-8">
  <title>How Random!</title>
  <style type="text/css">
    body { font-family:Verdana, sans-serif; }
  </style>
  <script src="jquery-1.9.1.min.js" type="text/javascript"></script>
  <script src="choose-random.js" type="text/javascript"></script>
  <script src="random-page.js" type="text/javascript"></script>
</head>
<body>
<h1>How Random!</h1>
<p>
This page has some very random stuff on it!
</p>
<div class="rand-quote">
  <h2>Random Quotes</h2>
  <div>Well, this is really random!</div>
  <div>I have been randomly selected!</div>
  <div>That's the amulet!</div>
  <div>Did you randomly arrive here?</div>
  <div>Serendipity is a happy happenstance.</div>
</div>
<div class="rand-quote">
  <h2>Random Quotes</h2>
  <div>Another set of random quotes? Really?</div>
  <div>I can't believe there could be more random quotes!</div>
  <div>Why?</div>
  <div>John put you up to this, didn't he?</div>
  <div>Please let this be the last random quote!</div>
</div>
</body>
</html>
```

2. Use the *choose-random.js* file that you have been using in this chapter and update it so that it allows the user to update two additional properties named *hLevel* and *hText*. Add these properties to the plugin so that they will allow the user to specify the level of the heading included with the random quote and the text within the heading. The default value for *hLevel* will be 2, and the default value for *hText* will be "Random Quote".

3. Save the file. When complete, the code should look like this:

```
(function($) {
  $.fn.chooseRandom = function(custom) {
    return this.each(function() {
      var defs = {
                  weight: "normal",
                  style: "normal",
                  hLevel: 2,
                  hText: "Random Quote"
                  },
          custOps = $.extend(defs, custom),
          $elmt = $(this),
          $coll = $elmt.children("div"),
          items = $coll.length,
          rQuote = $coll.eq(Math.floor(Math.random() * items)).text();
      $elmt.html('<h' + custOps.hLevel +'>' + custOps.hText + '</h' +
      custOps.hLevel + '><div style="font-weight:' + custOps.weight +
      '; font-style:' + custOps.style + ';">' + rQuote + '</div>');
    });
  }
}) (jQuery);
```

4. In the *pr11-01.js* file, write code so that the chooseRandom plugin is used and displays a random quote in italics and with the heading text "Cool Quote." Save the file. When complete, the code should look like this:

```
$(document).ready(function() {
  $(".rand-quote").chooseRandom({ style: "italic", hText: "Cool Quote"});
});
```

5. Open the *pr11-01.html* file in your Web browser. Both headings should now say "Cool Quote" and both quotes should be in italics. You can go back and alter options as desired to obtain different results.

Try This Summary

In this project, you used your knowledge of option maps and plugins to update your plugin method so that it could use two additional options, giving the user some additional flexibility when using your plugin.

Adding a Callback Function

Another way to allow customization is to allow users of your plugin to use callback functions. The jQuery library implements these often, as you have seen throughout the book. Often, a callback function is used so that code can be run once the operation of the main method has completed.

You can add any number of named callback functions to your plugin. While you may have other callbacks that allow users to do things such as calculate values, you would most commonly add only one callback that would run when the other plugin tasks are complete.

To begin, you will need to add another option to your default options list: an empty function. You then need to call the function once your other tasks have completed. This is shown in the following code (update your *choose-random.js* file to use this code and save it):

```
(function($) {
  $.fn.chooseRandom = function(custom) {
    return this.each(function() {
      var defs = {
                  weight: "normal",
                  style: "normal",
                  complete: function() {}  ◄——— An empty function is added and
                  },                             assigned to the complete() property
          custOps = $.extend(defs, custom),
          $elmt = $(this),
          $coll = $elmt.children("div"),
          items = $coll.length,
          rQuote = $coll.eq(Math.floor(Math.random() * items)).text();
      $elmt.html('<h2>Random Quote</h2><div style="font-weight:' + —————
      custOps.weight +'; font-style:' + custOps.style + ';">' + rQuote
      + ' </div>'); —————————————————————————————————
      custOps.complete.call(this);  ◄——————————————— Calls the callback function
    });
  }
})(jQuery);
```

An empty function is added and assigned to the *complete()* property

Calls the callback function

These lines should be on a single line in your editor

As you can see, a new property, *complete*, is added to the default map. It is simply an empty function that will do nothing by default. However, if the user supplies a function to the *complete* property when calling the plugin with an options map, the function supplied by the user will be run when it is called by the plugin. Since the callback function needs to run after the other tasks have completed, it is placed at the end of the plugin code. Instead of calling it normally, it is called using the JavaScript *call* method, with a reference to *this*, which allows the user to make use of the jQuery $(this) selector when coding the callback function.

NOTE

If you are using a jQuery method within your plugin method that takes time or retrieves information, such as *animate()* or *$.get()*, simply calling your callback function at the end of the plugin method code may not work (it may get called before the jQuery method completes). To adjust for this, you can place the code to call your callback function within the callback function of the jQuery method you are using.

With the callback setup in place, the user can use it to perform additional tasks once your plugin tasks have completed. For example, the following code will call the plugin with two options set: the *style* property and the *complete* property, which will be assigned a function, and trigger it as the callback function within your plugin (update your *random-page.js* file to use this code and save it):

```
$(document).ready(function() {
  $(".rand-quote").chooseRandom({ style: "italic", complete:
  function() {
        $(this).css("font-size", "+=10");
    }
  });
});
```

In this case, the callback function is used to increase the font size of text within the <div> elements with a class of *.rand-quote*. Since there was no font size adjustment option yet, the user was able to do this by using the jQuery *css()* method within the plugin's callback function. As you can see, this offers a great deal of flexibility to users of your plugin to extend options or perform additional tasks when needed.

Reload the *random-page.html* file in your browser and view the result. Once the page loads, you should have random quotes in italics for both "Random Quote" sections, and the font size for these sections should be larger. Figure 11-6 shows one of the possible results of loading this page in a browser.

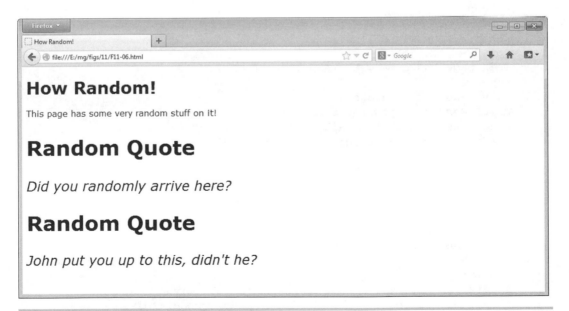

Figure 11-6 The font size is now larger.

Try This 11-2 Practice with Callbacks

pr11-02.html
pr11-02.js
choose-random.js

This project allows you to practice using the callback function you created in this chapter by having you perform a task after the plugin code completes.

Step by Step

1. Insert the following HTML code into your editor and save the file as *pr11-02.html*:

```html
<!DOCTYPE html>
<html>
<head>
  <meta charset="utf-8">
  <title>How Random!</title>
  <style type="text/css">
    body { font-family:Verdana, sans-serif; }
  </style>
  <script src="jquery-1.9.1.min.js" type="text/javascript"></script>
  <script src="choose-random.js" type="text/javascript"></script>
  <script src="random-page.js" type="text/javascript"></script>
</head>
<body>
<h1>How Random!</h1>
<p>
This page has some very random stuff on it!
</p>
<div class="rand-quote">
  <h2>Random Quotes</h2>
  <div>Well, this is really random!</div>
  <div>I have been randomly selected!</div>
  <div>That's the amulet!</div>
  <div>Did you randomly arrive here?</div>
  <div>Serendipity is a happy happenstance.</div>
</div>
<div class="rand-quote">
  <h2>Random Quotes</h2>
  <div>Another set of random quotes? Really?</div>
  <div>I can't believe there could be more random quotes!</div>
  <div>Why?</div>
  <div>John put you up to this, didn't he?</div>
  <div>Please let this be the last random quote!</div>
</div>
</body>
</html>
```

2. Use the *choose-random.js* plugin file you have been using in this chapter. The code should now include the callback function and look like this:

```
(function($) {
  $.fn.chooseRandom = function(custom) {
    return this.each(function() {
      var defs = {
                    weight: "normal",
                    style: "normal",
                     complete: function() {}
                    },
          custOps = $.extend(defs, custom),
          $elmt = $(this),
          $coll = $elmt.children("div"),
          items = $coll.length,
          rQuote = $coll.eq(Math.floor(Math.random() * items)).
          text();
      $elmt.html('<h2>Random Quote</h2><div style="font-weight:' +
      custOps.weight +'; font-style:' + custOps.style + ';">' +
      rQuote + '</div>');
      custOps.complete.call(this);
    });
  }
}) (jQuery);
```

3. Create a JavaScript file and save it as *pr11-02.js*. Write code so that the chooseRandom plugin is called, sets the *weight* property to a value of "bold", and so the *complete* property executes a callback function that will fade out the elements that use the plugin over 10 seconds. When complete, the code should look like this:

```
$(document).ready(function() {
  $(".rand-quote").chooseRandom({ weight: "bold", complete:
  function() {
        $(this).fadeOut(10000);
    }
  });
});
```

4. Open the *pr11-02.html* file in your Web browser. The random quotes should display, then begin fading out slowly.

Try This Summary

In this project, you used your knowledge of callback functions and plugins to perform an additional task when the tasks within the plugin were completed.

Chapter 11 Self Test

1. To make use of _____ internally for your jQuery plugin, you can use what is called an immediately invoked function expression.

    A. &

    B. ()

    C. $

    D. %

2. An important thing to remember when naming your plugin method(s) is that you want to avoid _____ with other jQuery or plugin method names.

    A. working

    B. conflicts

    C. searching

    D. executing

3. The _____ method can be used to generate a random number in JavaScript.

    A. Math.round()

    B. Random()

    C. Math.ceil()

    D. Math.random()

4. What will this code produce? *Math.floor(Math.random() * 5)*

    A. A random number from 1 to 5

    B. A random number from 0 to 4

    C. A random number from 10 to 50

    D. Five random numbers returned as an array

5. With each additional global method, you increase the chances that one of the method names will conflict with another global name or plugin that will be used on the page.

    A. True

    B. False

6. What will this code produce? *Math.floor(Math.random() * 5) + 2*

   A. A random number from 2 to 6

   B. A random even number

   C. A random number from 1 to 5

   D. Two random numbers in an array multiplied by 5

7. Global methods are the best way to create a plugin, even if the plugin will act on elements within a collection.

   A. True

   B. False

8. To create a new jQuery object method, you will need to extend the jQuery object using *jQuery.fn*, which can be shortened to _____ when you assign the $ shortcut to your plugin code.

   A. $jQfn

   B. $fn

   C. $.fn

   D. $jFn

9. Within your plugin method, the bare keyword _____ will refer to the current jQuery object, which is the collection of elements that was used to call it.

   A. that

   B. this

   C. current

   D. element

10. You need to be aware of how _____ _____ will affect your plugin.

   A. implicit iteration

   B. iterative implicits

   C. italic iteration

   D. indirect implicits

11. Your plugin should return a _____ object so that it can be chained to other jQuery methods.

    A. null

    B. deleted

    C. new

    D. jQuery

12. The jQuery library gives you a helpful method named _____, which takes in two arguments: a map of default values and a map that will overwrite any default values with the new ones supplied while leaving any unchanged values alone.

    A. $.extend()

    B. $.enhance()

    C. $.overwrite()

    D. $.insert()

13. While you may have other callbacks that allow users to do things such as calculate values, you would most commonly add only one callback that would run when the other plugin tasks are complete.

    A. True

    B. False

14. Your plugins should never allow users to submit an options map to change your default values.

    A. True

    B. False

15. A _____ _____ can be used to allow further customization by the user or to execute code after your plugin tasks have completed.

    A. callback function

    B. return function

    C. done function

    D. callforwarding function

Chapter 12

Advanced Techniques and Further Resources

Key Skills & Concepts

- Debugging
- Unit Testing
- Additional Resources

The jQuery library does a lot of work, but once you have your code in place, it is a good idea to test the code to ensure that it does what it needs to do. In this chapter, you will look at methods that can be used for debugging and testing your code, which can help you develop coding standards for your team or organization.

First, you will look at some tools available for debugging JavaScript/jQuery code. Next, you will look at some tools that allow you to perform unit testing on your code. Finally, you will be given some resources to enhance your knowledge of JavaScript/jQuery should you choose to pursue it further.

Debugging

Often, code doesn't quite work as intended. While some issues are easy to resolve, others may require quite a bit more time and effort to get fixed. There are numerous methods and tools you can use to debug your code; and you will cover some of these in this section.

Simple Alerts

For some issues, using the JavaScript *alert()* method can be a handy way to quickly see where the problem may be. You can use *alert()* to pop up one or more values to see if they are the type of values you are expecting (a number, a string, a Boolean, and so on).

For example, suppose you are having an issue where you are trying to add one to a number, but you're getting unexpected results. For example, consider the following code:

```
$(document).ready(function() {
  var time = 0,
      x = 400,
      y = 400,
      z = "400";
  function sum(x, y, z) {
    return x + y + z;
  }
  time = sum(x, y, z);
  $("#my-element").hide().show(time);
});
```

Running this code, you will likely find that the *show()* method seems to be moving at a pace that is much quicker than you had intended (which should be 1200 milliseconds). It appears that something is not working correctly. Either the *show()* method is receiving a much lower number than intended, or it is receiving a string that it does not recognize and is thus simply displaying it with its default time delay.

In this case, you can probably see the problem already, but if there were more code separating the variable definitions and the function call, this might not be as immediately apparent. Here, you can see what value is being sent to the *show()* method by alerting the value of the *time* variable just prior to your use of *show()*, as in the following code:

```
$(document).ready(function() {
  var time = 0,
      x = 400,
      y = 400,
      z = "400";
  function sum(x, y, z) {
    return x + y + z;
  }
  time = sum(x, y, z);
  alert(time);  ←
  $("#my-element").hide().show(time);
});
```

This alert will tell you the value that will be used on the next line for the *show()* method

When this code is run, you will receive an alert with a value of 800400! Figure 12-1 shows an example of how this alert may display from a browser.

Since *show()* is not working at an incredibly slow speed of 800,400 milliseconds, it looks like this must be a string value that is causing *show()* to use a default time. Going back to the function you call to set the time, you will see that it appears to be OK. It simply adds the values sent to it: *x*, *y*, and *z*. This should lead you to check the values of those variables. When you do, you will notice that the value for *z* is enclosed in quotes, which is making it a string value. This means that JavaScript will add 400 + 400 + "400": The first two will be added as numbers (giving 800), while the last will be added as a string that will concatenate the numeric 800 with the string "400", giving you "800400".

To fix this, you can simply remove the quote marks from the value of the *z* variable and the *show()* method will work as expected. This is shown in the following code, which fixes the issue and removes the alert:

```
$(document).ready(function() {
  var time = 0,
      x = 400,
      y = 400,
      z = 400;  ←
  function sum(x, y, z) {
    return x + y + z;
  }
```

The quote marks have been removed, making this a valid number

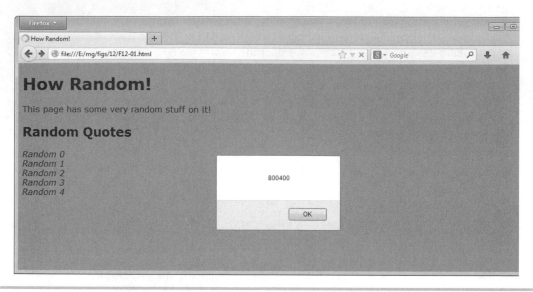

Figure 12-1 The alert displayed when the code is run

```
    time = sum(x, y, z);
    $("#my-element").hide().show(time);
});
```

Browser Developer Tools

All of the major browsers now offer their own set of developer tools that can be opened from the browser menu or via one or more shortcut keys (depending on the tool you want to open). Each of these tools offers a JavaScript console, which can aid you in debugging JavaScript/ jQuery code. They also offer tools to help you find DOM nodes, look at your HTML, test CSS code, and more.

Which one you use may depend on your browser of choice. However, if you test in multiple browsers (which is a good practice), you may become familiar with each one of them as you work on different projects. Figure 12-2 shows the "Web Console" in Mozilla Firefox (Firefox Menu | Web Developer | Web Console). Figure 12-3 shows the "Developer Tools" when opened in Google Chrome (Menu | Tools | Developer Tools).

No matter which you choose, you can use it to help you figure out where any issues may be in your code (whether HTML, CSS, or JavaScript/jQuery). For JavaScript/jQuery, each one offers a JavaScript console, which you can use to log values or display information as needed while developing or debugging.

For example, using the *console.log()* method in JavaScript, you could simply display a value on the console screen when needed. In many cases, this is far more convenient than an alert, because it does not interrupt the task at hand with an alert pop-up box. Instead, the value can be sent to the console for you to view while still having the code run as normal otherwise.

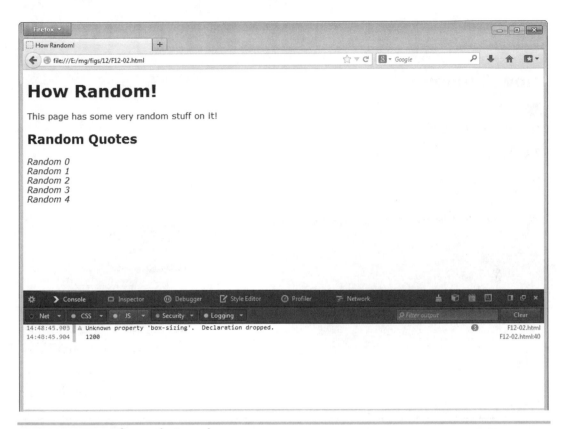

Figure 12-2 Firefox Web Console

You can alter the code you used for an alert to log the same value to the console, as shown in the following code:

```
$(document).ready(function() {
  var time = 0,
      x = 400,
      y = 400,
      z = 400;
  function sum(x, y, z) {
    return x + y + z;
  }
  time = sum(x, y, z);
  console.log(time);
  $("#rand-quote").hide().show(time);
});
```

The *console.log* method is used to log a value on the JavaScript console in the browser

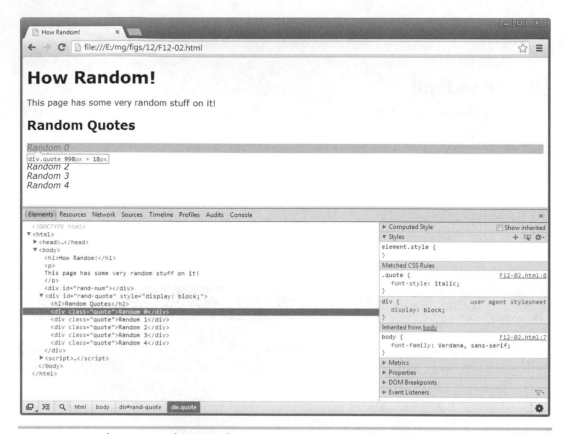

Figure 12-3 Chrome Developer Tools

Figure 12-4 shows how this looks when displayed in the Google Chrome JavaScript console.

As you can see, using the developer tools within a Web browser can certainly be helpful and less invasive than inserting alerts in your code. In addition, the ability to work with HTML, CSS, and the DOM of the document can be extremely useful when the issue may lie in one of those areas rather than in the script itself.

Using a Lint Tool

A lint tool is a program that checks your code against a set of standards and returns anything it finds that may be problematic. Not only can this help you find errors, but it can help you write better and more efficient code as well.

Two popular JavaScript lint tools are

- **JSLint**   www.jslint.com
- **JSHint**   www.jshint.com

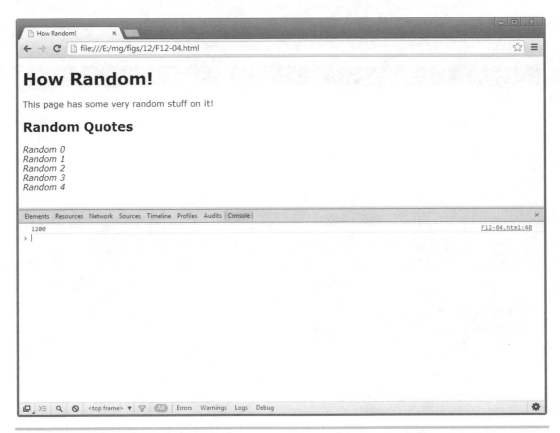

Figure 12-4   The value is logged to the JavaScript console.

Both tools allow you to check your JavaScript code for any number of issues. You can select various options to tailor the tool to your specific needs (for example, assuming the code is being run in a Web browser, a particular library is being used, or that the code is in development). Figure 12-5 shows the options available in JSHint.

Since JSHint allows you to select an option that tells it jQuery is being used, this is a good option for a jQuery example. Go to www.jsHint.com and paste the following code into the input area:

```javascript
$(document).ready(function() {
  x = 2;
  if (x == 2) {
    $("#my-element").show(1000);
  }
});
```

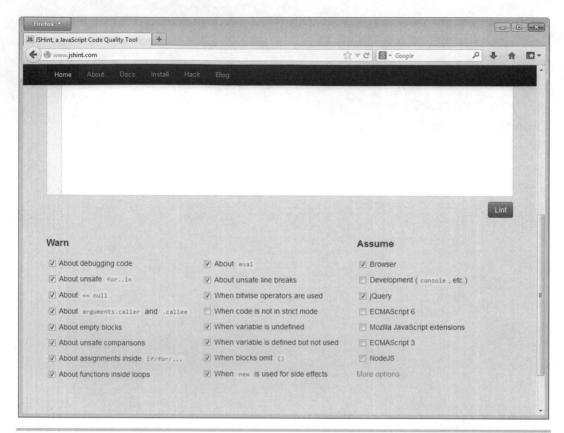

Figure 12-5 JSHint options

Make sure the "Browser" and "jQuery" check boxes are checked, make sure the "When code is not in strict mode" check box is unchecked, and click the "Lint" button. You will receive a set of errors.

The first error is shown in the following code:

```
Line 3: if (x == 2) {
Expected '===' and instead saw '=='.
```

Here, the lint tool is picking up on the use of == rather than === for comparison. Since == performs type coercion, unexpected results can occur. It is considered best practice to use === when checking for equality, since it requires both values to be equal and have the same data type.

The second error is shown in the following code:

```
Line 2: x = 2;
'x' is not defined.
```

Oops! It looks as though the *var* keyword was left off here. While it may not hurt in this case, this can become problematic, especially when functions are added. Declaring a variable like this within a function will make it global or overwrite the value of the global variable by the same name. In either case, this can cause your code to have numerous issues if it is not fixed. It is best to always include the *var* keyword when defining a variable.

The third and final error is shown in the following code:

```
Line 3: if (x == 2) {
'x' is not defined.
```

Since the variable *x* was not defined with the *var* keyword, the lint tool sees it as undefined here, which is helpful when debugging, as JavaScript will let this proceed as normal (it will define *x* with a value of *2* in the global scope, which causes this comparison to run as though there were no errors). Since JavaScript attempts to fix things as best it can, it may be difficult to find an error like this. However, the use of a lint tool can help you find such issues and resolve them quickly.

Ask the Expert

Q: **Where can I learn more about browser developer tools?**

A: Here are some resources:

- **Chrome DevTools**   https://developers.google.com/chrome-developer-tools/
- **Mozilla Developer Tools**   https://developer.mozilla.org/en-US/docs/Tools
- **F12 Developer Tools – Internet Explorer**   http://msdn.microsoft.com/en-us/library/ie/hh673541%28v=vs.85%29.aspx

Q: **Are there other JavaScript lint tools available? I would like to try out different tools to see what works best for me.**

A: Those listed already are popular, but you may find the following tools helpful as well:

- **JavaScript Lint**   www.javascriptlint.com
- **JSON Lint for JSON Syntax**   http://jsonlint.com

Q: **Is there anything else I can do to test my code?**

A: Yes! You can perform unit testing as you proceed through the development of your program. The next section will discuss this topic in more detail.

Try This 12-1 Practice Using a Lint Tool

`pr12-01.js` This project allows you to practice working with a lint tool to test your jQuery code and ensure that it does not contain any potential errors or pitfalls.

Step by Step

1. Save the following code as *pr12-01.js*:

```
$(document).ready(function() {
  var x = 2;
  if (x != 2) {
    var y = 3;
  }
  else {
    var y = 5;
  }
  $("#my-element).hide().show(1000);
});
```

2. Go to www.jshint.com and paste the code into the input area. Make sure the "Browser" and "jQuery" check boxes are checked, make sure the "When code is not in strict mode" check box is unchecked, and click the "Lint" button.

3. Based on the errors presented, attempt to fix anything that seems like it may be an issue. When complete, your JavaScript code should look something like this (this is one possible solution):

```
$(document).ready(function() {
  var x = 2,
      y = 0;
  if (x !== 2) {
    y = 3;
  }
  else {
    y = 5;
  }
  $("#my-element").hide().show(1000);
});
```

4. Run the test again with the new code to ensure it passes the test.

Try This Summary

In this project, you used your knowledge of JSHint to test whether a piece of JavaScript/jQuery code had any potential issues. Upon finding the issues, you were able to correct them and rerun the test to ensure there were no further issues with the code.

Unit Testing

While alerts, console logs, and browser tools can do quite a bit, sometimes programs become quite large and it becomes necessary to perform some automated testing to ensure that any current code is operating as expected and that any new code introduced does not break the code that is already in place. This can be done using what is known as unit testing.

Unit testing allows you to specify some tests that will be run on the JavaScript/jQuery code you have. These tests can do anything from testing values to testing whether a node was added to the DOM. To perform unit testing, it is helpful to have a unit testing tool. Some of these are listed next, with links to further information on each tool so that you can download and use it if you choose to do so.

- **QUnit**   http://qunitjs.com/
  (This one is highly recommended for unit testing jQuery code, and is used by jQuery, jQuery Mobile, and jQuery UI for testing. It can also test regular JavaScript code.)

- **Jasmine**   http://pivotal.github.io/jasmine/

- **Mocha**   http://visionmedia.github.io/mocha/

- **YUI Test**   http://developer.yahoo.com/yui/yuitest/

Additional Resources

When you are done with this book, you may find you want to learn more about jQuery or some of the other topics mentioned in the book. This section includes a list of resources that may be helpful to you as you delve further into Web development.

jQuery Resources

- **jQuery API**   http://api.jquery.com/

- **jQuery Forum**   http://forum.jquery.com/

- **jQuery Learning Center**   http://learn.jquery.com/

- **jQuery Cheat Sheet**   http://oscarotero.com/jquery/

JavaScript Resources

- **Mozilla MDN**   https://developer.mozilla.org/en-US/docs/Web/JavaScript

- **2ality**   www.2ality.com/

- **NCZOnline**   www.nczonline.net/

- **JavaScript Weekly**   http://javascriptweekly.com/

Contacting the Author

If you would like to contact me, I am available through my Web site, Twitter, Google Plus, and a Web development help forum. These are all listed here:

- **Web Site: Script the Web**   www.scripttheweb.com

- **Twitter**   https://twitter.com/ScripttheWeb

- **Google Plus**   https://plus.google.com/111287143870905163936/posts

- **Web Xpertz Help Forums**   www.webxpertz.net/forums/forum.php

Chapter 12 Self Test

1. For some issues, using the JavaScript _____ method can be a handy way to quickly see where the problem may be.

    A. Math.round()

    B. alert()

    C. Math.random()

    D. view()

2. You can use JavaScript to test one or more values to see if they are the _____ of values you are expecting.

    A. type

    B. total

    C. number

    D. minimum

3. Adding 400 + 300 + "100" in JavaScript will yield _____.

    A. 800

    B. 800100

    C. "700100"

    D. "800"

4. All of the major browsers now offer their own set of _____ _____.

    A. measuring utensils

    B. cup holders

    C. special foods

    D. developer tools

5. Testing your code in multiple browsers/platforms is a good idea.

    A. True

    B. False

6. No matter which browser's developer tools you choose, you can use them to help you figure out where any _____ may be in your code.

    A. issues (bugs)

    B. food

    C. drinks

    D. pixels

7. Browser developer tools will only help you if you are using JavaScript or jQuery.

    A. True

    B. False

8. Each of the browser developer tools offers a JavaScript _____.

    A. snippet

    B. game

    C. console

    D. variable

9. You can use the _____ method in JavaScript to display a value on the console screen when needed.

    A. console.write()

    B. console.log()

    C. console.show()

    D. console.fadeIn()

10. In many cases, placing a value in the console is far more convenient than an alert because it does not _____ the task at hand with an alert pop-up box.

    A. taunt

    B. enhance

    C. interrupt

    D. perform

11. In addition to JavaScript, the ability of browser developer tools to work with HTML, CSS, and the _____ can be extremely useful when the issue may lie in one of those areas rather than the script itself.

    A. DOM

    B. pizza

    C. TV

    D. phone

12. A _____ tool is a program that checks your code against a set of standards and returns anything it finds that may be problematic.

    A. check

    B. cool

    C. lint

    D. dirt

13. Since JSHint allows you to select an option that tells it jQuery is being used, this is a good option for testing jQuery code.

    A. True

    B. False

14. Forgetting the *var* keyword never presents any problems in JavaScript.

    A. True

    B. False

15. Learning how to use the jQuery library is _____.

    A. fun

    B. dreadful

    C. awesome

    D. OK I guess

Appendix

Answers to Self Tests

Chapter 1: Getting Started with jQuery

1. B. C#

2. A. A Web browser

3. C. John Resig

4. A. True

5. D. MIT License

6. B. False

7. B. <script>

8. A. <head>

9. D. <script src="jquery-1.9.1.min.js" type="text/javascript"></script>

10. B. The file is loaded from the server that is closest to the user, improving the speed of the file download.

11. C. $()

12. A. True

13. C. anonymous function

14. A. addClass

15. C. reusable

Chapter 2: Selecting Elements in the Document

1. The $() function returns a jQuery **object**, which points to all of the selected elements.

2. B. Curly braces { }

3. A. It selects elements by id.

4. C. all

5. A. True

6. C. $(".more").addClass("even-more");

7. B. False

8. A. $("div p")

9. B. >

10. D. $("p:not(.about-me)")

11. B. $("img[alt]")

12. A. attribute equals

13. B. False

14. A. True

15. B. element at index

Chapter 3: Event Handling

1. The *ready()* method allows you to begin running your script as soon as all of the elements have been loaded, but it does not wait for **images** or other media to finish loading.

2. C. load

3. B. noConflict()

4. D. click()

5. B. False

6. A. $("#my-element").click(function(event) {

7. A. True

8. B. keypress

9. D. mouseenter, mouseleave

10. A. bind()

11. D. on()

12. C. off()

13. B. False

14. A. True

15. A. trigger()

Chapter 4: Working with Styles

1. When working with CSS code, you define the selector and then define a rule within a set of **curly brackets ({}).**

2. B. css()

3. D. var eColor = $("#code").css("color");

4. D. shorthand

5. B. False

6. A. $("#text-box").css("background-color", "#FFFFFF");

7. A. True

8. C. +=, −=

9. D. function

10. A. removeClass()

11. C. chaining

12. B. toggleClass()

13. A. True

14. B. offset()

15. D. scrollTop()

Chapter 5: JavaScript and the Document Object Model

1. A single-line comment begins with two **forward slashes** (**//**) and ends at the end of the line.

2. C. /*, */

3. A. keywords, reserved words

4. D. null

5. A. True

6. C. backslashes (\)

7. B. False

8. A. equal, data type

9. B. else

10. C. declaration

11. B. length

12. A. nodes

13. B. False

14. C. before(), insertBefore()

15. B. detach()

Chapter 6: Animations and Effects

1. The **show()** method displays an element by increasing its width, height, and opacity.

2. C. toggle()

3. D. slideUp()

4. A. opacity

5. A. True

6. C. fast

7. B. False (uses milliseconds)

8. A. eq()

9. B. function

10. B. indexOf()

11. D. callback function

12. A. animate()

13. A. True

14. B. False

15. A. stop()

Chapter 7: The Event Object

1. The **Event** object contains properties and methods that are helpful when certain events are triggered.

2. B. type

3. C. milliseconds

4. D. Math.random()

5. A. True

6. A. which

7. B. False

8. C. key

9. C. the *preventDefault()* method has been called

10. B. isPropagationStopped()

11. A. stopPropagation()

12. C. preventDefault()

13. B. False

14. A. True

15. D. cancelable

Chapter 8: The DOM and Forms

1. The **val**() method allows you to get or set values for matched elements.

2. B. $("#yourname").val();

3. D. $("input[type=text]").val("Enter Value");

4. A. blur

5. B. False

6. C. focus()

7. A. True

8. D. select

9. B. "cool"

10. A. test()

11. C. i

12. B. before

13. A. True

14. B. False

15. C. required

Chapter 9: Working with AJAX

1. C. Asynchronous JavaScript and XML

2. A. server

3. A. XMLHttpRequest

4. B. load()

5. A. True

6. D. asynchronously

7. A. True

8. C. find()

9. B. JavaScript Object Notation

10. A. $.getJSON()

11. C. $.get(), $.post()

12. B. callback

13. B. False

14. A. True

15. D. serialize()

Chapter 10: Using Plugins

1. B. plugins

2. A. JavaScript

3. A. a callback function

4. D. first

5. A. True

6. B. names, values

7. B. False

8. C. $("#my-element").start({ time: 1000, repeat: "none" });

9. A. desktop

10. B. jquery-ui.min.css, jquery-ui.min.js

11. C. animate

12. B. widgets

13. A. True

14. A. True

15. D. jCanvas

Chapter 11: Creating Plugins

1. C. $

2. B. conflicts

3. D. Math.random()

4. B. A random number from 0 to 4

5. A. True

6. A. A random number from 2 to 6

7. B. False

8. C. $.fn

9. B. this

10. A. implicit iteration

11. D. jQuery

12. A. $.extend()

13. A. True

14. B. False

15. A. callback function

Chapter 12: Advanced Techniques and Further Resources

1. B. alert()

2. A. type

3. C. "700100"

4. D. developer tools

5. A. True

6. A. issues (bugs)

7. B. False

8. C. console

9. B. console.log()

10. C. interrupt

11. A. DOM

12. C. lint

13. A. True

14. B. False

15. Any answer is correct!

Index

Symbols/Numbers

A

X

Y

Essential Web Development Skills—Made Easy!

The Beginner's Guide series provides everything you need to get started in modern web development. Featuring a practical, hands-on approach, these fast-paced tutorials contain expert insights, sample projects, and downloadable code to help you create dynamic websites quickly and easily.

HTML5: A Beginner's Guide, Fifth Edition
Willard | 0-07-180927-9

JavaScript: A Beginner's Guide, Fourth Edition
Pollock | 0-07-180937-6

**PHP and MySQL Web Development:
A Beginner's Guide**
Matthews | 0-07-183730-2

jQuery: A Beginner's Guide
Pollock | 0-07-181791-3

Follow us on Twitter @MHcomputing